T&T Clark Studies in Systematic Theology

Edited by

John Webster, King's College,
University of Aberdeen, UK

Ian A. McFarland, Candler School of Theology,
Emory University, USA

Ivor Davidson, University of Otago,
New Zealand

t & t clark

HUMANITY IN THE MYSTERY OF GOD

The Theological Anthropology of Edward Schillebeeckx

Jennifer Cooper

t&t clark

Published by T&T Clark
A Continuum imprint
The Tower Building
11 York Road
London SE1 7NX

80 Maiden Lane
Suite 704, New York
NY 10038

www.continuumbooks.com

First published 2009
This paperback edition published 2011

British Library Cataloguing-in-Publication Data
A catalogue record for this book is available from the British Library

ISBN: HB: 978-0-567-03408-3
       PB: 978-0-567-03653-7

Typeset by Newgen Imaging Systems Pvt Ltd, Chennai, India

for Bernard

CONTENTS

PREFACE

Edward Schillebeeckx has never written a theological anthropology. In fact it is even possible from his own writings to suggest he has deliberately not done so. Instead his theology is a sustained and varied reflection on the nature of God who is both creator and redeemer. His theology is a 'treatise' on the God who is God for humanity. This means of course his theology is always a reflection on the nature of God and at the same time, a reflection on the meaning of humanity. So for Schillebeeckx what it means to be fully human is discovered in the relationship between the mystery of God and the mystery of humanity. In Schillebeeckx's own words:

> I discover myself in this mysterious condition which I cannot change: I am really myself in and of this world, becoming myself more and more therein, and yet at the same time created, even to the most deli-cate fibres of my being; completely of God, from whom I borrow myself and by whom I am continually given to myself. I am myself in dependence on God: the more I am God's, the more I become myself in transcending myself. In this constitutive relationship to God, who is a mystery, I am a mystery. The whole crux of my definition is precisely the mystery of God.[1]

For Schillebeeckx the full meaning of humanity is revealed and established in the mystery of God. We are defined ultimately as being a vocation to intimacy with God. Our human vocation to intimacy with the divine is defined as a dependence upon God and as a situated freedom. This vocation

---

[1] Edward Schillebeeckx, 'Dialogue with God and Christian Secularity', in *God and Man*, trans. by Edward Fitzgerald and Peter Tomlinson (London: Sheed and Ward, 1969), pp. 210–233 (pp. 215). 'Ik bevind mij in deze geheimnisvolle toestand waar ik niet buiten kan: waarlijk mezelf te zijn in en aan deze wereld, daarin steeds meer mezelf wordend, en toch tevens, tot in de fijnste weefsels van mijn bestaan, geschapen te zijn; volkomen van God, aan wie ik mezelf ontleen en door wie ik voortdurend aan mezelf word geschonken. In de afhankelijkheid van God ben ik mezelf: hoe meer ik van God ben, des te meer word ik, mezelf overstijgend, mezelf. In deze constitutieve verhouding tot God, die een mysterie is, ben ik een mysterie. De 'fine pointe' van mijn definitie is precies het mysterie van God.' 'Dialoog met God en Christelijke Seculariteit', in *God en mens* (Bilthoven: Nelissen, 1965), pp. 150–166 (pp. 153–154). First published in *Verslagboek v. d. Theologische week over de mens* (Nijmegen: 1958), pp. 3–21.

to intimacy with God describes not only our relationship with God but also and at the same time, our relationship to the world, ourselves and others. Hence the description of humanity which emerges from Schillebeeckx's treatise on God holds together humanity's metaphysical and moral significance.

At the heart of Schillebeeckx's theocentric anthropology is a christological structure. More particularly, Schillebeeckx develops a sacramental christology in light of his interpretation of Christ's incarnation; and the relation of incarnation to the death, resurrection and glorification of Christ establishes a sacramental theological anthropology. The meaning of humanity is given in its creative, salvific, sanctifying, participative and personal relation to the God who is God both of creation and of covenant.

This book focuses on the work of Edward Schillebeeckx in the earlier stage of his career from the late 1940s until just after the Second Vatican Council. Schillebeeckx's theology is significant in its own right. Yet even more than this, it is perhaps his approach to theology which will prove to be his enduring legacy. When I first undertook this research on his theological anthropology I was already familiar with his later theology and convinced of the importance of his theology both in itself and as a resource for the future of theology. However, I had assumed at the outset of my research I would focus my attention on his later theology, using his earlier work simply to prepare the ground for the more interesting and significant later work. I fully expected to read through his early works fairly speedily and move quickly on.

The project changed as I read. Not only is his earlier theology richly rewarding in itself, it is an invaluable resource for questions of theological method and the history of theological ideas at a pivotal time in the development of theology. There is a great wealth of theology here which rewards patient reading. This earlier work deserves more attention than it has received, and so I have undertaken a careful reading of the essays and books written up to and just after the Second Vatican Council. During this period his theology reflects his strengths as both a speculative theologian and as a positive theologian: much of his own originality as a theologian is developed in his *ressourcement* of the tradition. He recovers from within the tradition neglected and misinterpreted strands of thought and offers a creative and constructive reading of some of the most fascinating periods of theology. In particular I have examined his interpretation of Thomas Aquinas in this light, his use of a kenotic christology, and the influence of Dominic De Petter and Marie-Dominique Chenu. I have also considered Schillebeeckx's reflections on his Dominican formation and its influence within his theology; and I have discussed Schillebeeckx's own analysis of contemporary phenomenology and its contributions to theology. Above all else Schillebeeckx is a pastoral theologian: his theology is always at the service of the contemporary needs of church and world. In this service, he combines his knowledge of the tradition with a commitment to contemporary intellectual insights, both from within theology and from without.

PREFACE

The earlier period of Schillebeeckx's own theology is sometimes misinterpreted or too quickly dismissed. This later work is widely regarded as marking a substantive rupture with his earlier output but I am convinced that the continuities in his thought are far more significant. And so, in a very modest fashion, this book is a *ressourcement* of what is a very rich time in Schillebeeckx's theology. For a study of theological anthropology it is particularly rewarding: a study of Schillebeeckx's theological description of humanity is in itself a study of his theology of creation, revelation, grace, and salvation. And from this a definition of humanity emerges in light of the mystery of God: humanity is defined as vocation.

This book develops an interpretation of Schillebeeckx's theological anthropology by analysing his theology of revelation and grace, and by examining the christological structure of his theology. This christology centres on an interpretation of the incarnation in which the fully personal nature of Christ's humanity is key. This christology establishes the sacramental nature of humanity and hence Schillebeeckx's description of the meaning of human nature is also a theological description of the meaning of human action.

This book itself is a lightly revised version of my Oxford doctoral dissertation. I am grateful to the Religious of the Sacred Heart for supporting me over many years and making doctoral studies a possibility, most especially my communities in Oxford and Ottawa who have been my home on either side of the Atlantic. For their love and *cor unum* I am more grateful than I can say. Professor John Webster supervised my research for the doctorate with great wisdom, graciousness and humour, and has been a source of encouragement and inspiration. This book does little justice to the debt of learning I owe to him. I am indebted to the Warden and Fellows of Keble College, Oxford for electing me to the Liddon Fellowship in Theology during the final stage of research, and to the Master and Fellows of St Benet's Hall, Oxford for electing me to a College Lectureship as I prepared the manuscript for this book. My study of Schillebeeckx's theology has been enriched by many conversations and the insights of many friends. I am particularly indebted to Professor Fergus Kerr, Dr Philip Kennedy, Dr James Hanvey, Professor Mary Catherine Hilkert, Dr Eric Borgman, Professor Herwi Rikhof, Dr Stephan van Erp, Huub Stegeman, Dr Holger Zaborowski, Don Bolen and Dr Raymond Lafontaine. Dr Paul Roberts and Thomas Seville provided invaluable assistance at critical moments. I am very grateful to them. I remember with gratitude George Schner. Above all I owe thanks to Professor Edward Schillebeeckx for the privilege of our conversations, and for giving so generously of his time and his books during my visits to Nijmegen. Finally, it remains only to thank Dr Bernard Green. For this I have no words and so this book is dedicated to him.

Jennifer Cooper
College of the Resurrection, Mirfield
Feast of St Thomas Aquinas, 28 January 2009

1

REVELATION AND
HUMAN BEING

Introduction

Edward Schillebeeckx's theology of revelation gives a particular shape to his theological anthropology; this is the subject of this chapter. Schillebeeckx's theology of revelation has two fundamental characteristics: one is a trust in the capacity of created nature to know God, and the other is the conviction that God has revealed himself within history as human salvation. Revelation is concerned with the knowability of God where knowledge of God depends on the self-revelation of God in salvation history. For Schillebeeckx revelation sets the agenda for theology with respect to both content and method. The subject of theology is the God who is God for humanity. Based on this Schillebeeckx describes theology as theocentric in content and Christological in method.[1] For him this description of theology, which is at the same time an accurate description of his own theological project, follows from the structure of revelation

---

[1] Edward Schillebeeckx, 'What is Theology?', in *Revelation and Theology, I: Revelation, Tradition and Theological Reflection*, 2nd ed. (London: Sheed and Ward, 1987), pp. 95–183 (p. 104; pp. 138–143). 'Wat is Theologie?' in *Openbaring en Theologie* (Bilthoven: Nelissen, 1964), pp. 71–121. First published under the title 'Theologie' in *Theologisch woordenboek, III* (Roermond: Maaseik, 1958), col. 4485–4542. See also, 'Life in God and Life in the World', in *God and Man*, trans. Edward Fitzgerald and Peter Tomlinson (London: Sheed and Ward, 1969), pp. 85–209 (pp. 151–154; 153): '[I]n the revelation through salvation history the absolute meaning of God communicates itself.' 'Leven in God en leven in de wereld', in *God en mens* (Bilthoven: Nelissen, 1965), pp. 66–149. First published as two articles: 'Evangelische zuiverheid en menselijke waarachtigheid', *Tijdschrift voor Theologie* 3 (1963), 283–325; 'Herinterpretatie van het geloof in het licht van de seculariteit', *Tijdschrift voor Theologie* 4 (1964), 109–150.

itself. Theology, he suggests, proceeds by listening to 'the eternal symphony of revelation'.[2]

This relation between theology and revelation is a critical one. It must not be naïve. Theology is an activity of both listening and conversion. Theology must allow itself to be corrected by revelation.[3] As Schillebeeckx understands it, theology is 'a hazardous business because the theologian establishes [herself] completely in the reality of revelation with the whole of [her] human spirit and thinking mind'.[4] With Thomas Aquinas, Schillebeeckx describes theology as a *habitus*: theology follows from inhabiting 'revelation itself in its inner intelligibility'.[5]

Theological Anthropology: Intention and Condition

The above introduction is a very brief and preliminary sketch of Schillebeeckx's theology of revelation – each of these ideas will be returned to in greater depth – and it is intended only to set the stage for the more specific topic of this chapter: the contribution and significance of his theology of revelation for his theological anthropology. Here a question presents itself at the outset: why begin a study of theological anthropology with a discussion of the theology of revelation? The answer to this question, at least with respect to the theological anthropology of Schillebeeckx, is found in what he describes as the 'intention' – *bedoeling* – and 'condition' – *voorbehoud vooropstellend* – of theological anthropology itself.

---

[2] Edward Schillebeeckx, 'Salvation History as the Basis of Theology: *Theologia* or *Oikonomia?*', in *Revelation and Theology, II: The Concept of Truth and Theological Renewal*, trans. N. D. Smith (New York: Sheed and Ward, 1968), pp. 79–105 (p. 87). 'De heilshistoriche basis van de theologie: *theologia of oikonomia?*', in *Openbaring en Theologie*, pp. 265–281. First presented as a conference paper: *Vlaams Werkenootschap voor Theologie*, Brussels, 1953.

[3] Schillebeeckx, 'What is Theology?', p. 132: '[T]he whole of speculative theology is subject to the constant correction of the divine mystery of salvation.'

[4] Edward Schillebeeckx, '*Theologia* or *Oikonomia*', p. 84. See also 'Is the Church Adrift?', in *The Mission of the Church*, trans. N. D. Smith (London: Sheed and Ward, 1973), pp. 20–42 (esp. p. 35). 'De kerk op drift?', in *De zending van de kerk* (Bilthoven: Nelissen, 1968), pp. 25–39. First published in *Tijdschrift voor Geestelijk Leven* 22 (1966), 533–554.

[5] Schillebeeckx, 'What is Theology?', pp. 109–110: '[T]heology is concerned with the supernatural reality as it *is* in itself. It is important, therefore, to stress the *religious* character of theology as a science ... [T]heology is a science that is concerned with a *religious* reality, with the result that to live in this religious reality, which is possible only through faith, remains the basis of the scientific value of theology'. Schillebeeckx references Aquinas: 'Fides est quasi habitus theologiae'. *In Boethium de Trinitate*, q. 5 a. 4, ad 8.

First, what is the intention of theological anthropology? For Schillebeeckx the 'intention' of theological anthropology is to 'discover what God in his grace intends' for humanity:

> It is our intention to discover what God in his grace intends for humanity . . . What does the Word of God say about man? *How does God see man?* That God sees man does not mean simply that he knows what man is making of his life here below. On the contrary, it is the gaze of one who is personally interested, who calls us to salvation and participates with us in a personal, creative and sanctifying way: he is involved in the fortunes of man.[6]

The intention of theological anthropology is not to 'define' humanity, at least not in the sense of a closed or definitive description, rather its intention is to describe the meaning of human existence in light of its relationship to God – the God who calls us to salvation. The nature of this relationship between God and humanity defines humanity itself.

The task of theological anthropology is to explore the question: what does God intend for humanity? This means primarily that the full meaning of humanity is given in the divine–human relationship. In other words, the terms used to describe the full meaning of humanity are the same terms that describe the relationship between God and humanity. In Schillebeeckx's work the terms used to describe the human–divine relationship are creative, salvific, sanctifying, participative and personal. These are therefore the terms that form the most meaningful description of human being. It is not surprising then that the one place in all of Schillebeeckx's writings where he attempts what he specifically calls a 'theological definition' of humanity is an essay on divine Providence. In his own words, 'we cannot approach', the essence of humanity 'better than by doing so through reflection on divine Providence'.[7] The intention of theological anthropology is to discover what God intends for humanity.

By describing theological anthropology as a reflection on what God intends for humanity, that is, by situating the theological discourse on the meaning of human life within an understanding of divine Providence, Schillebeeckx has revealed what he considers to be the 'condition' for a theological anthropology:

> Even though we can only speak about God on the basis of our relationship with him, especially insofar as it has been made manifest in the man Jesus, our affirmations concerning God are nevertheless no

---

[6] Edward Schillebeeckx, 'Dialogue with God and Christian Secularity', in *God and Man*, trans. Edward Fitzgerald and Peter Tomlinson (London: Sheed and Ward, 1969), pp. 213–214.

[7] Schillebeeckx, 'Dialogue with God and Christian Secularity', p. 214.

mere anthropological affirmations; they are not just things said about man, but things also said about God himself. Having set up this condition we cannot approach man's essence better than by doing so through reflection on divine Providence.[8]

Here Schillebeeckx is clearly situating theological anthropology within a reflection on God's self-revelation as the God 'who calls us to salvation and participates with us in a personal, creative and sanctifying way' and does this in a particular manner. This is underscored by a comment he makes contrasting his anthropology with that of Bultmann. Bultmann, he suggests, 'identifies' theology, that is, the discourse on God, with a 'Christian anthropology'.[9] Schillebeeckx distinguishes this from his own anthropology which, although it is grounded in the conviction that 'the question as to the meaning of human life coincides with that regarding divine Providence', describes the relationship between these two realities in a manner that does not negate the human or the divine terms of the relationship but maintains their distinctiveness. This is the importance of Schillebeeckx's caveat: 'especially insofar as it has been made manifest in the man Jesus'. This Christological revelation and therefore structure of the human–divine relationship is precisely what Schillebeeckx means when he speaks of the human and the divine 'coinciding'.[10] This is consistent with his statement: 'In this constitutive relationship to God, who is a mystery, I am a mystery' – neither

[8] Ibid.
[9] Schillebeeckx does not elaborate on his critique of Bultmann. However, from his more general critique of existentialist theologies, and of Robinson in particular, it is clear that he considers a theology which 'identifies' the discourse on God with anthropology as reductive. This is in part why he is insistent upon the importance of metaphysics for theology. Theology is the discourse on God in which we encounter the reality – the being of God – and in this encounter we are revealed – human being – to ourselves. Revelation, and hence theology, is an intersubjective rather than reductive activity. For Schillebeeckx's general critique of existentialist theology see 'The New Trends in Present-Day Dogmatic Theology' in *Revelation and Theology*, II, pp. 106–154. 'De nieuwe wending in de huidige dogmatiek', in *Openbaring en Theologie*, pp. 282–312. First published in *Tijdschrift voor Theologie* 1 (1961), 17–46; for the critique of Robinson see 'Life in God and Life in the World'; for the importance of metaphysics see 'The Concept of "Truth"' in *Revelation and Theology*, II, pp. 5–29. 'Het begrip "waarheid"', in *Openbaring en Theologie*, pp. 185–200. First published in *Katholiek Archief* 17 (1962), 1169–1180. See also 'The Non-conceptual Intellectual Dimension in Our Knowledge of God According to Aquinas', in *Revelation and Theology*, II, pp. 157–206. 'Het niet-begrippelijk kenmoment in onze Godskennis volgens Thomas van Aquino', in *Openbaring en Theologie*, pp. 201–232. First published in *Tijdschrift voor Philosophie*, 14 (1952), 411–453.
[10] Schillebeeckx, 'Dialogue with God and Christian Secularity', p. 214: '[God] is involved in the fortunes of man (so much so indeed that in the *theophania* of the man Jesus he personally devotes himself in solidarity with human beings to the formation and construction of the "essence" of man in himself).'

the full reality of what it means to be human nor the full reality of the divine is negated in this relation.[11]

At stake then, in the theological definition of humanity, is the definition of the human–divine relationship, which is intersubjective and has a particular dynamic. It holds together both the human and the divine in an irreducible and non-reductive manner. Theological anthropology is the description of what it means to be human in light of the creative, salvific, sanctifying, participative and personal nature of the relationship between God and humanity. Each of these terms – creative, salvific, sanctifying, participative and personal – is therefore of fundamental importance in anthropological terms. As Schillebeeckx phrases it:

> The definition of humanity will only be seen clearly when we consider humanity in light of the dogma of creation and salvation; that is to say, in terms of our whole experience of existence, which includes a history of salvation.[12]

This is what Schillebeeckx intends when he says, 'In this constitutive relationship to God, who is a mystery, I am a mystery. The whole crux of my definition is precisely the mystery of God'[13]. Humanity is defined in relation to the God who is both creator and redeemer. As this exploration of Schillebeeckx's theology develops it will become clear that humanity can be described as both an absolute dependence – 'I am myself in dependence upon God' – and as a situated freedom – 'I am really myself in and of this world' – and these two terms are related and non-contradictory in the same manner as creation and redemption are related and non-contradictory.[14]

---

[11] Schillebeeckx, 'Dialogue with God and Christian Secularity', p. 215.

[12] Ibid.

[13] Ibid.

[14] Schillebeeckx, 'Dialogue with God and Christian Secularity', p. 215. Schillebeeckx uses the phrase 'situated freedom' to describe human existence. This is a statement not only of essential contingency and temporality, but also a statement which defines humanity in terms of agency: humanity realises itself within history as it makes history. Schillebeeckx often refers to this agency as the activity of humanization. Schillebeeckx, 'Dialogue with God and Christian Secularity', pp. 212–213; 217: 'This concept of man as a personal subject whose essence it is to be, or to construct himself in freedom by giving meaning to the world of people and things, is one which we shall assume from the outset as a forward-looking, open-ended definition of man in which believers and non-believers alike can find a common ground for dialogue.' Theological anthropology does not override this description of humanity but defines it more fully in terms of its ultimate possibilities: 'The opposition in views between partners in the dialogue – the believers and the non-believers – does not then consist in a denial by the believers of the possibilities of which the non-believers speak; rather it consists in the fact that the believer is taking into account possibilities which give it an entirely new significance to the intramundane possibilities with which the non-believer is concerned: the ultimate possibilities implied by a fundamental relationship with God.'

This has important consequences particularly for a theology of human action.

In essence theological anthropology is derived from the relationship between God and humanity: the meaning of humanity coincides with God's intention for humanity. In setting up his theological anthropology in this manner, Schillebeeckx has clearly made a significant assumption: if the theological definition of humanity is found in the description of what God intends for humanity, this definition cannot be given in the manner of a closed or definitive definition because at its heart, theological anthropology is concerned with the ultimate fulfilment of humanity. This fulfilment of humanity is given in the present in relationship with God and at the same time it is given in an eschatological manner as the ultimate 'possibility': the 'ultimate possibilities implied by a fundamental relationship with God'.[15] Humanity's fundamental relationship to God is actually constitutive of its being in the world and at the same time it is a dynamic and open relationship where humanity comes more and more to itself, the more and more it deepens in its dependence upon God.

This idea of 'dependence' upon God that is axiomatic to humanity's definition, both in its created nature and in salvation history, is one Schillebeeckx describes as being in the world *together with* the living God – *samen met de levende God*. This is constitutive of humanity's present and historical existence and constitutive of the ultimate and eschatological meaning of human life: humanity experiences this dependence upon God now by dwelling with God in the world and at the same time humanity experiences its dependence upon God as 'the ultimate possibility' which is the fulfilment of humanity. Theological anthropology considers what it means to be human in light of

> [T]he ultimate possibilities implied by a fundamental relationship with God. For being-in-and-present-to-the-world takes on a completely different meaning if humanity experiences this presence in the world and in history not as an isolated individual – that is, in a radical personal loneliness which persists even in face of the fact that personal existence is co-existence – but as a dwelling in and with the living God in the historical situation of this world. And then the question becomes urgent as to whether an adequate definition of humanity can ultimately be given without making any reference to our relationship with God, which we can freely assent to or feely deny. In the final analysis the definition of man is *vocational*: he is defined by God's call.[16]

---

[15] Schillebeeckx, 'Dialogue with God and Christian Secularity', p. 213.

[16] Ibid. p. 213. The original Dutch text describes humanity in history 'together with' God – 'samen met' – rather than 'in and with' God as it is given in the official English translation. 'Dialoog met God en Christelijke Seculariteit', p. 152: 'Het-in-en-bij-de-wereld-zijn krijgt immers en heel andere betekenis indien men deze tegenwoordigheid

The key point here is the intrinsic relation between human historical existence and the eschatological or ultimate possibilities for humanity – between the human capacity for self-definition and ultimate dependence upon God for definition. Schillebeeckx captures this intrinsic relation between humanity's existence as a situated freedom – finite, temporal, contingent – and the ultimate meaning or possibilities for humanity – being together with God – by defining human life as 'vocation'. Humanity is defined by its possibilities, and this implies divine promise: 'In the final analysis the definition of humanity is vocational: humanity is defined by God's call'.

The choice of the concept of 'vocation' as the definition of humanity is an interesting one and is of key significance for interpreting Schillebeeckx's anthropology. The central importance of this idea is that it ensures a non-dualistic theology of human life. To define humanity as a vocation suggests that the essence of what it means to be human cannot be defined in a dichotomy of body–soul or in any other set of dualistic terms. Vocation suggests that the definition of what it means to be human rests in the nature and the dynamism of a call and a response, and this in turn implies the essentially personal reality of humanity: body and soul, social and individual, receptive and creative. Indeed, Schillebeeckx attaches such significance to the concept of vocation precisely because it ensures 'the personal meaning' of human life. It is an active, dynamic and open term suggesting the involvement of the whole person. Defining human being as a vocation therefore suggests an anthropology that privileges the concept of person and therefore implies a non-dualistic anthropology generally. It also suggests a non-dualistic anthropology in more specifically theological terms: divine and human, infinite and finite, grace and nature, eschatological and temporal. All human action within the world 'becomes personally meaningful only in the context of humanity's theologal relationship with God'.[17]

The concept of vocation as the theological or ultimate definition of human life is conditioned by the doctrines of creation and salvation, for as Schillebeeckx maintains: 'The definition of humanity will only be seen clearly when

in de wereld en in de geschiedenis effectuerend beleeft niet alleen vanuit een radicale persoonlijke eenzaamheid (hoe innig deze dan ook moge aanleunen bij het "*Mit-sein*" der medemensen), maar ook *samen met de levende God* in deze wereld en in haar geschiedenis staat.' 'Together with' gives a more accurate sense of the personal and intersubjective relationship between humanity and God in history in which Schillebeeckx places emphasis upon humanity's freedom, capacity and responsibility to construct a meaningful history. See 'Dialogue with God and Christian Secularity', p. 212: 'This concept of man as a personal subject whose essence it is to be, or construct himself in freedom by giving meaning to a world of people and things, is one which we shall assume from the outset.' It also places greater emphasis on the distinctiveness and difference between the human and divine in this relation, and that is something Schillebeeckx underlines consistently.

[17] Schillebeeckx, 'Dialogue with God and Christian Secularity', p. 217.

we consider humanity in light of the dogma of creation and salvation'.[18] Hence the vocation that is definitive of humanity – the dynamism of call and the response – has a certain content and structure that binds together being in the world with being together with God. For this reason Schillebeeckx calls this the only 'adequate definition of humanity':

> We describe the human person according to his horizontal dimension as a being who must define himself in and towards this world in community with his fellow men through the exercise of his freedom. Thus, from a theological point of view . . . we could describe him as a free being who must define himself in and towards the world in dialogue with God.[19]

In short, humanity is a 'situated freedom' – being in the world – whose definition is 'primarily a dialogue with God' – being together with God in the world. Here Schillebeeckx gives further shape to the concept of vocation by defining it more precisely as a 'dialogue'.

Dialogue of course suggests the personal and participative nature of the definition of humanity, one that is consonant with the description of the human–divine relation. Recalling that the terms that define humanity are the terms that describe the divine–human relationship – creative, salvific, sanctifying, participative and personal – Schillebeeckx's definition of humanity primarily as a dialogue with God is consistent with his understanding that the intention of a theological anthropology is to define humanity in light of this specific relation. In other words, humanity defined as dialogue with God follows from the question: what does God intend for humanity?

Schillebeeckx goes on to develop the idea of vocation as dialogue further by describing this dialogue as a particular kind of intimacy – 'theologal intimacy':

> The theological definition of man's personhood is his theologal intimacy with God; man is primarily a dialogue with God. The theological definition of his essential incarnation or dialogue with the world then becomes the following: in his intimacy with God man approaches the world and his fellow men.[20]

With this even more specific description of vocation as intimacy with God, Schillebeeckx draws together the idea of vocation with both the content and the structure of the dogma of creation and salvation, and in doing this the definition of humanity becomes more clearly creative, salvific and sanctifying

[18] Ibid. p. 215.
[19] Ibid. p. 214.
[20] Ibid. pp. 216–217.

as well as personal and participative. The concept 'theologal' is used by Schillebeeckx in his theology to denote the relationship between humanity and God that is creative, salvific and sanctifying: it is constitutive of humanity's existence; it is the fulfilment of this existence; and it begins the work of this fulfilment within history.[21] It also underscores the intersubjective nature of this relationship and therefore is consistent with, and contributes to, the personal and participative characteristics of the human divine relation.[22] The vocation to be human is a vocation to a dialogue with God, where this dialogue is intimacy with God; furthermore, because of the nature of this intimacy, it is constitutive of humanity's relation to the world itself.

The nature of the intimacy with God that defines humanity is established by the realities of creation and redemption, and most important for Schillebeeckx, it is defined by holding these truths together: theologal intimacy and hence the definition of humanity is 'the consequence of [holding] the dogma of creation in connection with the dogma of redemption'.[23]

---

[21] This idea recurs in Schillebeeckx's theology. There is a helpful explanation provided in a translator's note. Edward Schillebeeckx, *Christ the Sacrament of the Encounter with God* (London: Sheed and Ward, 1963), pp. 15–16; n 14: 'By "theologal attitude of existence" we mean a vital human activity of which God himself is the object and the motive, and in the perfecting of which God is coactive: namely the life of grace in faith, hope and love, the only virtues which of their nature bring about a personal relationship with God.' This is given its fullest expression in Schillebeeckx's christology: 'Personally to be approached by the man Jesus was, for his contemporaries, an invitation to a personal encounter with the life-giving God, because personally that man was the Son of God. Human encounter with Jesus is therefore the sacrament of the encounter with God, or of the religious life as a theologal attitude of existence towards God.' The Christological structure of human life and hence the sacramental nature of human life is explored in more depth in the second half of this book. The English translation is taken from *Christus-Sacrament van de Godsontmoeting* (Bilthoven: Nelissen, 1959). This is the third revised and expanded edition of the original 1958 text published under the title *De Christusontmoeting als sacrament van de Godsontmoeting. Theologische begrijpelijkheid van het heilsfeit sacramenten* (Bilthoven: Nelissen, 1958).

[22] The intersubjective emphasis of the term 'theologal', and his preference for this term, is explained by Schillebeeckx. 'Faith Functioning in Human Self-Understanding', in *The Word in History: The St Xavier Symposium*, ed. Patrick Burke (London: Sheed and Ward , 1966), pp. 41–59 (p. 59 n 1): 'The word *"theologal"* . . . refers to the communion with the living God. This communion surpasses the "natural" capacities of man, and is possible only through the gratuitous self-communication of God. Consequently, it is equivalent to the traditional word "supernatural" which, however refers explicitly only to the surpassing of human powers. Thus, I prefer the term "theologal" to express this mutual communion or inter-subjectivity of God and man.'

[23] Edward Schillebeeckx, 'Religion and the World: Renewing the Face of the Earth', in *World and Church*, trans. N. D. Smith (New York: Sheed and Ward, 1971), pp. 1–18 (pp. 10–11). 'Godsdienst en Wereld: het aanschijn der aarde vernieuwen', in *Wereld en kerk* (Bilthoven: Nelissen, 1966), pp. 58– 71. First published in *Het geestelijk leven van de leek* (Tilburg: Drakenburgh-conferenties, 1951), pp. 7–27.

There are two central concepts here. The first is 'the relationship with God is not something added, it is constitutive of man'; and the second being that this relationship is realized 'in and through a completely new and free initiative of God, who calls theologal intersubjectivity into life through his grace'. However, in another description that Schillebeeckx uses, humanity 'exists for God' yet 'does not hold the personal meaning of his existence within himself, and cannot realise it of himself.'[24]

These two theological concepts – creation and redemption – are pivotal for an interpretation of Schillebeeckx's theological anthropology. An exploration of his writings on the dogma of creation reveals an anthropology that is theocentric – an interpretation of what it means to be human in light of humanity's relationship of absolute dependence upon the God who is cause, transcendence and difference. An exploration of his understanding of the dogma of redemption reveals an anthropology that is theocentric and Christological – an interpretation of what it means to be human in light of humanity's personal relationship with the God who reveals himself as personally immanent in human history as salvation. Humanity is defined by the nature of this human–divine relation.

The vocation to which humanity is called is intimacy with God. This is the 'primary task' of human life.[25] In this sense, human life is theocentric and Christological:

> Theologically, it is certain that man becomes himself only in moving outwards from his own centre of life towards God. Or, to express this another way, in a deeper introversion, so as to press on in grace through the most profound depths of his subjectivity to God; more accurately, to experience personally God's presence within him.[26]

The first two chapters of this book, on revelation and grace, explore this idea that intimacy with God is constitutive of humanity. The third and fourth chapters, on incarnation and death, and resurrection and glorification, explore the 'nature of this intimacy with God'. The idea of intimacy with God is developed by Schillebeeckx 'in more detail by considering the man Jesus'.[27] From the Christological nature of human intimacy with God a 'definition' of human life as kenosis takes shape: Schillebeeckx's theocentric and Christological definition of human life describes humanity as the vocation to intimacy with God in self-emptying. The 'primary task' of humanity is 'radical love' of the other: this is the sacramental – human and

---

[24] Schillebeeckx, 'Dialogue with God and Christian Secularity', pp. 215–216.
[25] Ibid. p. 220.
[26] Ibid. p. 211.
[27] Ibid. pp. 220–221.

historical – nature of the vocation to intimacy with God.[28] This is a thoroughly sacramental anthropology: kenotic intimacy with God defines humanity's 'metaphysical and moral significance' – I discover myself in dependence upon God in the world.[29]

What does God intend for humanity? Schillebeeckx's response to this question is the thesis that determines his theological anthropology. God defines humanity as the vocation to an intimacy with God, which is creative salvific, sanctifying, personal and participative. Humanity is defined by God's intention. It follows from this for Schillebeeckx that theological anthropology is conditioned by the following claim: whatever can be affirmed of God is at the same time an affirmation of the meaning of human life.

Returning to the earlier question: but why begin this anthropology with a theology of revelation? From Schillebeeckx's own writings on the nature and task of theology and its relation to revelation, there are two phrases that focus an answer to this question with particular acuteness. The first of these is his statement, 'The infinite is disclosed in the finite, without destroying it' – *'In het eindige ontsluit zich het oneindige, zonder dit eindige teniet te doen'*.[30] The second is, 'God gives man an insight into his own conditions, God reveals man to himself precisely by revealing himself as love to man' – *'God door zichzelf als liefde te openbaren aan de mens, juist daardoor de mens een inzicht geeft in zijn eigen condities, hem aan zichzelf openbaart'*.[31] Between these two theological assumptions, there is an interpretation of revelation that holds together creation and redemption – the God of creation who is utterly different and separate from creation is the God who is personally immanent within history: 'the same God who is the creator is also the redeemer; the same God is also both the Lord of the history of man and of the history of salvation'.[32] At the same time these assumptions indicate a theology of revelation that establishes the intersubjective relationship between humanity and God, and this is critical for Schillebeeckx's

---

[28] Schillebeeckx, 'Christian Faith and Man's Expectation for the Future on Earth', in *The Mission of the Church*, pp. 51–89 (p. 78). 'Christelijk geloof en aardse toekomstverwachting', in *De zending van de kerk*, pp. 46–72. First Published in *De kerk in de wereld van deze tijd* (Antwerp: Hilversum, 1967), pp. 78–109.

[29] Schillebeeckx, 'Dialogue with God and Christian Secularity', p. 215.

[30] Schillebeeckx, 'What is Theology?', p. 109; 'Wat is Theologie?', p. 79. The Dutch text is particularly helpful here because it places emphasis on the irreducibility of the finite in relation to the infinite. This idea is developed by Schillebeeckx at length in his interpretation of revelation, especially with respect to the relation between conceptual and non-conceptual knowledge. See 'The "Concept of Truth"'; 'The Non-conceptual Intellectual Dimension in Our Knowledge of God According to Aquinas'.

[31] Schillebeeckx, 'Christian Faith and Man's Expectation for the Future on Earth', p. 54; 'Christelijk geloof en aardse toekomstverwachting', p. 48.

[32] Schillebeeckx, 'Christian Faith and Man's Expectation for the Future on Earth', p. 55.

foundational insight: 'Every theological statement, that is everything that is said about God is at the same time a statement about man'.[33]

Schillebeeckx's interpretation of the doctrine of revelation is a good starting point for an interpretation of his theological anthropology precisely because it introduces his understanding of the nature of God: in Schillebeeckx's theology, the structure and content of revelation hold together the dogma of creation and redemption and begin to describe the relation of creation to redemption, and of human history to the history of salvation. Revelation also introduces the theological interpretation of human life as a dialogue with God, as vocation to an intersubjective intimacy with God that is creative, salvific, sanctifying, participative and personal. Both of these ideas – the nature of God and the definition of humanity – are explored in the following four sections of this chapter: (1) humanity *and* God – a distinctively Dominican theology; (2) humanity created by God: God as cause, transcendence and difference; (3) humanity addressed by God: God as personal and immanent; and (4) humanity revealed to itself by God: God as ultimate human meaning. From this a picture begins to emerge of a theological anthropology in light of 'the eternal symphony of revelation': 'In this constitutive relationship to God, who is a mystery, I am a mystery. The whole crux of my definition is precisely the mystery of God'.[34]

Humanity and *God: A Distinctively Dominican Theology*

One of the consistent preoccupations of the very many studies of Schillebeeckx's theology is the question of continuity and discontinuity within his work. This is not a surprising preoccupation in light of the length and breadth of Schillebeeckx's own career and of the context in which this has unfolded. Certainly the second half of the twentieth century was one of the most creative and contentious periods of Roman Catholic theology, reflecting a time of monumental change and renewal, of argument and debate, within the church as a whole. With the Second Vatican Council not a single aspect of the life of the church remained untouched. Vatican II was a council of *aggiornamento* – it saw at least the beginning of a massive reappraisal of the relation between church and world; and it was also a council of *reformation* – it initiated a renewal of church life from within. In very general terms two insights shaped the Council and are reflected in the final versions of the documents it produced: the fundamental historicity of human life, and faith and the recovery of Scripture as the unique source and expression of the Christian faith.

---

[33] Ibid. p. 54.
[34] Schillebeeckx, 'Dialogue with God and Christian Secularity', p. 215.

Behind the aggiornamento and reformation of Vatican II – in the preparations for the Council, in the debates during the conciliar sessions themselves, and most important, in the documents that are the Council's lasting legacy – lies an enormously fruitful and tumultuous period of theology. The aftermath of modernism gave rise to a remarkable flourishing in all areas of theology, and this flourishing contributed most creatively to the quite singular achievements of Vatican II. Never before in the history of the church have so many changes so directly and so immediately affected the life of the church as a whole.

In the years preceding the Council, in the sessions of the Council, and in the turbulent years following, Schillebeeckx was actively engaged in the pastoral and theological preparation and reception of Vatican II's aggiornamento and reformation.[35] This engagement is characteristic of his theology as a whole. His theology consistently shows rigorous academic engagement with the tradition and with wider contemporary intellectual developments, and at the same time it also represents a faithful and energetic pastoral commitment to the church in and with the world. Schillebeeckx is essentially a pastoral theologian. He works from the conviction that theology must place itself at the service of the pastoral needs of the world even as it seeks to articulate the 'truths of faith'. It is the pastoral nature of his theology that accounts for his refusal to ignore points of conflict or confrontation, either between theology and church or between church and world, and his commitment to the prophetic nature of both theology and church is never far from the surface of his writings.[36] In this, as in a great deal that shapes his

[35] Schillebeeckx's involvement in the preparations of the Council, during the Council itself and in the years immediately following is discussed fully by Erik Borgman, *Edward Schillebeeckx: een theoloog in zijn geschiedenis. Deel I: Een katholieke cultuurtheologie (1914–1965)* (Baarn: Nelissen, 1999), pp. 352–450. Borgman, a Dutch theologian, has been appointed by the Dutch Dominican Province to write an intellectual biography of Schillebeeckx. This is the first volume of a projected two-volume work. It has been translated into English under the title, *Edward Schillebeeckx: A Theologian in his History. Volume I: A Catholic Theology of Culture (1914–1965)*, trans. John Bowden (London: Continuum, 2003). There are some inaccuracies in the translation and in particular in the references to the original Dutch texts of Schillebeeckx's earlier works. For this reason the Dutch edition of Borgman's book will be followed. Borgman's other articles on Schillebeeckx include 'Theologie tussen universiteit en emancipatie: De weg van Edward Schillebeeckx', *Tijdschrift voor Theologie* 26 (1986), 240–258; 'Op zoek naar Maria . . . en verder', *Tijdschrift voor Theologie* 33 (1993), 241–266; and 'Van cultuurtheologie naar theologie als onderdeel van de cultuur', *Tijdschrift voor Theologie* 34 (1994), 335–360.

[36] The prophetic responsibility of theology is expressed most eloquently in his later christology: 'To put it starkly: whereas God is bent on showing himself in human form, we on our side slip past this human aspect as quickly as we can in order to admire a "divine Ikon" from which every trait of the critical prophet has been smoothed away. Thus we "neutralise" the critical impact of God himself and run the risk simply of

13

theology and his engagement with church and world, he reflects his Dominican heritage: the dilemma of 'God *or* humanity', 'church *or* world', is quite simply a false one.[37]

Schillebeeckx often acknowledges the formative influence his Dominican vocation holds for his theological work.[38] Indeed, in acknowledging the importance of his Dominican heritage he indicates that theology is always a contextual or historical activity, and hence he is quite unapologetic about the biographical characteristics of his own work.[39] Amongst these characteristics, he identifies his Dominican context as central:

> For the most part people live by stories. I myself live by my own story. When I became a Dominican I linked my life story with the family story of the Dominicans; as a result, my life story took on a new orientation and I picked up the thread of the story of the Order in my own way. So my own life has become part of the Dominican family story: a chapter in it. Through the story of the Order I have attained my own identity.[40]

adding a new ideology to those which mankind already possesses in such plenty: that is to say, Christology itself! I fear at times that with the keen edge of our creedal utterances about Jesus we dull the critical vision of his prophecy, having as it does real consequences for our society and politics. A one-sided apotheosis of Jesus that restricts him exclusively to the divine side actually has the effect . . . of silencing Jesus the prophet.' Schillebeeckx, *Jesus: An Experiment in Christology* (London: Collins, 1979), p. 671. *Jezus, het verhaal van een levende* (Bloemendaal: Nelissen, 1974).

37 Schillebeeckx, 'Non-religious Humanism and Belief in God', in *God and Man*, pp. 41–84 (p. 47). 'Niet-godsdienstig humanisme en het godsgeloof', in *God en mens*, pp. 36–65. First published in *Modern niet-godsdienstig humanisme* (Nijmegen, 1961), pp. 74–112.

38 Schillebeeckx, *God is New Each Moment: in Conversation with Huub Oosterhuis and Piet Hoogeven*, trans. David Smith (Edinburgh: T&T Clark, 1983). *God is ieder ogenblik nieuw: gesproken met Edward Schillebeeckx* (Baarn: Ambo, 1982); Schillebeeckx, *Theologisch testament: notarieel nog niet verleden* (Baarn: Nelissen, 1994).

39 Philip Kennedy draws attention to the 'biographical' nature of Schillebeeckx's theology: 'Explaining Edward Schillebeeckx's distinction as a Christian thinker necessarily calls for attention to his biography. Rephrased somewhat, his theology is biographical. His publications cannot really be prised apart from his life's history. Although anecdotal material is rarely evident in his writings, every article and book he has written has been produced from, and responds to, a specific circumstance impinging on his life. If he is not responding to an event or experience in his publications, then he is addressing an individual or current of thought. In short, his texts have contexts. Familiarity with the latter assists comprehension of the former.' Philip Kennedy, *Schillebeeckx* (Collegeville: Liturgical Press, 1993), p. 13. Kennedy describes Schillebeeckx's theology as a 'biographically determined theology'. Kennedy, *Deus Humanissimus. The Knowability of God in the Theology of Edward Schillebeeckx* (Fribourg: Fribourg University Press, 1993), p. 29.

40 'Dominican Spirituality', in *God among Us: the Gospel Proclaimed*, trans. John Bowden (London: SCM, 1983), pp. 232–248 (p. 232). 'Dominicaanse spiritualiteit', in *Evangelie Verhalen* (Baarn: Nelissen, 1982).

Schillebeeckx's Dominican identity shows itself directly in his theology in at least two ways: in its indebtedness to certain characteristics of the Dominican spirit and equally in the influence of specific Dominican mentors. And so, this section of the chapter has two 'subdivisions': Schillebeeckx's Dominican identity as this is reflected in his description of Dominican spirituality and life, and his Dominican identity as he has inherited this from three particular mentors: Thomas Aquinas, Dominic De Petter and Marie-Dominique Chenu. Turning first to the Dominican characteristics of a specifically Dominican spirituality and life, the source for his conviction that theology is both a pastoral and an intellectual discipline becomes evident.

There are certainly a number of good 'biographies' of Schillebeeckx that discuss his Dominican vocation and its influence upon his theology in some depth.[41] There are also a number of essays and sermons in which Schillebeeckx himself writes of Dominican life and spirituality.[42] This is therefore not an exhaustive account of his Dominican life. The premise underlying this brief biographical intermezzo is that Schillebeeckx's theology of revelation – its content and structure – receives some of its characteristics from his own Dominican formation. This is in turn significant for his theological anthropology whose essential features of a non-dualistic, non-reductive, non-competitive relation between the divine and human provide him with a definition of humanity as the vocation to intimacy with God within history. In this context it is interesting to note in particular three of his own reflections on his Dominican vocation and tradition because they are clearly indicative of his understanding of the relation between church and world and between the divine and human.

The first of these reflections is taken from Schillebeeckx's recollections of his initial choice for the Dominican life. Schillebeeckx underlines the centrality given both to human friendship and to the graciousness of God as decisive factors in his choice of this religious order.[43] He contrasts this with the austerity of the Jesuits.[44] In light of this contrast it is particularly

---

[41] See especially Borgman, *Edward Schillebeeckx: een theoloog in zijn geschiedenis*, pp. 40–50; Kennedy, *Deus Humanissimus*, pp. 39–40.

[42] Schillebeeckx, 'Dominican Spirituality'; 'Dominicaanse spiritualiteit', *Biekorf* (1954), 154–162; 'Domingo de Guzmán, Founder of the movement of "the Dominican family"', in *For the Sake of the Gospel*, trans. John Bowden (New York: Crossroad, 1990), pp. 119–124 (p. 123); 'Domingo de Guzmán. Stichter van de beweging "de dominicaanse familie"', in *Om het behoud van het evangelie* (Baarn: Nelissen, 1989).

[43] In recalling his initial decision for the Dominicans, Schillebeeckx highlights the importance of the value given to friendship. Borgman underlines the theological interpretation, which Schillebeeckx would later attach to this value given to human friendship: the profound harmony between the natural and supernatural. *Edward Schillebeeckx: een theoloog in zijn geschiedenis*, p. 53.

[44] For Schillebeeckx's description of the contrast between Jesuit and Dominican life, see *Theologisch testament*, pp. 19–22; *God is New Each Moment*, pp. 4–9. Borgman

15

interesting to note the austerity of the Dominican novitiate itself in Ghent during the time when Schillebeeckx was there, and he comments on this himself.[45] Yet it is the stress placed upon God's grace and the genuine openness to the world that attracted him to the Dominican life and distinguished the austerity of religious life as it was when he began as a novice at Ghent from the Jesuit austerity he had observed as a student at Turnhout. These same features distinguish his theology from the theologies of some of his contemporaries. A fundamental confidence in God's graciousness, an openness to the world and a commitment to the human are the constant threads that give his work its continuity in general.[46] They also account for the non-dualistic and non-competitive characteristics of his theological anthropology in particular. For Schillebeeckx the 'dilemma of God *or* humanity' is always a false one, a truth underlined in his comments on the principles of renewal for religious life in the wake of Vatican II:

> We of course tend spontaneously to think of adapting the religious life to the modern age rather than adapting it to the gospel, but the problem arises at once – what should function as the principle of adaptation? Should it be the modern age itself, or the gospel? My question, however, is this – is this a false dilemma?'[47]

Schillebeeckx considers any theology that allows for the dilemma of God *or* humanity is mistaken, a conviction evident in his reflections on his own formation to religious life.[48]

offers an analysis of the factors influencing Schillebeeckx's decision for the Dominicans: *Edward Schillebeeckx: een theoloog in zijn geschiedenis*, pp. 40–50.

[45] Schillebeeckx, *Theologisch testament*, p. 23.

[46] Schillebeeckx often draws a contrast between theologies coloured by a human–divine dualism, frequently identifying these as 'Augustinian', or 'medieval'. By 'medieval' he means later than Thomas, or those modern misinterpretations of Thomas that attribute this dualism to Thomas himself. Particularly good examples of this are found in his commentary on *Gaudium et spes* and in one of his essays on Christian humanism. See 'Christian Faith and Man's Expectation for the Future on Earth'; 'Humble Humanism', in *World and Church*, pp. 19–31. 'Nederig humanisme', in *Wereld en kerk*, pp. 71–80. First Published in *Kuulterleven* 16 (1949), 12–21.

[47] Schillebeeckx, 'Religious Life in a Secularised World', in *The Mission of the Church*, pp. 132–170 (pp.132–133). 'Kloosterleven in een geseculariseerde wereld', in *De zending van de kerk*, pp. 235–262. First published under the title, 'Het nieuwe mens-en Godsbeeld in conflict met het religieuze leven', in *Tijdschrift voor Theologie* 7 (1967), 1–27.

[48] This is an interesting point when considering that Schillebeeckx's own formation to religious life took place many years before its renewal in the wake of Vatican II. Religious life prior to this renewal tended to place greater emphasis on a more dualistic interpretation of the church/world relation.

It is worth remarking here upon the particular relation between the priority of God's grace and the value accorded to the human that Schillebeeckx describes in his reflections on his vocation. He draws a connection between the Dominican emphasis placed on the graciousness of God, the stress placed on the 'priority of grace' that allows 'God to be God' – 'de prioriteit van de genade en het "God God laten zijn"' and the importance given to human friendship and a pastoral openness to the world.[49] What emerges from his reflections on his own vocation is the conviction that the balance between church and world and between the divine and human, which he found so compelling in the Dominican charism, is achieved precisely because of the priority given to God's grace.[50] It is not surprising therefore that Schillebeeckx will later describe the task of theology as primarily the task of letting 'God be God'.[51] His own theological anthropology, especially his writings on the meaning of human action and temporality, will develop from – and be grounded in – his understanding of God's transcendence.[52] Indeed for him the meaning of human action is dependent upon an interpretation of the transcendent, that is, upon an interpretation of the nature of God. This is consistent with his conviction that theological anthropology is the discourse on 'God close to humanity in grace' – and in this he is entirely consistent with his Dominican tradition.[53]

From Schillebeeckx's writings on his own Dominican vocation certain key theological ideas emerge: the priority of God's grace and the value of the human in light of God's graciousness. These are symbolized for him in the importance given to human friendship within Dominican life. His writings on Dominican spirituality more generally also indicate the influence of particular Dominican ideals on his theology. In an essay on Dominican spirituality, Schillebeeckx describes the essentially pastoral and evangelical

---

[49] Schillebeeckx, *God is New Each Moment*, p. 9; *God is ieder ogenblik nieuw*, p. 20.

[50] Schillebeeckx makes this connection in a conversation in which he contrasts the 'balance' of Dominican life with the 'competitive' or 'combative' nature of Jesuit life, a contrast that he attributes to the Dominican stress placed on the priority of God's grace – letting 'God be God'. *God is New Each Moment*, pp. 8–9.

[51] 'Thomas Aquinas: Passion for Truth as Loving Service to Men and Women', in *For the Sake of the Gospel*, pp. 125–129 (p. 125). 'Thomas van Aquino – passie voor de waarheid als liefdedienst aan mensen', in *Om het behoud van het evangelie*, pp. 57–60.

[52] This comes into focus most clearly in his critique of humanism. A particularly good example is his essay 'Religion and the World: Renewing the Face of the Earth'. It is also at the heart of his analysis of the strengths and weaknesses of contemporary theology and forms the basis of his criticism of certain existentialist theologies. Substantive examples of this critique can be found in the essays: 'Life in God and Life in the World'; 'New Trends in Present day Dogmatic Theology'.

[53] Schillebeeckx, 'Christian Faith and Man's Expectation for the Future on Earth', p. 73. Schillebeeckx attributes atheism in part to false understandings of God's nature as transcendence that result then in the human–divine relation collapsing into competition or negation. See 'Religion and the World: Renewing the Face of the Earth'.

nature of Dominican life and tradition.[54] Here the twofold commitment to serious intellectual engagement with the tradition and pastoral engagement with the needs of the contemporary church and world is identified as an important aspect of Dominican life. At the heart of this reflection is the evangelical imperative, which gives the Dominicans the title of Order of Preachers. In essence, as Schillebeeckx summarizes the Dominican tradition, 'Evangelism without the church or the church without evangelism is essentially un-Dominican'.[55]

This twofold commitment to the richness of tradition and to the needs of the present Schillebeeckx describes as the grace of the Dominican foundation:

> Dominic wove a new fabric, created a new religious programme. Thus the Dominican order was born from the charisma of the combination of admonitory and critical recollection of the spiritual heritage of the old monastic and canonical religious life with the 'modernistic' religious experiment of the thirteenth century. Dominic had a fine sensitivity both to the religious values from the past and to the religious promise for the future emanating from the modern experiments of his time. The Dominican Order was born out of this two-fold charisma. I would say that this is our *gratia originalis*, the grace at the origin of our Order.[56]

It is quite clear from Schillebeeckx's own theology that this twofold charism – a sensitivity to the values of the past and the promise or possibilities of the present – defines not only religious life but also the task of the theologian; and the common thread is the evangelical nature.

The essay in which Schillebeeckx describes this twofold Dominican charism is a reprise of an earlier article on Dominican spirituality, expanded to include some reflections of the renewal of religious life more generally as discussed in the Vatican II document on religious life, *Perfectae caritatis*. The principle insight of *Perfectae caritatis* to which he turns is the Christological and hence evangelical norm for religious life: 'to follow Jesus is the ultimate and supreme norm of any form of religious life.' This is a summary of the following text:

> The sensitive renewal of religious life involves: the constant return to the source of Christian life in general and the original genius of the

---

[54] Schillebeeckx,'Dominican Spirituality'. Incorporating reflections on the renewal of religious life in light of the Vatican II document *Perfectae caritatis*, this includes much of the material of the 1954 essay 'Dominicaanse spiritualiteit'.

[55] Schillebeeckx,'Dominican Spirituality', p. 246.

[56] Ibid. p. 238.

religious foundations in particular; together with the modifications of such foundations to accommodate new circumstances. This renewal, open both to the influence of the holy [*sic*] Spirit and to the guidance of the church, should be furthered according to the following principles:

a) the essential characteristic of religious life is that following of Christ enjoined by the gospel. All foundations are to regard this as their fundamental rule

Although this Christological and therefore evangelical norm seems obvious enough for a theology of religious life, it is worth remarking upon because it indicates very clearly the extent to which a particular theology of revelation had been taken up by the work of the Second Vatican Council in all of its aspects.[57] The ultimate norm of religious life as it is described in *Perfectae caritatis* is in line with the work of renewal in all areas of the life of the church in light of the rediscovery of the scriptures as a unique source of God's self-revelation.[58] Schillebeeckx's commitment to this theology of revelation is clear: 'Dominican spirituality is only valid in so far as it takes up the story of Jesus', which means therefore that Dominican spirituality is 'subject to the criterion of the sources of Christian life', namely 'the Gospel of Jesus Christ', as 'the source which is never exhausted and always offers new possibilities'.[59]

The evangelical nature of religious life in which the following of Christ as enjoined by the gospel is the norm, means the twofold charism, which is the Dominicans' *gratia originalis,* has a critical function, not necessarily always a conciliatory one and certainly never a passive one. Dominican religious

---

[57] *Dei verbum*, art. 2: 'It has pleased God in his goodness and wisdom to reveal himself and to make known the secret purpose of his will (see Eph. 1, 9). This brings it about that through Christ, God's Word made flesh, and in his Holy Spirit, human beings can draw near to the Father and become sharers in the divine nature (see Eph. 2, 18; Pt 1, 4). By thus revealing himself God, who is invisible (Col. 1, 15; 1 Tim. 1, 17), in his great love speaks to humankind as friends (see Ex 33, 11; Jn 15, 14–15) and enters into their life (see Bar. 3, 38), as to invite and receive them into relationship with himself. . . . By this revelation the truth, both about God and about the salvation of humankind, inwardly dawns on us in Christ, who is in himself both the mediator and the fullness of revelation.' See Tanner, *Decrees of the Ecumenical Councils,* II, pp. 971–981 (p. 972).

[58] *Dei verbum*, art. 25: 'Likewise the synod strongly and specially urges all the faithful, particularly religious, to learn by frequent study of the scriptures "the surpassing worth of knowing Jesus Christ" (Ph 3, 8), for "ignorance of the scriptures is ignorance of Christ"'. Tanner, *Decrees of the Ecumenical Councils, II,* p. 980.

[59] Schillebeeckx, 'Dominican Spirituality', p. 233. For Schillebeeckx's critique of the early schemata of *Dei verbum* and his influence in the discussions leading to the final text see Guiseppe Alberigo and Joseph Komonchak, eds, *History of Vatican II*, vols I–II (Maryknoll: Orbis, 1995–1997), pp. 426–429; 73–75; 236–246.

life as *présence à Dieu* and as *présence au monde* is founded upon a critical norm, God's self-revelation:

> It is essential for Dominican spirituality to attend to God as he has already revealed himself to us in the past and to attend to the present-day 'signs of the times' in which the same God, who is faithful to us, makes his appeal. Any one-sidedness – in one-track, uncritical judgement either of the past or of what prove to be the symptoms of the future in the present – is un-Dominican. Dominic submits the present, with its own possibilities, to comparison with the dangerous recollection of certain events and legacies from the past. . . this must remain its genius. The *présence à Dieu* and the *présence au monde* describe the very nature of Dominican spirituality throughout the history of the order.[60]

At the centre of this spirituality there is an understanding of the historical and personal nature of God's revelation, and hence the Dominican life is lived in relation to God and to the world according to the 'dangerous recollection' of its source, which is the gospel. This relation to the world is open, dynamic and above all, critical – defined by the 'dangerous recollection' of God's self-revelation incarnate within history. Above all, it is a relation to the world that is confident and hopeful, grounded in trust in God's faithfulness.

The nature of Dominican spirituality – *présence à Dieu* and *présence au monde* – is reflected in Schillebeeckx's description of epistemology as it is appropriate to theology. The development or dynamism of theological insight involves a process of conversion: 'The growth of insight into the content of the evangelical message is not simply a growth of knowledge, but always a conversion.'[61] This epistemology of conversion is the consequence of theology's dependence upon God's self-revelation in history and it is founded upon two convictions. The first is that God is faithful in this historical revelation. That is to say, God's revelation in history is the revelation of God's self; hence it is essential for theology 'to attend to God as he has already revealed himself to us in the past and to attend to the present day "signs of the times" in which the same God, who is faithful to us makes his appeal.'[62] The second is that God has revealed himself as the meaning or 'value' of human life and hence attending to this revelation is a critical

---

[60] Schillebeeckx, 'Dominican Spirituality', p. 240.
[61] Schillebeeckx, 'Is the Church Adrift?', p. 35.
[62] Schillebeeckx, 'Dominican Spirituality', p. 240.

activity that interrogates our interpretation both of the past and of the present:[63]

> The fact is that what is new, and profoundly experienced, can obscure earlier truths which remain believable only insofar as they are thoroughly rethought right down to the core of their original formulation and become . . . newly discovered. It may appear paradoxical, but the recognition of old truths sometimes demands a more profound conversion than the recognition of attractive, freshly discovered truths which have the advantage of a new and surprising brilliance. . . . Although theological reflection can help us in the renewed discovery of old truths, it is nevertheless only a subordinate servant.[64]

Schillebeeckx goes on to describe all theology as a subordinate servant to the 'breakthrough of a new appreciation of God, of God as a value in and of himself worthy of love – and the heart and centre of all other values'.[65] This is the nature of the growth in theological insight as a 'conversion' that allows theology to reinterpret the past and appropriate the present critically; or, in a language that echoes his comments on Dominican spirituality: being attentive to the *présence à Dieu,* and the *présence au monde* requires an epistemology of conversion.

In his reflections on his Dominican life there are some clear indications of important features of Schillebeeckx's theological anthropology, both in its content and method. In terms of its content, the priority of God's grace allows Schillebeeckx room for considerable hope and confidence in human being and in human action within his theological anthropology. In his theology grace is always described in relation to nature; and here in his reflections on Dominican spirituality, grace is described particularly in relation to human action:

> Belief in the absolute priority of God's grace in any human action: the theologal direction of the Dominican life and its programme in relation to ethics, the world, society and the betterment of people. No cramped self-concern but trust in God: I can trust God more than myself. Therefore a tranquil and happy spirituality. God still gives an unexpected future to the limited meaning and scope of my own actions.[66]

---

[63] Schillebeeckx, 'What is Theology?', p. 108; 'Theologia *or* Oikonomia?', p. 84.
[64] Schillebeeckx, 'Life in God and Life in the World', p. 95.
[65] Ibid.
[66] Schillebeeckx, 'Dominican Spirituality', p. 241.

This relation between grace and human action – divine and human freedom – which Schillebeeckx transposes into the relation between human activity within our history and the future of this history, is the centrepiece of his theological anthropology, as will emerge in this chapter from a reading of his critique of *Gaudium et spes*.[67]

The other feature of his theological anthropology that is central, and to which this first is clearly related, is a non-dualistic and non-reductive relation between the human and the divine. Schillebeeckx holds consistently to this relation in his description of the human. In his essay on Dominican life it is captured in his reflection on the meaning of apostolicity:

> Religious life in the light of the gospel (*vita apostolica*) as the atmosphere in which the Dominican is *apostolic* (*salus animarum*, salvation as the aim of the activity of the Order): through preaching in all its forms. The result of that is *contemplari* and *contemplata aliis tradere* (i.e. the agreement between what a person proclaims and their own life.)[68]

The reference here to Thomas' maxim: *contemplari et contemplata aliis tradere* is the classic Dominican understanding that apostolicity means the 'essential insertion of study into the structure of Dominican evangelism'.[69] What is so important for Schillebeeckx's theological anthropology is the non-dualistic nature of the human person upon which this apostolicity depends: the agreement between what a person proclaims and his or her own life. There is an intrinsic relation between what it means to be human in relation to God and what it means to be human in the world – between humanity's 'metaphysical' and 'moral' significance. This thread runs throughout Schillebeeckx's theology generally and is a particular emphasis of his theological anthropology.[70]

A further comment on Dominican spirituality and Schillebeeckx's theological anthropology concerns the centrality of the humanity of Jesus, and this touches upon both the content of the anthropology and its method. In Schillebeeckx's Christology, the humanity of Jesus is presented as

---

[67] Schillebeeckx, 'Christian Faith and Man's Expectation for the Future on Earth'.

[68] Schillebeeckx, 'Dominican Spirituality', p. 241.

[69] Ibid.

[70] Here the influence of Chenu for Schillebeeckx on the relation between contemplation and incarnation is telling; this is examined in Chapter 3 of this book. Chenu's *St Thomas d'Aquin et la théologie* (Paris: Editions de Seuil, 1959), provides a thoughtful discussion of Thomas' understanding of theology as a contemplative and apostolic vocation. For a description of Chenu's own understanding of the Dominican vocation as the 'mixed life' of contemplation and apostolate see Christophe Potworowski, *Contemplation and Incarnation: The Theology of Marie-Dominique Chenu* (Montreal: McGill-Queen's University Press, 2001), esp. pp. 3–40.

'the personal manifestation of God's love for humankind'.[71] This is developed through a particular systematic exposition of the doctrine of the incarnation and will be discussed at length in Chapters 3 and 4. The particular manner in which Jesus is the personal manifestation of God's love gives Schillebeeckx's theological anthropology its 'structure'; consequently a kenotic Christology becomes normative for a theology of human action. It emerges from Schillebeeckx's understanding of incarnation that Christology is the 'method' for a theocentric anthropology. The groundwork for that discussion has been laid in his theology of revelation from which he describes theology as 'theocentric on its content and Christological in its method'.[72] This will be discussed further in this chapter in the section on the personal and immanent nature of God in dialogue with humanity.

The final comment here on Dominican spirituality and Schillebeeckx's theological anthropology follows from the centrality of the humanity of Jesus and the importance this places on the personal and historical nature of human being. This importance of the person is captured in the Dominican 'principle of dispensation'. Schillebeeckx describes this principle as 'the respect for the particular personal charisma of a fellow Dominican within the Dominican community, bearing in mind the purpose of the order.' Acknowledging that this can be 'an extremely dangerous principle, which has been abused to disastrous effect', he makes the telling observation that 'Dominic would rather take that risk than give up', its 'human and Christian significance'.[73] This is a rather startlingly clear indication of the non-dualistic and non-reductive nature of the relation between the divine and the human: the formative influence on Dominican religious life, as Schillebeeckx recounts it, is the relationship between the 'human and Christian significance' of religious life. In light of this 'principle of dispensation' it is unsurprising that an important feature of Schillebeeckx's own theological anthropology is the importance of the personal nature of human being in which both the individual and the individual in relation to others are central to a fully Christian anthropology. Nor is it surprising that in his theology of revelation there is value given to the historical nature of human self-knowledge or self-awareness. Revelation is addressed to a human 'consciousness' that is not *a*historical but is historical – temporal and contingent – and therefore dynamic and changing.[74]

What emerges from Schillebeeckx's reflections on his own personal vocation to Dominican life and on the tradition and spirituality of the Order is a

---

[71] Schillebeeckx, 'Dominican Spirituality', p. 242; *Christ the Sacrament*, esp. pp. 2–45; 'The New Trends in Present-Day Dogmatic Theology', pp. 123–127.

[72] Schillebeeckx, 'What is Theology?', pp. 138–143.

[73] Schillebeeckx, 'Dominican Spirituality', p. 243.

[74] Schillebeeckx, 'What is Theology?'; 'Christian Faith and Man's Expectation for the Future on Earth'.

description not only of the spirit of Dominican life but equally of his own theology. At its heart Schillebeeckx's theology is characterized by a trust in the graciousness of God; and founded upon this priority of grace is a commitment to a genuine openness to the world. The ground for this theology, in both its trust in grace and openness to the world, is a spirituality centred on the humanity of Jesus. The importance of the human is the focus of both the priority of grace and openness to the world.[75]

Turning now to those Dominicans who have influenced Schillebeeckx's approach to theology, the best place to start is with Dominic himself. In a brief essay on Dominic and his personal qualities and their corresponding influence on the Order he founded, Schillebeeckx draws particular attention the critical and prophetic nature of theology's engagement with both church and world.[76] His reflection on Dominic is interesting as it reveals again something of the character of his own theology.

The first half of the twentieth century was an immensely rich period for theology. It was also a period of great turbulence and conflict; and it is remarkable that this period has emerged as one of such theological flourishing. It is in this context of conflict and of intellectual creativity and richness that Schillebeeckx's own theology developed. Indeed Schillebeeckx himself identifies such flourishing in a time of ferment as a peculiarly Dominican characteristic – one that he traces back to Dominic:

> Judged by the ups and downs in our Dominican history, Dominicans, like Dominic, seem only to be at their best when a particular dominant culture is in process of disappearing and a new culture is making progress but is not yet dominant. Outside periods of crisis Dominicans seem regularly to go to sleep and rather to endorse uncritically the prevalent culture, even giving it theological justification. In this respect too we were often great teachers, and alas even grand inquisitors. Like Dominic, Dominicans only become awake, alert and evangelical when something in the world is in process of springing up or bursting out

[75] Schillebeeckx, 'Dominican Spirituality', pp. 241–242. The nature of religious life and its tradition is clearly dynamic rather than static. It is therefore not at all surprising that Schillebeeckx does not attempt to offer a comprehensive list of particularly Dominican characteristics. Rather he offers a brief description of some of these characteristics without suggesting that these are exhaustive of a living tradition and spirituality. Indeed the characteristics he highlights are rather 'autobiographical' in nature and therefore draw attention to significant features of his own theology. These particular characteristics are: belief in an absolute priority of God's grace; commitment to an apostolic life in light of the gospel through preaching in all its forms; a spirituality and mysticism centred on the humanity of Jesus; and a genuine openness to the world.

[76] Schillebeeckx, 'Domingo de Guzmán'.

and new signs of hope and freedom are announcing themselves on the horizon of society and culture. There are in fact people who are at their best in times of crisis and opposition; perhaps we are people of that ilk.[77]

This reflection on Dominic, delivered as a homily for the Feast of St Dominic, has an autobiographical ring to it. In its title Schillebeeckx refers to his religious community as the 'Dominican family', and it is not hard to imagine he is implicitly drawing a parallel between the thirteenth and twentieth centuries.

Schillebeeckx's own writings are grounded in a confidence in God's graciousness and in human action; hence they reflect his hope in both the life of the church and the world, yet this is never an uncritical hope. Side by side with his conviction that humanity is creatively making its own history – 'humanizing the world' – lies an acknowledgement of the 'abrasive history of suffering'.[78] Alongside his theology of church in which he describes the church as the 'sacrament of the risen Christ', there is a critically restless sense that the church stops short of its evangelical task.[79] In all of this, Schillebeeckx is consistently reflecting strands of his Dominican tradition.

[77] Ibid. p. 123.
[78] On the capacity of humanity to make history by 'humanizing the world', see the essays on secularism: 'Non-Religious Humanism and Belief in God'; 'Dialogue with God and Christian Secularity'; 'Religion and the World: Renewing the Face of the Earth'; 'Humble Humanism'. For Schillebeeckx's description of history as, 'a motley collection of arrant nonsense complicated by abrasive suffering,' see 'The Search for the Living God', in *God and Man*, pp. 18–40 (p. 22). 'Op zoek naar de levende God', in *God en Mens*, pp. 20–35. This text was delivered as his inaugural lecture in Nijmegen in 1958. For a discussion of the idea of suffering in Schillebeeckx's theology see Kathleen McManus, 'Suffering in the Theology of Edward Schillebeeckx', *Theological Studies* 60 (1999), 476–491. McManus offers a brief analysis of the influence of Thomas for Schillebeeckx in this context.
[79] This is the ecclesiology which emerges from his *Christ the Sacrament*, p. 56. Schillebeeckx's critique of the church emerges in his analysis of several of the documents of Vatican II where he registers his concern over the inherent ambivalence and incompleteness of these texts. His criticisms of particular texts, most notably those concerning the laity and religious life, can be read as a general commentary on the work of the Council. See Edward Schillebeeckx, 'The Typological Definition of the Christian Layman according to Vatican II', in *The Mission of the Church*, pp. 90–116. 'De typologische definitie van de christelijke leek volgens Vaticanum II', in *De zending van de Kerk*, pp. 134–153. First published in *De kerk van Vaticanum II: Commentaren op de concilie constitutie over de kerk, II*, ed. G. Baraúna (Bilthoven: Nelissen, 1966), pp. 285–304. See also: 'Religious Life in a Secularised World'; 'Christian Faith and Man's Expectation for the Future on Earth'. His most substantive criticism is directed at the prevailing ecclesiology of Vatican II, and he remains convinced that the failure of the Council to achieve a full expression of collegiality, and the extent to which it compromised on this, is its most critical weakness: 'It was the conciliar assembly of the church itself which on a large

This initial outline of Schillebeeckx's theology and its anthropology – a theology characterized by a trust in the graciousness of God and an anthropology characterized by profound hope in the human that is founded upon this priority of grace can be filled in now more substantively by considering the influence of three further Dominican mentors who have been most significant in his theological formation: Thomas Aquinas, Marie-Dominique Chenu and Dominic De Petter. Schillebeeckx's theology is influenced by his own formation and experience of Dominican life, and it also undoubtedly receives something of its distinctively Dominican character from these fellow Dominican theologians and philosophers.

The following remarks concerning the influence of Thomas, Chenu and De Petter are not exhaustive. As with the material on the Dominican tradition just discussed, the following comments on his Dominican mentors are taken from Schillebeeckx's own writings, either explicitly or implicitly. What is most interesting here is Schillebeeckx's own interpretation and appropriation of the works of these thinkers because this provides important indications of his own theological convictions.[80] Although this is most especially the case with respect to Thomas – Schillebeeckx is carefully selective in his interpretation of Thomas from among a great plurality of possible interpretations – his interpretation of the significance of Chenu and de Petter reveals much about his theological development, both in its areas of continuity and areas of change and discontinuity.

For Schillebeeckx the theologian acts as a 'catalyst' for the church: the theologian is 'called to stand at a dangerous crossing of the roads – at the point where faith comes into contact with modern thought and the whole new philosophical situation.'[81] This is precisely his interpretation of Thomas: 'As Aquinas himself said, nothing is so paralysing as habitual thought which

scale, after sensitive concessions to a minority which was powerful in church politics but theologically one-sided (fixated on Trent and Vatican I), promised its believers, and explicitly also the theologians among them, Christian freedom within the open space of the binding gospel of Jesus Christ. And when this Christian freedom recognised by the Council was not subsequently guaranteed and protected by church law, this promise became an empty gesture, without any evangelical influence in our history. Then the breath of the Council was cut off and its spirit, the Holy Spirit was extinguished. Then, by virtue of various concerns (which were often matters of church politics), church hierarchies achieved an uncontrolled power over men and women of God.' Edward Schillebeeckx, *Church: The Human Story of God*, trans. John Bowden (London: SCM, 1990), p. xiv. *Mensen als verhaal van God* (Baarn: Nelissen, 1989).

[80] These comments are neither an assessment of the adequacy of Schillebeeckx's interpretations of Aquinas, De Petter or Chenu, nor are they intended to suggest that these are the only Dominican influences on his theology (it is impossible to imagine that Yves Congar has not influenced Schillebeeckx). They are simply the debts which he acknowledges most transparently in his own writings – an indication that the importance which he attaches to their work tells us something significant of his own.

[81] Schillebeeckx, 'What is Theology?', p. 163.

26

makes us adhere firmly to traditional views that, on critical analysis, frequently turn out to be false views.'[82] Schillebeeckx's most significant mentors – after Thomas himself – are two fellow Dominicans who deliberately interpreted Thomas in light of modern thought and the 'new philosophical situation'. De Petter read Thomas in light of contemporary phenomenology, and Chenu read Thomas in light of modern historical consciousness. Significantly, what De Petter and Chenu hold in common, and Schillebeeckx with them, is the commitment to reading Thomas himself rather than relying on scholastic commentaries. Schillebeeckx's own interpretation of Thomas is clearly influenced by De Petter – in the interpretation of Aquinas' epistemology – and by Chenu – in the emphasis placed on Thomas as a positive theologian – and at the same time he follows their commitment to reading Thomas himself and hence has his own interpretation to offer.[83]

Interestingly, Schillebeeckx entitles his reflection on the essentially liturgical nature of Thomas' theology: 'Thomas Aquinas: Passion for Truth as loving Service to Men and Women'.[84] In this essay Schillebeeckx depicts Thomas' understanding of the work of theology as an *opus divinum* in which theology is a 'distinctive kind of liturgical praise'; the activities of study and writing are likened by Thomas to the liturgical signing of the psalms in the Divine Office. Schillebeeckx's clear intention is to present Thomas as a pastoral theologian, one for whom ethical practice, worship and theology as an intellectual discipline are bound inextricably together. At the same time, Schillebeeckx draws attention to the fact that Thomas did not conflate these aspects of human life.[85] Schillebeeckx clearly

---

[82] Ibid.

[83] Schillebeeckx's commitment to reading Thomas himself is clearly evident from his attention to Thomas' own context. He is careful not to attribute to Thomas 'modern' insights. This is true in his interpretation of Thomas' epistemology. See Schillebeeckx, 'The Non-conceptual Intellectual Dimension in Our Knowledge of God according to Aquinas'. It is also the case in his discussion of Thomas as both a speculative and as a positive theologian. See Schillebeeckx, 'What is Theology?', pp. 99–100; 124–126.

[84] Schillebeeckx, *For the Sake of the Gospel*, pp. 125–129.

[85] Schillebeeckx, 'What is Theology?', pp. 112–113: 'The christian experience of life harmonises the mind with the reality of revelation, which is precisely the field of the theologian's work. This unity of intimate christian life and theological acumen was precisely what formed the deep "theological sense" of which those saints who were also theologians were so often living witnesses. But we must be careful not to confuse these issues. The influence of the personal spiritual life on theology is formally only an inspirational power, the most suitable sphere from which to enter the field of theology. But it cannot replace the scientific work of theology and, from the theological point of view, it is of no value unless these affective insights are translated into theological terms. However much they may influence each other, it would be wrong to identify such different levels of life. The great contribution made by Aquinas, in making for the first time the necessary distinctions here should not be ignored'. The key phrase here is

interprets Thomas as a theologian for whom faith and reason are related, yet related in a manner that quite deliberately maintains the distinctiveness of both: 'theology, although it proceeds from faith, although it constantly presupposes this faith and serves it, is formally a question of scientific activity and insight, of research and of methodical precision'.[86] This relation of faith to reason and hence of the spiritual life to theology is grounded for Thomas, as for Schillebeeckx, in the sacramental structure of revelation.[87]

Schillebeeckx's interpretation of Aquinas on the nature of theology – its pastoral orientation that holds together intellectual discipline with an ethics of service to others – says as much about his own understanding of the vocation to theology as it says about Thomas:

> Thomas experienced the general call to serve God in the service of one's fellow human beings as being realised for him in this form: to serve God by expressing him as God to fellow men and women; to let God be God by letting him speak to others through his own human words. The *raison d'être* of his life lies in this service to his fellow men and women, which consists *ex professo* of being occupied with God, in order to let others share in these experiences and reflection on them. . . . For Thomas, being occupied in religious thought with God, human beings and the relationship between them is both a service to humankind and a distinctive kind of liturgical worship of God. Theological thought itself becomes both worship and apostolate.[88]

In this understanding of theology as both worship and apostolic activity, there is more than a suggestion that the vocation to theology is sacramental. Schillebeeckx makes this explicit: 'For Thomas, thought is the human material which he sanctifies as a christian and dedicates to God and at the same time that with which he seeks to be of service to his fellow human beings.'[89] This sacramental structure of theology mirrors the religious spirit of the

'the reality of revelation' by which Schillebeeckx underlines Thomas' understanding of both the objective and subjective nature of the knowing that is related to faith. 'What is Theology?', p. 104: 'Faith is conditioned by this revelation, in which we are addressed by God. Faith is therefore a way of knowing.'

[86] Schillebeeckx, 'What is Theology?', p. 113.

[87] Schillebeeckx, 'What is Theology?', p. 117: 'Revelation is accomplished in and through history, and we live now from this revelation in word and revelation in reality – in and through the sacramental reality of the church and through the church's service of the word. The history of salvation and the word give us, by virtue of the light of faith, a view of the revealed reality, with which we associate ourselves in faith.'

[88] Schillebeeckx, 'Thomas Aquinas', pp. 125–126.

[89] Ibid. p. 126.

Dominicans, the mixed life of contemplation and apostolate captured by the *devise*: '*contemplata aliis tradere*' – a phrase first used by Thomas and, on Schillebeeckx's interpretation, so well reflected in Thomas' own life.[90]

For Schillebeeckx, following Thomas, theology takes the 'form' of allowing 'God [to] be God by letting God speak to others through human words'. This form reflects the structure of revelation itself: revelation is always both 'a saving event and a preaching which bears upon this event'.[91] In this sacramental structure of revelation, the description of the vocation to theology finds its proper context in the vocation of humanity: the vocation to worship and to apostolic activity, to intimacy with God and to self-emptying as radical love of the other. In Schillebeeckx's brief remarks about Thomas and the vocation to theology, the relation between this one particular form that the human vocation might take, and the general form of human being defined as vocation, is apparent. For Thomas, on Schillebeeckx's telling, the theologian's vocation is simply a particular expression of the definition of human being as vocation. In other words, the remarks Schillebeeckx makes concerning the nature of theology in light of revelation are particular expressions of a more general theological anthropology that Schillebeeckx constructs from the nature of revelation itself. The vocation to intimacy with God – worship – is at the same time the vocation to intimacy with others – love. This theological anthropology in which humanity is defined as vocation holds together both the 'metaphysical' and 'moral' significance of human being.

The sacramental structure of revelation, the 'reality' of revelation in human and historical form, and hence of theology, faith incarnate in human reason, indicates Schillebeeckx's debt to two fellow interpreters of Thomas: De Petter and Chenu. Taught philosophy by De Petter, Schillebeeckx learned from him both the value of reading Aquinas in light of contemporary philosophy, phenomenology in particular, and also the value of a certain kind of metaphysics for theology, a non-essentialist metaphysics: 'metaphysics not centred upon concepts'.[92] This is perhaps best explained via an

---

[90] Schillebeeckx, 'Thomas Aquinas', p. 126. Schillebeeckx's interpretation of Thomas' understanding of the vocation to theology is interesting: the sacramental structure with which Schillebeeckx describes Thomas' understanding of the activity of theology is grounded in the sacramental structure of revelation itself, and it is this interpretation of revelation that gives Schillebeeckx's theology its own structure. This interpretation of Thomas reveals the real nature of Thomas' mentorship for Schillebeeckx.

[91] Schillebeeckx, 'The Lord and the Preaching of the Apostles', in *Revelation and Theology, I*, pp. 27–35 (p. 27). 'De Heer en de verkondiging der Apostelen', in *Openbaring en Theologie*, pp. 27–32. First published as 'De kyriale waardigheid van Christus en de verkondiging', in *Vox Theologica* 29 (1958), 34–38.

[92] Philip Kennedy, 'Continuity underlying Discontinuity: Schillebeeckx's Philosophical Background', *New Blackfriars* 70 (1989), 256–277 (p. 269). For a brief description of De Petter's interpretation of Aquinas and his subsequent epistemology see Mary

illustration – a passage in which Schillebeeckx interprets Thomas along the lines of De Petter's non-essentialist metaphysics. This epistemology hinges upon the relation between the conceptual and the non-conceptual in the act of knowing:

> [T]he most profound inspiration of Thomism absolutely refuses to apply the conceptual content itself to God and prefers to speak of intending God through the objectively referential value of our conceptual contents ... the entire objective, true, and speculative value of our concepts of faith resides in their *objective projection* in the direct line or the direction (and in no other line or direction) which is indicated by the content itself of these concepts (which are accessible to us), with the restriction however, that we have no suitable conception of the specifically divine manner of realisation of this content. The entire argument is based on the view that knowledge implies more than merely 'explicit, conceptual' knowledge. The mystery is preserved, but we have an objective view of it.[93]

Here the objective value of non-conceptual knowledge is developed: the objective value of non-conceptual knowledge resides in its objective projection that reflects the concept itself. In this way De Petter developed an epistemology that allowed for the objective knowledge of reality while also safeguarding the idea that reality itself cannot be grasped or circumscribed by concepts: the mystery is preserved, at the same time, we have an objective view of it.

Schillebeeckx holds to this 'metaphysics of reality' in his theology: faith is the knowing that comes from being addressed by the 'reality of revelation', that is, by the reality of the being of God. This transcends human knowing and is also available to human knowing. Schillebeeckx also holds to the essentially historical nature of revelation, and thus of theology, and here his debt to Chenu is clear. From Chenu Schillebeeckx learned a love of theology. Chenu, a medievalist and undeniably one of the greatest Thomists of the twentieth century, combined his academic explorations of the thirteenth century with a committed pastoral engagement with the twentieth century. He was arguably the most formative influence for Schillebeeckx, in his approach to theology, in his interpretation of Thomas and in his pastoral

---

Catherine Hilkert, 'Hermeneutics of History in the Theology of Edward Schillebeeckx', *Thomist* 51 (1987), 97–145 (pp. 100–102 ; esp. p. 100 n 9). De Petter's epistemology and its use by Schillebeeckx is described clearly and at length in Philip Kennedy, *Deus Humanissimus*, pp. 79–142. For De Petter's influence on Schillebeeckx's philosophical formation see Borgman, *Edward Schillebeeckx: een theoloog in zijn geschiedenis*, pp. 53–62.

[93] Schillebeeckx, 'What is Theology?', p. 137; p. 137 n 2.

commitment to the world around him.[94] From Chenu, Schillebeeckx learned that theology is never an *a*historical discipline, and Schillebeeckx's commitment to the intrinsic relation between speculative theology and positive theology is part of his debt to Chenu. The Christological structure that he develops as his theological method bears a very strong resemblance to the incarnational method of Chenu's own work.[95]

One brief hermeneutical caveat before turning from Schillebeeckx's Dominican heritage to a more formal analysis of revelation: Schillebeeckx's interpretation of Thomas, along with the influence of De Petter and Chenu, provide important hermeneutical keys to his own theology. Much of this is closest to the surface of his work in the earlier monographs and essays. Yet precisely because this influence of Thomas and Chenu, and to a lesser extent, De Petter, remains important to Schillebeeckx throughout his theological career, his earlier writings are interesting in their own right certainly and are also important source material for interpreting his later theology. However, Schillebeeckx's early work is not always received in his light. Much of the secondary literature on Schillebeeckx suggests that there are two prevailing tendencies when treating the earlier work, if it is treated at all. One tendency is to read these texts as forming a worthy but dull prelude to the later work, which is by contrast more interesting or important.[96]

---

[94] On the enduring influence of Chenu in current Aquinas studies see Jean-Pierre Torrell, *Initiation à St Thomas d'Aquin: Sa personne et son oeuvre* (Paris: Editions Cerf, 1993). On the pastoral nature of Chenu's theology see T. van den Hoogen, '"Pastoral Theologie": het theologisch procédé volgens Chenu', *Tijdschrift voor Theologie*, 33 (1993) 396–416. This article is a discussion of Chenu's theological reflection on pastoral engagement. At the heart of this reflection is the idea which is especially relevant to his influence on Schillebeeckx: his incarnational understanding of history. Salvation is revealed in history and hence history becomes the body of Christ. The important point here is that Chenu does not restrict his definition of the body of Christ to the church but expands this to include the world. For the influence of Schillebeeckx and the theological reading of Thomas which he acquired from Chenu on current Dutch studies of Thomas see Herwi Rikhof, 'Thomas at Utrecht', *Contemplating Aquinas. On the Varieties of Interpretation*, ed. Fergus Kerr (London: SCM, 2003), pp.105–136 (pp. 107–108).

[95] For a study of the incarnational method of Chenu's theology, see Potoworowski, *Contemplation and Incarnation*. This is examined at some length in Chapter 3 of this study.

[96] One of the great contributions of Borgman's intellectual biography of Schillebeeckx, *Edward Schillebeeckx: een theoloog in zijn geschiedenis*, is its analysis of the early material, much of which is in the form of lecture notes and remains unpublished. The English translation of this text makes available material which is otherwise only available in the original Dutch. Yet, while Borgman acknowledges the importance of this early work by Schillebeeckx, and also acknowledges the openness with which he approached interpretations of Thomas, largely as the result of the influence of Chenu and De Petter, he still leaves the reader with the impression that Schillebeeckx's 'Thomistic' phase is somewhat static and almost entirely left behind in his later theology. He contrasts the freedom and more dynamic nature of Schillebeeckx's post-Vatican II

The early phase is characterized as 'pre-critical' or 'dogmatic' by contrast with the later 'critical' and experience centred phase.[97] The second tendency is to privilege the early texts as belonging to Schillebeeckx's 'orthodox phase' when he is concerned with the truths of dogma.[98] The later works are then dismissed as not sufficiently concerned with the 'truths' of the Christian faith.

The difficulty is that neither of these readings does full justice to the earlier writings of Schillebeeckx and hence undermines interpretations of the later works. The first tendency fails to recognize the full significance of Chenu's influence insofar as it fails to recognize the importance of history and experience from the very beginning of Schillebeeckx's work. Far from interpreting Thomas as a closed system that gives rise to an ahisorical theology, the early Schillebeeckx interprets Thomas as a pastoral and biblical theologian who incorporated the understandings of history, tradition and experience, available in his own time, into his theology. In an essay on the nature of theology, Schillebeeckx quite pointedly interjects an interpretation on Thomas and his positive (historical) theology:

> It has frequently happened that Aquinas has been falsely interpreted because of his differently orientated terminology. Aquinas was a great theologian above all because of his positive theological output. It was astonishing for his period, especially as he was often unable easily to obtain certain positive works – such as the commentaries of a father of the church. . . [I]t is characteristic of Aquinas that he seldom used the term *theology*, but usually employed the term *sacra doctrina*. And for him *sacra doctrina* included very much more than pure speculative theology. Every scientific activity that was concerned with 'holy scripture' was, for Aquinas, genuine theology. Holy scripture was really the centre of all theological activity. But the method of dealing with it was always dependent on the new techniques of thought.[99]

writings with the more constrained and technical tone of the pre-conciliar work. This is not an entirely fair reading of Schillebeeckx whose early interpretation of Thomas is in itself dynamic and innovative. See Borgman, *Edward Schillebeeckx: een theoloog in zijn geschiedenis*, pp. 219; 234–240.

[97] For this distinction see Hilkert, 'Hermeneutics of History in the Theology of Edward Schillebeeckx'.

[98] For this approach to Schillebeeckx see Jean Galot, 'Schillebeeckx: What's he really saying about Jesus' ministry?' *The Catholic Register*, October 1983, p. 1; Leo Scheffczyk, 'Christology in the context of Experience: On the interpretation of Christ by E. Schillebeeckx', *Thomist* 48 (1984) 383–408. For analyses of the methodological issues involved see *The Schillebeeckx Case*, ed. Ted Schoof (New York: Paulist Press, 1983); Herwi Rikhof, 'Of Shadows and Substance: Analysis and Evaluation of the Documents in the Schillebeeckx Case', *Journal of Ecumenical Studies* 19 (1982), 244–267.

[99] Schillebeeckx, 'What is Theology?', p. 124.

This is not the description of an uncritical, abstract or *a*historical theology, and it belongs to the early phase of Schillebeeckx's career. There is no doubt here that Chenu's interpretation of Thomas as theologian is the driving force behind this description, and Schillebeeckx notes three of Chenu's works in this regard.[100]

The second tendency undermines the influence of De Petter insofar as it negates the importance of metaphysical realism and in doing this it misinterprets the meaning of 'truth', especially in relation to 'dogma', in Schillebeeckx's early work. For Schillebeeckx, as for both De Petter and the Aquinas he interprets, orthodoxy arrives at truth not as a series of propositions but at truth as 'reality':

> Orthodoxy is not primarily a question of adherence to the precise conceptual formulation of the articles of faith but of assent to the intent expressed in the formulation. As St Thomas Aquinas says: 'the act of faith has its term not in the proposition as it is enunciated – that is, in the conceptual image – but in the *reality itself*.' It is primarily the assent in faith to the saving reality of the gospel which makes anyone's faith 'orthodox'.[101]

In this description of orthodoxy, Schillebeeckx brings together the influences of Aquinas, De Petter and Chenu. It illustrates De Petter's epistemological concern to express human knowing as an objective activity of the intellect that extends via the capacity for non-conceptual knowledge – implicit intuition – to knowledge of reality. This is in contrast with conceptual knowledge. Faith, in this model, is a real knowledge of God. This is one point of interest in this passage. A further point of interest is that Schillebeeckx identifies this 'reality itself' – '*de werkelijkheid zelf*' – as 'the saving reality of the gospel' – '*de evangelische heilswerkelijkheid*' – and in doing this, he brings a historical and soteriological reference to De Petter's metaphysical realism. The reality faith knows is the God of revelation who acts in history. Reality is defined as the personal God of biblical revelation and here Chenu's interpretation of Thomas as a biblical theologian for whom the one God is the personal and Trinitarian God of revelation finds expression. In his own doctrine of God, Schillebeeckx will combine this metaphysical realism with the encounter in history of the personal God of revelation. He does this by holding together the doctrines of creation and salvation.

From this discussion of Schillebeeckx's Dominican heritage – its spirituality and tradition and the influence of Dominican fellow travellers – the characteristic features of Schillebeeckx's own theology have emerged.

---

[100] Ibid. p. 14 n 1. See Marie-Dominique Chenu, *La théologie comme science au XIIIe siècle* (Paris: Vrin, 1957); *La théologie au XXIIe siècle* (Paris: Vrin, 1957); *Introduction à l'étude de saint Thomas d'Aquin* (Paris: Vrin, 1950).

[101] Schillebeeckx, 'Life in God and Life in the World', p. 105.

His theology is characterized by a fundamental confidence in God's graciousness, which in turn grounds a commitment to an equally fundamental conviction that the life of faith, and hence theology, must be lived in openness to the world. Yet this is not an uncritical openness. Wedded to a confidence in God's graciousness is a spirituality founded upon the humanity of Jesus; hence Dominican life and theology are evangelical activities.

The implication for Schillebeeckx's theology of revelation and the theological anthropology it fashions are clear. Theology in light of revelation is the reflection on the transcendent as it is revealed in the immanent. God's graciousness has a Christological structure – the divine is given in the human and historical – and this is the ground for a theological anthropology which is sacramental and hence non-dualistic. Theological anthropology will reflect the creative, salvific, sanctifying, participative and personal nature of the human in its relation to the divine insofar as it is a theology that explicates the sacramental nature of grace: God's graciousness as both transcendent and immanent. As a result, Schillebeeckx's theological anthropology embraces both humanity's moral and metaphysical significance. The relation of the infinite to the finite is constitutive of the finite and presupposes the finite. The manner in which Schillebeeckx explicates this in light of the structure of revelation itself – in conversation with Thomas on the nature of God – is developed in the following three sections of this chapter: in the section on creation the influence of De Petter is clear; in the section on immanence the influence of Chenu is quite telling; and in the section on eschatology, Schillebeeckx's own interpretation comes most clearly into its own.

Humanity Created by God: God as Cause, Transcendence and Difference

Edward Schillebeeckx's theology is distinctively Dominican. In it many of the characteristics of Dominican life that first attracted him to the Order, and many of the features of its tradition and spirituality, are present. Some of these characteristics are very close to the surface of his writings; of these, the confidence in God's graciousness is paramount. For Schillebeeckx this is the ground for human knowledge of God and for the meaning of human life itself in all of its metaphysical and moral significance. Contra the death of God philosophies – and theologies – of the mid-twentieth century, he is convinced that the meaning of human life is grounded in – and hence can only be understood in relation to – the mystery of God.[102] Most important

---

[102] See Schillebeeckx, 'God in Dry Dock', in God and Man, p. 17. 'God op de helling', in God en mens, pp. 11–19. First published in Tijdschrift voor Geestelijk Leven 15 (1959), 397–409.

for him, it is the correct interpretation of God's transcendence, and not its negation, which allows for a definition of human being that adequately describes the ultimate meaning of humanity. Theological anthropology begins with the mystery of God. In other words, it begins from the point at which humanity encounters God: God's self-revelation.

As noted above in the opening section of this chapter on revelation, there are two key features to Schillebeeckx's theology of revelation that are especially apposite to a theological definition of human being: the first is the truth that 'the infinite is disclosed in the finite without destroying it'; the second is that 'God reveals himself by revealing humanity to itself'.[103] To understand Schillebeeckx's theological anthropology this means two things: the starting point and ground of theological anthropology is the mystery of God, and the mystery of God and of humanity are intrinsically related in a non-reductive, non-dualistic and non-contradictory manner. More specifically, the mystery of God reveals humanity to itself in a relation to God that is creative, salvific, sanctifying, participative and personal.[104]

In Schillebeeckx's words, the theological discourse on human being is to be determined by 'no cramped self-concern but trust in God.'[105] Attending to the mystery of God establishes the meaning of human being – it neither negates nor threatens it. Schillebeeckx's own understanding of the mystery of God can be found in his interpretation of Thomas' treatise on God in which he identifies and underlines a 'tripartite division' as a 'constant feature in all of Aquinas' works': 'We know God as *cause* and by his *transcendence* and by his utter *difference*'.[106] This same division is also a constant feature of Schillebeeckx's own theology and hence there are a number of ideas here that are important for any interpretation of his theological anthropology. The first is the concept of the relation to God as a relation of dependence that does not negate the human: 'I am myself in dependence upon God'. The second is the fundamental affirmation of the finite and contingent: 'I am myself in and of this world'. The third is the importance of metaphysics: the theological definition of human being holds together humanity's 'metaphysical and moral significance'.[107] The importance of metaphysics for a theological anthropology for Schillebeeckx can be inferred from the importance he attaches to a metaphysics of reality in his writings on the epistemology appropriate to theology and therefore his interest in De Petter, and it can be inferred from his critique of theologies

[103] Schillebeeckx, 'What is Theology?', p. 109; 'Christian Faith and Man's Expectation for the Future on Earth', p. 54.
[104] Schillebeeckx, 'Dialogue with God and Christian Secularity', p. 214.
[105] Schillebeeckx, 'Dominican Spirituality', p. 241.
[106] Schillebeeckx, 'The Non-conceptual Intellectual Dimension in Our Knowledge of God according to Aquinas', p. 163.
[107] Schillebeeckx, 'Dialogue with God and Christian Secularity', p. 215.

that abandon metaphysics.[108] It can also be inferred from his description of humanity as 'mystery' defined in relation to the 'mystery' of God.

Schillebeeckx's commitment to the human in its relation to God, to the human in its relation to the world and to a metaphysics of reality that impinges on both the doctrines of the being of God and the being of humanity, are all at play in his adoption of Thomas' tripartite distinction: 'We know God as *cause* and by his *transcendence* and by his utter *difference*.' Schillebeeckx's expansion upon this text is important:

> Aquinas shows . . . how creatures are always the basis of human knowledge of God, so that all that we can attain of God is what creatures tell us about him. Aquinas distinguishes three complementary aspects of this theophany. In his view, the theophany or creatureliness implies: (1) *the habitudo Dei ad creaturas*, or, more correctly, the *habitudo creaturarum ad Deum*, which forms the basis of the *via affirmationis*; (2) the *differentia creaturarum ab ipso*, through which God's complete difference from the world of creatures is affirmed: "he is not of those things which are caused by him," with the result that the affirmation is continually corrected by the *via negationis vel remotionis*; and (3) the affirmation of the fullness of being of the divine being-Other: "these things are not separated from him by any deficiency in him, because he transcends them," that is the supreme check on the negative correction of the *via affirmationis* exercised by the *via eminentiae*.[109]

This is a statement primarily concerned with epistemology and the knowability of God. This epistemology centres on the manner in which created nature is essential to knowledge of God who is not created and therefore complete difference; central to this argument is the idea that real knowledge of God is possible – *via affirmationis* – yet this knowledge is always conditioned by the *via negationis*. That is to say, real knowledge of God is possible, and this knowledge is at the same time an unknowing. Real knowledge of God is always conditioned by God's transcendence and difference. This epistemological tension between knowing and unknowing, between the *via affirmationis* and the *via negationis* says something definitive about the

---

[108] This idea receives fuller consideration in Chapter 2 of this book, and then comes to its fullest expression in his sacramental christology. Christ, as the sacrament of the encounter with God is the ground for human being – *zijnsgrond* – which establishes the meaning of human life as theologal – participation in the life of God. From his sacramental christology Schillebeeckx argues that the Christian life cannot be divorced from the ethical life, but nor can it be reduced to ethics.

[109] Schillebeeckx, 'The Non-conceptual Intellectual Dimension in Our Knowledge of God according to Aquinas', pp. 162–163.

relation between created nature and creator: it is real insofar as it is 'distinct yet complementary'. This is precisely the 'condition' for a theological anthropology: 'every theological statement, that is, everything that is said about God, is at the same time a statement about man.'[110] Humanity is neither absorbed into the mystery of God nor is the mystery of God anthropomorphized. The relation is real in its distinction and in its complementarity. It is precisely God's transcendence and difference – 'the fullness of being of the divine being-Other' that grounds this relation.

The importance of the definition of God's nature as cause, transcendence and difference here, and illustrated epistemologically via the possibilities and limits for knowledge of God, is that it begins to describe a relation between the infinite and the finite with a particular structure: a relation of distinction and complementarity that is dependent upon God's being-Other. Hence the relation here of created to creator can be described as absolute dependence. Human being in relation to God on this definition – creature to creator – experiences its meaning as absolute dependence upon God in a manner that at the same time affirms the value of created nature. This is what it means to be created by God:

> The fact that man is created by the living God means that he is constantly receiving himself from God; that he is real in himself, firmly fixed in his own inviolable independence, and nevertheless wholly from, in and of God both in his thought and his will and his essential existence in this world. I find myself in this mysterious state and I am unable to extricate myself from it: on the one hand I am really and truly myself; I stand freely and courageously in this world and take my life in my own hands . . . thus becoming more and more myself. On the other hand, in this whole being I am at the same time, and into the finest warp and woof of my being, wholly from God, from whom I derive myself and from whom I am constantly given to myself.[111]

Humanity is itself in absolute dependence where this dependence does not negate the human, but establishes it: I am myself in dependence upon God. Further this dependence is the ground of my identity as person: 'man comes from the hand of God as a person and therefore under all aspects possesses an immediate relationship to God which calls him forth as a person'. Equally this dependence is the ground of my freedom: 'man possesses an immediate relationship with God which calls him forth as a person – a situated freedom – into existence'. Absolute dependence upon God describes

---

[110] Schillebeeckx, 'Christian Faith and Man's Expectation for the Future on Earth', p. 54; 'Dialogue with God and Christian Secularity', p. 214.
[111] Schillebeeckx, 'God in Dry Dock', pp. 8–9.

both the nature of my relation to God and the nature of my relation to the world: 'man belongs first to God and only secondly to himself. He exists for God. This is his metaphysical and moral significance.' Hence it is the relation to God who is cause, transcendence and difference which establishes and does not negate the human: 'man comes from the hand of God as a person and therefore under all aspects possesses an immediate relationship to God which calls him forth as a person – a situated freedom – into existence'.[112]

Humanity's relationship to God is one of absolute dependence: this is the meaning of the truth that 'the relationship with God is not something added, it is constitutive of humanity'. Humanity 'comes from the hand of God as a person', and therefore absolute dependence – the 'immediate relationship to God' – is constitutive of what it means to be human – human being. The relationship between created nature and the God who is cause, transcendence and difference is described by Schillebeeckx as one of absolute dependence: humanity 'comes from the hand of God'; 'exists first for God'; 'receives itself from God'. This relation of dependence is constitutive both of humanity's metaphysical and moral significance. In this immediate relationship to God, humanity is established as a 'situated freedom': personal, contingent and temporal. Schillebeeckx's epistemology – the tension between the *via affirmationis* and the *via negationis* – is illustrative of this relationship: divine difference and transcendence is the ground and not the negation for real human knowledge of God.

A further illustration of this relation of finite to infinite in which the finite is not negated but established is the idea of the relation of an effect to its cause. Schillebeeckx uses the terms similitude and dissimilitude to describe the human divine relation as one of participation:

> 'We know God . . . as *cause* and by his *transcendence* and by his *utter difference.*' These are three inseparable aspects of causality in which the effect is no different from the act itself of the cause in the other, so that the effect as such is *participative* the act of the cause itself. *Participatio obiectiva* and *participatio causalis* are thus always essentially connected in Aquinas. The participational character of the effect in respect of its cause consequently implies a *similitudo*, which is naturally accompanied by a basic *dissimilitudo*: 'in the effect is found something by means of which it is assimilated to its cause and something by means of which it differs from its cause.'[113]

---

[112] Schillebeeckx, 'Dialogue with God and Christian Secularity', p. 215.
[113] Schillebeeckx, 'The Non-conceptual Intellectual Dimension in Our Knowledge of God according to Aquinas', p. 163. Schillebeeckx summarizes Aquinas here.

What is interesting here for theological anthropology is that in this description of participation the human–divine relation is one of similitude as well as dissimilitude, and the concept of participation contains both of these aspects. The idea of divine difference and transcendence does not preclude the participative nature of the relation between the divine and human, rather it establishes the possibility of the relation and gives it a certain structure. As creature to creator, this structure is described as a participation that implies both a similitude and a dissimilitude. The idea of participation contributes to the understanding of Schillebeeckx's fundamental anthropological claim: 'In this constitutive relationship to God who is a mystery, I am a mystery. The whole crux of my definition is precisely the mystery of God.'[114] God's transcendence and difference – the tension between the *via affirmationis* and the *via negationis* – are terms that describe a particular relation between the infinite and the finite. Likeness and difference are both attributes of this relation, which is neither dualistic nor reductive but participative.

For Schillebeeckx, theological anthropology begins with the mystery of God: 'The whole crux of my definition is the mystery of God'.[115] In light of the mystery of God who is creator – cause, transcendence and difference – human being is defined in its dependence on God and as a situated freedom. This is the meaning of creation. In this, Schillebeeckx's interpretation of creation and Thomas' tripartite distinction in the treatise of God reveal two key ideas for his theological anthropology: 'I am myself in dependence upon God', and 'I am myself in and of this world.' Dependence upon God – human being as created – is constititutive of human being as person – a situated freedom. The relation to God as creator who is utter difference from creation is the ground and possibility of human being and action in the world. In this sense God as cause and as transcendence and difference is also the most 'immediate' relation to the human – more immediate than I am to myself and hence my definition as human being is given first in this relation: 'Humanity exists first for God'. This is consistent with and supported by his theology of revelation in which the infinite is disclosed in the finite without destroying it.

A third idea that emerges from Schillebeeckx's interpretation of Thomas' treatise on God is the importance of metaphysics for theology and for a theological anthropology. Already implicit in this brief overview of the meaning of creation – humanity defined in absolute dependence upon God – this becomes more explicit in his exploration of Thomas' epistemology via De Petter's understanding of non-conceptual knowledge. It is in some of the material in which Schillebeeckx explores the idea of 'concept' and its relation to human knowledge of God that the relation between creature and creator comes to its most acute expression. Not only is this relation

---

[114] Schillebeeckx, 'Dialogue with God and Christian Secularity', p. 215.
[115] Ibid.

constitutive of the finite but also, in the relation of infinite to finite, the infinite presupposes the finite. This further illustrates the constitutive relation between the finite and infinite in light of the relation between humanity and God's nature as cause, difference and transcendence.

The influence of Dominic De Petter on Schillebeeckx's interpretation of Thomas is very clearly apparent in one of the most philosophical of Schillebeeckx's essays, 'The non-conceptual intellectual dimension in our knowledge of God according to Aquinas'. This essay is certainly among the most difficult and complex of all of his writings. Its central concern is an epistemological question: in what sense is knowledge of God conceptual, and in what way does this knowledge of God transcend concepts? These epistemological questions have been analysed clearly and at length elsewhere, yet this essay deserves a brief analysis in light of questions particular to Schillebeeckx's theological anthropology.[116] On this front, it is particularly interesting because it demonstrates his commitment to a 'metaphysics of reality'. This is particularly important for his theological anthropology in light of his claim that humanity's metaphysical and moral significance have an intrinsic relation in light of humanity's relation to God. For Schillebeeckx, the 'metaphysics of reality' is founded upon the capacity of the creaturely to reveal the divine. This is at the centre of his discussion of the relation between concepts and non-conceptual knowledge.

The question Schillebeeckx tackles is one originally posed by Maréchal: given it is not possible for us to know God purely conceptually, how can we 'achieve a real knowledge of God, a knowledge that brings us into contact with him as a reality'?[117] At the heart of his argument, following De Petter, is a pivotal claim: there is knowledge of God that 'surmounts' the conceptual in a 'non-conceptual noetic contact of the spirit with God'. What is crucial for Schillebeeckx in this argument is maintaining the 'noetic value of a real objective contact with God' because to deny the possibility of an

---

[116] Kennedy, *Deus Humanissimus*, pp. 79–142. Kennedy provides a concise summary of Schillebeeckx's epistemology which is found in this essay and more generally in all of his writings: 'In effect Schillebeeckx's early way of describing God's knowability relies on a number of distinctions between (a) indivisible positive and negative moments in a single process of knowledge; (b) abstract or conceptual, and non-abstract or non-conceptual facets of cognition; (c) contingent and non-contingent realities; and (d) natural, creaturely concepts applicable to God, together with supernatural concepts of faith. Each of these distinctions is drawn, however, in association with a superintending metaphysical presupposition, namely, the notion that reality is constituted by a homogeneity between a divine Creator and contingent creatures.' Kennedy describes this homogeneity as 'a relational ontology' which he identifies as the 'heart and pre-eminent specificity of Schillebeeckx's thought'. *Deus Humanissimus*, p. 80.

[117] Schillebeeckx, 'The Non-conceptual Intellectual Dimension in Our Knowledge of God according to Aquinas', p. 159.

objective non-conceptual knowledge of God would lead to a 'surrender of a metaphysics of reality'.[118]

In the epistemology Schillebeeckx adopts, the 'objective and real value of our knowledge of God' is dependent upon the 'dynamism of the content of being' itself. This is a satisfactory epistemology for Schillebeeckx because it provides sufficient explanation of the objective value of knowledge; at the same time it escapes a purely conceptual knowledge and allows for a dynamic relation between the knowing subject and the objective content of knowledge. Returning again to the earlier illustration:

> [T]he most profound inspiration of Thomism absolutely refuses to apply the conceptual content itself to God and prefers to speak of intending God through the objectively referential value of our conceptual contents . . . the entire objective, true, and speculative value of our concepts of faith resides in their *objective projection* in the direct line or the direction (and in no other line or direction) which is indicated by the content itself of these concepts (which are accessible to us), with the restriction however, that we have no suitable conception of the specifically divine manner of realisation of this content. The entire argument is based on the view that knowledge implies more than merely 'explicit, conceptual' knowledge. The mystery is preserved, but we have an objective view of it.[119]

Here, Schillebeeckx has safeguarded two key principles: the dynamic nature of the human activity of knowing and the objective value of knowing, and he has done so in a manner which is consistent with his commitment to an epistemology founded upon a participative relation between similitude and dissimilitude – between the *via affirmationis* and the *via negationis*. The dissimilitude implies that the similitude is not graspable as 'concept'.

The whole of Schillebeeckx's interpretation of Thomas circles around the tripartite division by which we know God: as cause, transcendence and utter difference. It follows from the centrality of this particular interpretation of the treatise of God that Schillebeeckx's analysis of Thomas' epistemology identifies the Thomistic concept of similitude as pivotal – an understanding of similitude that coheres with the nature of God:

> Aquinas affirms on the one hand that we know that a likeness exists between the creature and God, and on the other hand that this creaturely likeness escapes the grasp of our specific, and even of our merely

---

[118] Schillebeeckx, 'The Non-conceptual Intellectual Dimension in Our Knowledge of God according to Aquinas', p. 161. The key concept here is the importance of the 'objective' nature of the knowledge of reality. For Schillebeeckx this is precisely the strength of De Petter's epistemology. See Schillebeeckx, 'What is Theology?', p. 137 n 1.
[119] Schillebeeckx, 'What is Theology?', p. 137; p. 137 n 2.

generic conceptual knowledge. It is, in his view, impossible to grasp this *similitudo* conceptually. The importance of this affirmation is that it is precisely *this* similitude (as the essential aspect of dependence on God or absolute participation) which, according to Aquinas, forms the basis of the objective value of our knowledge of God. The really existing *similitudo* of the creature to God is therefore an immanent *beyond* of our predicamental and conceptual knowledge, at the same time not confined by any specific and generic limitations. The 'likeness' of the creature to its creator is not a '*definite* proportion or measure,' because, though there is a real likeness, the *dissimilitudo* is infinitely great and God is incomparable. All our representations of God derived from the created world can certainly *signify* God, 'but not definitively or exhaustively'.[120]

Schillebeeckx builds his case for the nature of non-conceptual knowledge around one fundamental principle: 'the likeness which exists between the creature and God'.[121] Yet precisely because of the nature of this likeness, a likeness that is both similitude and dissimilitude, he must affirm the creaturely capacity to signify God objectively, and at the same time he must develop an understanding of signification that does not suggest that God is grasped by a precise conceptual definition.

In summary, because of the nature of the likeness between creature and creator, the nature of human knowledge is objective. It signifies and envisages reality, yet it does not grasp this conceptually. However, because this knowledge signifies the reality towards which it points objectively, the non-conceptual aspect of the act of knowing cannot be divorced from its objective conceptual content:

> According to Aquinas, we have no concepts of God, but only creaturely concepts, which we do not, however, attribute or assign to God, but via which we reach out for God without actually grasping him conceptually.[122]

Clearly, in Schillebeeckx's interpretation of Thomas, the task is to explain the relationship between conceptual knowledge and non-conceptual knowledge in which the act of knowing God is both conceptual and non-conceptual and the non-conceptual element is described in relation to creaturely concepts. For Schillebeeckx this is the epistemological implication of Thomas'

---

[120] Schillebeeckx, 'The Non-conceptual Intellectual Dimension in Our Knowledge of God according to Aquinas', p. 170.

[121] Ibid.

[122] Schillebeeckx, 'The Concept of Truth', p. 10.

premise: 'We know God from and in the created world'.[123] Significantly, it is consistent with the treatise on God.

At this point a picture of Schillebeeckx's anthropology has begun to emerge in which both the metaphysical and moral significance of humanity are held together in a relation that has its ground in God's graciousness. From his interpretation of Thomas' treatise on God, God's nature as cause, transcendence and difference is in itself the absolute affirmation of the contingent and the finite. Taking again from his analysis of Thomas, the basis of our objective knowledge of God is 'the really existing similitude of the creature to God' – '*de reëelbestaande "similitudo"*' – where similitude means 'dependence on God or absolute participation' – '*als wezenlijk moment van de Godsafhankelijkheid of de absolute participatie*'.[124] The relation between creator and creature is a relation of similitude that is also dissimilitude, or, a relation of absolute participation that is defined on the side of the creature as absolute dependence. By placing such emphasis on the capacity of the creaturely to signify the divine, Schillebeeckx, following Thomas, heightens rather than negates the importance of the contingent and finite, and hence the human. Knowledge of God, and participation in God as dependence does not depend on transcending the finite but rather presupposes the finite. This epistemology has anthropological consequences: 'I am myself in dependence upon God and I am myself in and of the world'.[125] I am absolute dependence and situated freedom, and because I hold both of these things at once my metaphysical and moral significance as human being are bound together.

Humanity created by God is defined in a relation to God that is creative, sanctifying, participative and personal. For Schillebeeckx, as for Thomas, humanity created by God is defined in a relation to God that is at the same time salvific. In Schillebeeckx's estimation, this is Thomas' crowning achievement – the God who is creator and who can be known in created nature is also the God of salvation:

> [W]hile conceptual thought in all its forms is not pernicious, not every form of such thinking can be approved . . . there is in other words a rationalising kind of conceptualism which attempts to enclose the

---

[123] Schillebeeckx, 'The Non-conceptual Intellectual Dimension in Our Knowledge of God according to Aquinas', p. 166. Kennedy has described Schillebeeckx's theology as one continuous commentary on this epistemological principle of Thomas. See Kennedy, 'Continuity Underlying Discontinuity: Schillebeeckx's Philosophical Background', pp. 265; 275.

[124] Schillebeeckx, 'The Non-conceptual Intellectual Dimension in Our Knowledge of God according to Aquinas', p. 170; 'Het niet-begrippelijk kenmoment in onze Godskennis volgens Thomas van Aquino', p. 208.

[125] Schillebeeckx, 'Dialogue with God and Christian Secularity', p. 215.

inexpressible in conceptual terms, and there is, on the other hand, a kind of conceptual thought which leaves the mystery *as a mystery* and tries somehow to express it precisely as a saving mystery, with the result that the concepts of faith radiate a value for life . . . Aquinas' crowning achievement in the sphere of theology may well be that he built the value of dogma for life on the basis of its meaning and value as truth, while at the same time remaining fully aware of the value of truth for human life.[126]

The God who is cause, transcendence and difference is the God who is personally immanent in history as salvation, and it is the history of salvation that reveals the fully personal nature of God, and the salvific nature of the relation between God and humanity. The definition of humanity is the mystery of God who is both creator and redeemer. Here the significance of God's self-revelation becomes definitive of the definition of humanity: 'God reveals himself by revealing humanity to itself'.

The structure of revelation has precise consequences for the method of theological reflection. Aquinas correctly emphasised the fact that the 'revealed God' – God as God – is the subject of theology but that we must also remain fully aware of how and where the divinity of God is revealed to us. It is in fact revealed to us in the inner light of faith, the objective content of which is given to us in the *theophaneia* of the history of salvation.[127] Theology and the theological discourse on humanity are the knowledge that comes from being addressed by God – God as God – as salvation within history.

Humanity Addressed by God: God as Personal and Immanent

Perhaps the single most important insight into the inspiration that drives Schillebeeckx's theology can be found in this somewhat wishful reflection: 'How splendid and illuminating a treatise on *de Deo Uno* could be if it were a theological reflection on the experience of the people of Israel with their God in the history of salvation which provides the clearest intimation of God's innermost being'.[128] For Schillebeeckx, theological reflection on the nature of God can reach its most adequate expression only when it is a reflection that holds together the God of creation and the God of the covenant, the Lord of history and the Lord of salvation.[129] Yet this conviction is

---

[126] Schillebeeckx, 'Theologia *or* Oikonomia?', pp. 83–84.
[127] Ibid. p. 93.
[128] Ibid. p. 96.
[129] Schillebeeckx, 'Christian Faith and Man's Expectation for the Future on Earth', p. 54.

much more than methodological wishful thinking on Schillebeeckx's part. He identifies this as the most profound insight of Thomas and his own commitment to a treatise on God that holds together both *de Deo Uno*, and the Triune God of salvation history is clear from his critique of contemporary theology, of which the following is a good example:

> This is something that is often forgotten nowadays. There are deviations here both to the right and to the left, and the central truth is forgotten – *either* that the living God, who is reached by the light of faith, has only expressed what is capable of being positively known about his being at the level of the historically situated economy of salvation, *or* that the mystery of the history of salvation is only the revelation of a supratemporal mystery of God himself . . . Is it therefore not typical, that in a recent theological *summa*, which is otherwise, in many respects, very striking, there is no genuinely *theological* treatise on God or the Trinity, although it contains all the other normal theological treatises?[130]

God both transcends history as utter difference and acts within history as human salvation. God is both transcendent and immanent in a manner that is non-contradictory and non-reductive. These are the realities in light of which it is possible to develop a 'genuinely theological treatise on God'.

Schillebeeckx's commitment to this particular approach to the treatise on God is much more than a critique; it also determines the content and method of his own theology. For Schillebeeckx the subject of theology is the one God of creation and covenant and therefore, as we have already noted, he describes his theology as a 'theocentric theology' that has a 'Christological method'.[131] The relation between human knowledge of God and salvation is established by the very structure of revelation itself. God's self-revelation occurs as salvation for humanity: God personally addresses humanity in the encounter that is itself salvation. Salvation history is quite simply the locus in which humanity encounters God: 'Salvation is the very act of encounter between God and man'.[132] In essence, every one of Schillebeeckx's monographs and the almost inexhaustible number of essays, lectures and homilies are an attempt to offer exactly this 'splendid and illuminating treatise on *de Deo Uno*' in light of the encounter between God and humanity, which is at the same time salvation.

Strictly speaking, of course, there is not one self-contained definitive 'treatise' dedicated exclusively to a reflection on the nature of God among Schillebeeckx's writings. Rather, it is the theme of his theological project in

[130] Schillebeeckx, 'What is Theology?', pp. 139–140.
[131] Ibid. p. 138.
[132] Ibid. p. 103.

its entirety, and in many ways it is most sharply focused in his essays. In fact, some of Schillebeeckx's best work is contained in his essays, and his strength as a writer is perhaps best expressed as an essayist. This is hardly surprising from the theologian who describes theology as 'always a "stammering" in the face of the transcendent mystery of faith'. Theology performs its task – 'a task full of conflicts and risks' – by 'stuttering out the great truths of God as best we can echo them', a humility theology should acknowledge:

> It is in theology a matter of good form constantly to acknowledge this humility, which is not merely apparent in the manner in which theology is practised. The attention of theology must always be directed to the mystery of salvation that is announced and not to the human means which help us approach it.[133]

Yet theology's stammering in the face of mystery is never an irrational or an unintelligible stammering, rather it is a stammering that reflects what Schillebeeckx describes as the 'tension between theological incarnation and disincarnation', between the 'meaningful intelligibility of faith' and a 'fundamental resistance to rationalisation'.[134] This tension has implications for a theological anthropology.

The risks and conflicts inherent in the task of theology are discernible in the history of theology's exploration of the tension between incarnation and disincarnation. The manner in which this tension is expressed, whether in epistemological or speculative questions or in areas of more pastoral and evangelical concern, will contribute to the understanding of what it means to be human in relation to the divine:

> The development of the synthesis between the tendency towards incarnation and the tendency towards disincarnation in theological thought will always be accompanied by painful conflicts. Harmony between

---

[133] Ibid. pp. 176–177.
[134] Schillebeeckx, 'What is Theology', p. 176. 'In the content of faith there is both a tendency towards incarnation in human thought and a fundamental resistance to rationalisation. On the one hand, theology should not sink into so-called evangelism, which is only aware of the mystery and the "folly of faith", nor should it tend towards an uncontrolled incarnation, which is only conscious of the meaningful intelligibility of faith. We know from the history of the church that "pure evangelism" which refuses to become incarnate in doctrine and institution results in the ultimate suicide of the genuine evangelical attitude. . . . But on the other hand we also know from church history, that whenever faith becomes too incarnate, as though it could be completely absorbed by human thought, there is always an imminent danger of naturalism and rationalism. Sound theology can only develop if it progresses diffidently between this Scylla and that Charybdis. It must actively maintain a constant tension between incarnation and disincarnation.'

nature and supernature, both at the level of human action and ascesis and at the level of theological thought, is not something that is automatically given; it is something that can only come about in a very laborious way.[135]

Schillebeeckx interprets the history of theology from this perspective, from the harmony between nature and supernature. His own theological anthropology is dependent upon how he develops and sustains a harmony between incarnation and disincarnation, between nature and supernature, between the finite and the infinite and between the temporal and the eschatological. For Schillebeeckx this points to the fundamental importance of the structure of revelation itself for a theological anthropology. The preoccupation at the centre of his anthropology is this conviction: 'The infinite is revealed in the finite without destroying it'.[136] This is the pivotal truth – the structure of revelation itself – which lies at the very heart of his theological anthropology and in light of which he makes his methodological choices.

In the preceding section of this chapter, this insight into the relation between the finite and the infinite was taken up primarily as an epistemological question, although one with clear anthropological implications: what is the relation between conceptual and non-conceptual knowledge of God? It emerged from this analysis that in Schillebeeckx's interpretation of Thomas, there is a clear understanding that non-conceptual knowledge of God presupposes conceptual knowledge. There is an intrinsic relation between conceptual and non-conceptual knowledge that is founded upon a theology of creation. In other words, human knowledge of God and therefore contingent and finite knowledge of the infinite, is not dependent upon overcoming the finite or contingent. Human knowledge of God depends upon our finitude and our contingency. The creaturely is not negated, rather it is in our created nature that we know God as 'cause, transcendence, and as utter difference'. Hence, in our knowledge of God, Schillebeeckx holds to the claim that the infinite is revealed in the finite, where both the nature of the finite – as creaturely knowledge of God – and the nature of the infinite – as cause, transcendence and difference – are maintained.

Over the course of his career, there have been significant shifts in some of Schillebeeckx's epistemological structures; at the same time, his pastoral commitments have meant that he has published and lectured on a wide range of topics. However, underlying this diversity and plurality there is deep continuity in his commitment to Thomas' tripartite distinction, which means that his theology always seeks to be coherent with the treatise on God where God is known as cause, transcendence and difference. Just as in his interpretation of Thomas on the nature of God and the relation

---

[135] Schillebeeckx, 'Theologia or Oikonomia?', p. 85.
[136] Ibid. p. 109.

between revelation and creation, and contra more existentialist theologies, Schillebeeckx does not develop a definition of theological reflection by denying metaphysics, so too does this hold for his theological anthropology. However, although he is clearly committed to metaphysics within theology, it is also equally true that he does not develop his theology along abstract, impersonal or *a*historical lines, and this comes more sharply into focus when he turns to the relation between revelation and salvation history. Schillebeeckx's theology is from beginning to end a 'treatise' on God, which is a soteriology, a treatise on the 'God who precisely under the aspect of his godhead is the God of our salvation'.[137] This is the subject of this section of the chapter. The definition of humanity as vocation is given in dialogue with the God who is both transcendence and immanence, difference and personal.

Thomas' doctrine of God has a twofold influence on Schillebeeckx: not only must theology sustain a treatise on the nature of God that holds to the tripartite description of the *Deus sub ratione Deitatis*, it must also hold this description of the nature of God together in a coherent manner with an understanding of the nature of God as God for humanity, the *Deus salutaris*. This is the consequence of determining that revelation itself establishes the theological method:

> If we accept, correctly, with Aquinas that the true subject of theology is the living God, the *Deus salutaris* or the *Deus sub ratione Deitatis* – that is, the saving God, God as seen under the aspect of his godhead – (for it is precisely as such that he is our salvation), then it is clear that we shall only be able to reach this living God where he revealed himself as such – in Christ Jesus, who is the public manifestation of God. This at the same time shows that theology which is orientated towards the history of salvation is not opposed to theology which accepts the *ratio Deitatis* ('aspect of godhead') as the principle of theological study and that a theology which, on the other hand, is directed towards the *ratio Deitatis* in everything cannot neglect the history of salvation in which God manifests himself precisely as God.[138]

All human knowledge of God is dependent upon revelation because revelation, as the event of our salvation, is not something we can come to through our own initiative; furthermore, revelation as the event of salvation is the revelation of the *ratio Deitatis* because it is 'precisely as such' that God is the

---

[137] Schillebeeckx, 'What is Theology?', pp. 138; 142: For Schillebeeckx the treatise on the nature of God is inseparable from soteriology and therefore it is 'wrong to contrast theology on the basis of the history of salvation with so-called abstract metaphysical theology.'

[138] Ibid. pp. 138–139.

Deus salutaris.[139] Therefore *theologia* – God's 'proper being' – can never be divorced from the salvation history in which God is revealed – *oikonomia*. Correspondingly neither may speculative theology be divorced from positive theology, nor may positive theology be reduced to history.[140]

The context for this description of the 'true subject of theology' is a discussion of the nature of theology in which Schillebeeckx is particularly anxious to address the 'unfortunate' divisions within theology, particularly the division between positive and speculative theology. The climate in which he takes up this question was one of suspicion on the part of the magisterium over the 'new theology' that placed emphasis on the essentially historical nature of theology.[141] In response to this suspicion Schillebeeckx develops his interpretation of the doctrine of revelation as the determining factor of theological method: 'The structure of revelation itself and of the act of faith associated with it must suggest the type of reflection to which faith in Christ can lead'.[142] From the structure and content of revelation itself, Schillebeeckx

---

[139] Ibid. p. 103: 'Religion is essentially a personal communion between God and men. This personal contact with the living God cannot be established by human effort. It can only be established by the initiative of grace with the divine revelation that is implied in it. Salvation is the very act of encounter between God and man, in which the first fundamental contact is established by faith. This divine revelation makes history.'

[140] Ibid. pp. 118–120: '[T]heological reflection about the content of revelation requires a positive examination of the way in which God allowed his divinity and the meaning of our humanity to be experienced by men in his saving activity ... It is not only the fact that something has been revealed that is of great importance for a deeper understanding of the intentions of God in revelation. It is also important to know how it was revealed and how it was made explicit in terms of faith. . . . The theologian does not, however, carry out this whole positive task formally as an historian. Positive theology is not a historical science, although it has to make use of strictly historical methods as an aid. But the theologian does this as a theologian ... the positive function of theology is not just a pre-theological preliminary stage of speculative theology. It is quite simply theology itself. Positive and speculative theology are not two types of theological thought, but two equally essential functions of one and the same science, the unity of which consists in the close co-operation between the light of the intellect and the light of faith, the latter always assuming the leading function.'

[141] This suspicion is the impetus behind the 1950 encyclical of Pius XII, *Humani generis*.

[142] Schillebeeckx, 'What is Theology?', p. 102. The most important influence here is Chenu whose work on the incarnational structure of theology is seminal to Schillebeeckx's thought. This is discussed in Chapter 3. Schillebeeckx's essay 'What is Theology?' clearly owes much to Chenu's book *La théologie est-elle une science?* (Paris: Arthème Fayard, 1957). For both of these theologians 'the act of faith' associated with revelation is a form of knowledge. 'What is Theology?', p. 104: 'Faith is conditioned by this revelation, in which we are addressed by God. Faith is therefore a way of knowing. This knowing has a distinctive character in that it is a knowledge which comes about by our being addressed, by our being confidentially informed through God's mercy. God speaks to us inwardly through the inward grace of faith, the *locutio interior*, and at the

argues that new developments in theology must not always be seen as 'a source of danger to theology and theological orthodoxy' but rather, if they are 'deeply and lovingly anchored in the whole of tradition', they may well be the source of theology's renewal and enrichment.[143] The almost creedal tone of Schillebeeckx's response to the magisterial suspicion of the *nouvelle théologie* signals his emphatic commitment to the historical nature of theology:[144]

> Within the church, we believe in the mystery of Christ as the revelation of God – we believe in the christian historical plan of salvation in which the trinitarian mystery of salvation which transcends history is realised for and in us. The entire theological method is determined by this structure of revelation.[145]

The importance of his doctrine of revelation for his own theology cannot be overestimated. It is here that the need within theology for a coherence between what is said of the nature of God as cause, transcendence and difference – the God who is creator – and the nature of God as immanent and personal – the God who is redeemer, is established.

With respect to the theological definition of humanity given in the relation to God who is both creator and redeemer there are clear implications. Just as Schillebeeckx understands the 'entire theological method' to be 'determined by this structure of revelation' so too he understands theological anthropology to be determined by this structure. The mystery of human being is revealed in relation to the mystery of God. For this reason Schillebeeckx has not written a theological treatise on anthropology: it is implicit in his doctrines of God and Christology or as he describes it himself: 'No Christian anthropology rather God is close to humanity in grace'.[146] Schillebeeckx's theological anthropology is theocentric with a Christological method. Furthermore, because the mystery of human being is revealed in relation to the

---

same time we are addressed from outside by the God of revelation – this is the aspect of *fides ex auditu*. This 'external address' is the Old Testament history of salvation, accompanied by the prophetic word, and its climax: the human appearance of Christ himself in word and deed as addressed to the apostles. Finally it is the life of the church, in her activity and in her kerygmatic word, by which man living now is addressed and in which the glorified Christ really lives'.

143 Schillebeeckx, 'Theologia *or* Oikonomia?', p. 86.
144 Schillebeeckx, 'What is Theology?', pp. 123–126. Schillebeeckx, like his mentor Thomas, devotes a great deal of his theology to the positive task of re-reading the tradition, from scripture to its present interpretations, and his speculative theology is always done in relation to this positive aspect of theology. Positive theology is a *locus theologicus*. He locates the 'pernicious division' between positive and speculative theology as a later development in theology, later than Thomas.
145 Schillebeeckx, 'What is Theology?', p. 104.
146 Schillebeeckx, 'Christian Faith and Man's Expectation for the Future on Earth', p. 73.

mystery of God where the mystery of God itself – *theologia* – is revealed in a particular action within history – *oikonomia* – human being – humanity's 'metaphysical significance' – must be inseparable from its agency within history – humanity's 'moral significance'. A thoroughly theocentric anthropology, one that was coherent with the structure of revelation itself, would hold together the 'metaphysical and moral significance' of humanity.[147]

Schillebeeckx wrote extensively on the theology of revelation, principally because for him the structure of revelation establishes the structure of human knowledge of God:

> Revelation is accomplished in and through history, and we live now from this revelation-in-word and revelation-in-reality. . . . [T]he history of salvation and the word give us, by virtue of the light of faith, a view of the revealed reality, with which we associate ourselves in faith. As we base the possibility of a theology of the objective and the subjective aspect of faith, so too are the positive and the speculative functions of theology justified in these two aspects. . . . [The] positive and speculative orientation of the human mind – two aspects of one and the same fundamental orientation towards reality – finds its corresponding point of contact in the structure of revelation.[148]

This structure of revelation that establishes the structure of human knowledge of God has two significant consequences for theological anthropology. The first is the personal nature of human knowledge of God and hence the determination of human meaning as personal in light of the relation to God. The second is a sacramental nature of human history and hence the sacramental meaning of human being, action, temporality and contingency. In other words, at the heart of Schillebeeckx's theological anthropology is the fundamental conviction that the God of creation is also the God of salvation. This is precisely the theological anthropology that follows from allowing revelation to determine the structure and content of theology. Theological anthropology must 'let the objective structure of revelation speak', and in doing this it becomes clear that the theological discourse on human being is theocentric and Christological.[149]

---

[147] Schillebeeckx, 'Dialogue with God and Christian Secularity', p. 215. The relation between the metaphysical and moral significance of humanity is explicated most fully by Schillebeeckx in his eschatology, which is the final topic addressed by this chapter.

[148] Schillebeeckx, 'What is Theology?', p. 117. Schillebeeckx expands upon the idea of the positive and speculative aspects of human knowing: 'The structure of the human mind possesses a double complementary orientation. The human mind seeks first to become conscious of the data that present themselves purely as data, but in addition it seeks to understand the sense, the intelligibility or the *quidditas* of these data – it seeks to know what *is* reality.'

[149] Schillebeeckx, 'Theologia *or* Oikonomia?', p. 87.

A theological anthropology that takes Schillebeeckx's interpretation of revelation as its starting point and as its content and structure is one that is ultimately non-dualistic and non-reductive: the relation between the finite and infinite is constitutive of the finite rather than reductive. The structure of revelation itself provides the structure for an anthropology, which is a definition of the 'being' or reality of humanity where this definition is inseparable from humanity's relationship to God within history. The dilemma of God *or* humanity is a false one because of the nature of revelation: 'The very structure of the reality of revelation must show us objectively whether we ought to follow a metaphysical, theocentric course or whether we should proceed along the christological lines of the history of salvation'.[150] The nature of theology in general, and the nature of theological anthropology itself, revolves around one question for Schillebeeckx: 'What is the mode of this revelation?' In other words, is it 'simply a question of a communicating of a knowledge of truths that are beyond our understanding, or is it primarily a question of sacramental revelation, a revelation in human and historical form?' [151] Revelation, for Schillebeeckx, is sacramental revelation. It is the communication of truths or knowledge of God where this knowledge is historical and personal.[152] The sacramental character of revelation determines a theological anthropology that defines human being as personal situated freedom. Ultimately the truth that 'the finite is revealed in the infinite without destroying it' depends on a sacramental interpretation of revelation.

The sacramental character of revelation is established by the truth that 'the *theologia* is given to us in an *oikonomia*, a history of salvation'. Following Aquinas:

> In the most proper sense, theology provides ideas about God as the highest cause, that is, not only insofar as he is capable of being known from the created world . . . but also insofar as he alone knows himself and as he communicates this knowledge to others by revelation.[153]

---

[150] Ibid.

[151] Ibid. p. 88.

[152] In his interpretation of revelation Schillebeeckx consistently maintains the importance of the conceptual aspect of revelation: revelation is a particular kind of knowing and it is this which establishes and sustains the scientific nature of theology. Schillebeeckx, 'Theologia *or* Oikonomia?', p. 87: 'I shall keep two aspects above all in mind – the aspect of theology as characterised by the history of salvation and the conceptual character of theology, both within the context of the Christological focus of a theology that is nonetheless essentially theocentric.' Here two things must be kept in mind: Schillebeeckx's understanding of conceptual knowledge – the relation between concept and the non-conceptual aspect of knowing – and the careful distinction – and relation – he draws from Aquinas between the spiritual life and the task of theology. See Schillebeeckx, 'What is Theology?', pp. 110–113.

[153] Schillebeeckx, 'Theologia *or* Oikonomia?', pp. 87–88.

This of course means that the question of the mode of revelation is *neither* 'a question of a communication of a knowledge of truths that are beyond our understanding', *nor* 'a question of revelation in human and historical form', rather, it is a question of the relation between knowledge of that which transcends history in utter difference and yet is immanent within history and therefore knowable. This relation is what is meant by the sacramental character of revelation: *theologia* given in *oikonomia*.[154] Schillebeeckx develops this with an example that is particularly apposite for anthropology: the relation between the God of creation and the personal God of revelation. In this relation not only is the divine constitutive of the finite, it presupposes the finite.

The one and the same God who is the God of creation – the God who does not enter into human history yet is constitutive of historical humanity – is the God of salvation – the God who freely intervenes in human history. Therefore, although it is this historical intervention – revelation – that reveals the personal nature of God this is not to say that God's nature becomes personal with revelation. This is what Schillebeeckx means when he asserts, 'It is then the history of salvation and not creation (which is, of course, the starting-point of the history of salvation) that reveals to us who God really is and his wish to be really our God.'[155] Creation, described as the 'starting point of the history of salvation' – '*de eerste aanzet*' – says something fundamental about the nature of God: 'The God of creation is also the personal God', although 'he does not reveal himself in his creative concern with the world as person to us'.[156] It also says something fundamental about created nature: 'Creation offers us the possibility of affirming the personal nature of God.'[157]

---

[154] Ibid. p. 88: Schillebeeckx illustrates this by making the distinction between an understanding of the knowledge of God that would consider knowledge of the supernatural to be something added to what can be known through natural knowledge. As distinct from this a sacramental interpretation of revelation understands knowledge of the supernatural to presuppose natural knowledge: 'We should at the very outset be misinterpreting the data of the problem if we were to take the assertion that Christianity involves revelation to mean that God has revealed certain truths that are beyond our natural understanding only as a kind of addition to an already acquired natural knowledge of God. It is of course, certainly true that the aspect of knowing in revelation is formal. Revelation of necessity addresses a consciousness ... how does this revelation, this process wherein the human consciousness is addressed by the living God take place concretely? We should not forget that the dispensing and receiving of grace, the supernatural order of life, by definition involves both salvation and history.'

[155] Schillebeeckx,'Theologia *or* Oikonomia?', p. 90: 'De heilsgeschiedenis en niet de schepping (die overigens de eerste aanzet is van die heilsgeschiedenis) openbaart ons wie God eigenlijk is en dat Hij, oor voor ons mensen, werkelijk God wil zijn.'; 'De heilshistoriche basis van de theologie: *theologia* of *oikonomia*?', p. 271.

[156] Schillebeeckx, 'Theologia *or* Oikonomia?', p. 88.

[157] Ibid. p. 89.

Schillebeeckx's interpretation of the reality that created nature 'offers us the possibility of affirming the personal nature of God' indicates in what sense he interprets the divine as presupposing the human, the infinite presupposing the finite:

> The act of creation is certainly the free act on the part of the personal God, but the true face of the living God does not emerge from his creation. Creation does, however, offer us the possibility of affirming the personal character of God as a mystery, and this recognition forms the basis of the possibility of associating with God in grace. For, if at a certain point which is not grace, our human freedom were not able to come into contact in some way with the personal God, then grace or revelation would be impossible. It is precisely because grace is *grace*, God's free gift of himself, that it implies a vis-à-vis [*sic*] with the God of grace, a subject who can accept grace, or refuse it – free man in the world.[158]

In other words, the doctrine of revelation, understood here as the activity of God that allows us to enter into a personal relationship with him – grace – establishes the personal nature of humanity very clearly: revelation presupposes an intersubjective relationship between God and humanity.

This means God not only reveals himself as person but also reveals human nature in itself as personal. In God's self-revelation humanity is revealed to itself in its created nature:

> Life led in the light of revelation is a life led in personal communion with the living God, man's encounter in faith with his God. Such an encounter presupposes a natural basis – the existence of two persons, God and man, who meet each other, with all of the natural implications of what is implied in the human state of being a person. If man does not make definite contact with God at one point that is not grace (in the theological sense of the word), then the God who reveals himself cannot address man meaningfully.[159]

---

[158] Ibid.

[159] Schillebeeckx, 'What is Theology?', p. 170. The reference here to 'not grace' does not infer a dualism between nature and grace but a specific 'existential unity of nature and supernature' in which human freedom is not negated. Schillebeeckx, 'Theologia *or* Oikonomia?', p. 89: 'It is precisely because grace is *grace*, God's free gift of himself, that it implies a vis-à-vis [*sic*] with the God of grace, a subject who can accept grace as grace or refuse it – free man in the world, who is therefore, in a certain respect, not graced. It is this that implies the distinction between nature and supernature, even though the existential unity of nature and supernature must be established.' This begins to anticipate the topic of the next chapter in which Schillebeeckx's interpretation of the relation between grace and nature is discussed.

Here another aspect of Schillebeeckx's theology of revelation becomes clear with respect to his understanding of the human–divine relation: for revelation to be revelation – God's personal self-revelation as human history – it must be received as a personal historical and salvific revelation. For God's revelation to address humanity meaningfully it presupposes 'all that is implied in the human state of being a person' and all that is implied in the divine being God.[160] This means that it is both human and historical, and transcendence and difference. Revelation is 'sacramental revelation': it is a communication of divine truths revealed in human and historical form.[161]

The ground for the sacramental nature of revelation is its theocentric and Christological nature: 'Throughout our history our only encounter with the *ratio Deitatis*, with God's own being, is in the man Jesus, in the saving history of the sacramental economy of salvation, in which God reveals himself personally'.[162] The importance of the personal nature of the humanity of Jesus here is essential for understanding what Schillebeeckx means by a theocentric and Christological theology and anthropology.

> This revelation reached its culminating point in Christ. God entered into personal relationships with us in and through his humanity, of which the Logos is the person. A fellow man who treats us personally, then, is personally God. Jesus' human treatment of his fellow men is therefore an invitation to us to encounter God personally . . . the gift and reception of grace, revelation, thus takes place within the framework of human intercommunication.[163]

---

[160] Schillebeeckx, 'Theologia *or* Oikonomia?', p. 89: 'Creation does allow us to affirm the personal God, but this personal character is not revealed in its personal life, its innermost aspect, in creation. In other words, the free activity of creation does not itself enter into human history, although it does constitute historical man. The activity of God's grace, on the other hand, is a free intervention on God's part in the history of man. This activity is itself historical, in the sense that God himself thereby enters into personal relationships with man in the (logically) already constituted history of man. It is moreover, only the history of salvation that gives any intimation of the true face of the trinitarian God. Therefore, whereas God does not, by definition, enter as creator into human history, which he transcends by being interior to it, the activity of his grace and revelation is, also by definition, resulting in his commencing an existential dialogue with his people as man's partner, a dialogue in which he opens up his inner life to us.'

[161] Schillebeeckx, 'Theologia *or* Oikonomia?', p. 88.

[162] Ibid. p. 91.

[163] Schillebeeckx, 'Theologia *or* Oikonomia?', p. 90. Schillebeeckx's interpretation of the incarnation is the ground or 'structure' from which he interprets the meaning of human life in relationship with God and hence the sacramental nature of human life. This Christological material is considered at length in the second half of this book.

This Christological definition of revelation as sacramental – divine revelation in human and historical form – brings Schillebeeckx to the relation between divine self-revelation and the revelation of humanity to itself: 'God gives man an insight into his own conditions, God reveals man to himself precisely by revealing himself as love to man.'[164] A theological anthropology that is true to the nature of God's revelation is both theocentric and Christological.

Schillebeeckx's interpretation of the doctrine of revelation leads him to a description of theology as 'theocentric (trinitarian) with a christological method'.[165] Understanding what Schillebeeckx means by this phrase is critical to interpreting his theology correctly. It also continues to fill in the picture of what Schillebeeckx means by an anthropology, which is a description of human life in light of the relation to God that is creative, salvific, sanctifying, participative and personal. In effect, there is a parallel between what Schillebeeckx does to express the doctrine of God – a theology that is theocentric with a Christological method – and what he does to describe the meaning of humanity – a vocation to relationship with God that is creative, salvific, sanctifying, personal and participative. Just as in the discourse on the nature of God there can be no contradiction between *Deus sub ratione Deitatis* and *Deus salutaris*, so too in the definition of humanity there can be no competition between the definition of humanity as a situated freedom and humanity defined in relation to God. Just as the doctrine of God is theocentric with a Christological method, so too is the theological discourse on human being. Similarly, just as the doctrine of revelation determines the shape and content of theology so too with theological anthropology. This is captured in two aspects of Schillebeeckx's theology of revelation: the first is the assertion that 'the infinite is revealed in the finite without destroying it'. The second deepens the meaning of this by introducing the specifically Christological and hence personal language of salvation: 'God reveals man to himself precisely by revealing himself as love to man'.[166]

Schillebeeckx's analysis of Thomas' treatise on God, and the theology of revelation he develops in light of this, begins to suggest the content and method of an anthropology 'in the mystery of God'. From God's nature as creator in relation to the creation, this is an anthropology in which what it means to be human is considered in relation to God as cause, transcendence and difference: human being is a situated freedom and is at the same time an absolute dependence upon God. From God's self-revelation as salvation this is an anthropology in which what it means to be human is considered in relation to a personal God who acts within history: human being is a situated freedom in personal dialogue with God. Because of his commitment to

---

[164] Schillebeeckx, 'Christian Faith and Man's Expectation for the Future on Earth', p. 54.
[165] Schillebeeckx, 'What is Theology?', p. 138.
[166] Schillebeeckx, 'Christian Faith and Man's Expectation for the Future on Earth', p. 54.

a particular relation between creation and redemption – a relation that rests in the nature of God: the God of creation is the God of the covenant – what is said of the meaning of human life in light of creation and of salvation history must cohere. Thus an anthropology that is consistent with this conviction defines human being as both freedom and absolute dependence: a vocation to intimacy with God. In constructing this anthropology Schillebeeckx is working in a manner that is faithful to his own understanding of the relationship between *theologia* and *oikonomia*, and between positive theology and speculative theology.

Here again his interpretation of Thomas is very telling. As noted above he describes just such coherence between *theologia* and *oikonomia* as Thomas' 'crowning achievement':

> Aquinas' crowning achievement in the sphere of theology may well be that he built the value of dogma for life on the basis of its meaning and value as truth, while at the same time remaining fully aware of the value of truth for human life.[167]

This idea of the 'value of truth for human life' that is central to both the doctrines of creation and redemption – and indeed describes the relation between these: God is God for humanity – has a further significance in Schillebeeckx's theology; here his theology finds a note of clear originality while remaining consistent with Thomas' tripartite distinction in God. For Schillebeeckx, 'the value of the truth for human life' is an eschatological reality: God is the truth of human life as the future of humanity. I am myself in absolute dependence upon God who is the 'absolute future' of humanity.[168] God reveals humanity to itself by revealing himself as ultimate human meaning.

Humanity Revealed by God: God as Meaning

Vatican II is often referred to in the secondary literature on Schillebeeckx's theology as the 'turning point' in his work. Although it is abundantly clear that the Second Vatican Council was an event of enormous significance for twentieth century Roman Catholic theology, and certainly no less so for Schillebeeckx, it is also true that by the time of the Council Schillebeeckx's theology had reached a certain maturity. One of the constant features of his theology is his insistence that the discourse on the nature of God and the nature of human being are inextricably bound together – the question of

---

[167] Schillebeeckx, 'Theologia *or* Oikonomia', pp. 83–84.
[168] Schillebeeckx, 'Christian Faith and Man's Expectations for the Future on Earth', p. 86.

God *or* humanity is simply a false dilemma. This is the conviction that he develops in his own speculative theology – in his doctrine of God and in his Christology – and it is also the truth that he traces in his positive theology – from his reading of the history of the tradition.[169] Both as a speculative and a positive theologian Schillebeeckx consistently works from one fundamental premise: God is God *for* humanity. The subject of theology is *Deus qui sub ratione Deitatis est salus nostra*. For Schillebeeckx this is the logical consequence of doing theology according to the content and structure of revelation:

> God revealed himself, not as a being existing somewhere far away, but as the God of salvation – as *my* and *our* God, who is personally concerned with my and our life. Theology has to do with the God of the covenant, 'Deus qui sub ratione Deitatis est salus nostra' ('God who under the aspect of his godhead is our salvation').[170]

This is the theology ratified by the Council: with Vatican II 'the problem of man's existence functions in the light of revelation'.[171]

That this theology had already come to maturity in Schillebeeckx's own thought is indicated quite strikingly by his critical assessment of the Council's strengths and weaknesses. God as God for humanity is the theological starting point from which Schillebeeckx both welcomes and critiques the results of Vatican II. The strengths of the Council can be found, in Schillebeeckx's judgement, in its 'attempt to integrate belief in man with belief in God'; he has spent the whole of his career doing theology in this spirit of the Council.[172] In his theology after Vatican II he continued to build upon this theology, which had come to a mature expression prior to the Council.[173]

---

[169] This has already been discussed in relation to Schillebeeckx's appropriation of Thomas within his own theology. It will be developed further in Chapters 2 and 3 that examine his interpretation of certain strands of patristic Christology, primarily the patristic interpretation of a kenotic Christology.

[170] Schillebeeckx, 'What is Theology?', p. 168. Here Schillebeeckx is distancing himself from the kerygmatic theologians: 'This clearly shows how incongruous was the position of the so-called "kerygmatic" theology, which claimed to deal in theology only with those truths of faith that have a saving value, as though there were other truths that do not have this saving significance – truths that ought preferably to be confined to the periphery of our theology and preaching.'

[171] Schillebeeckx, *Vatican II: The Real Achievement* (London: Sheed and Ward, 1967), p. 47.

[172] Ibid. p. 19.

[173] This is not to suggest that Schillebeeckx's theology does not continue to develop and to find new expressions after the Council. The point being made is that Vatican II illustrates the deep lines of continuity in Schillebeeckx's theology and hence it is misleading to suggest that there is profound discontinuity between Schillebeeckx's theology pre and post Vatican II.

Indeed, Schillebeeckx himself believed strongly at the time of the Council itself that the church needed a mature theology if it was to be of any real service to the world:

> The church must, so to speak, make God the Father and Jesus, his Son who becomes man, visibly present for all men, show herself in the power of the Holy Spirit. What is necessary is not a naïve faith, but a living, mature and lucid faith which is strong enough for martyrdom. In this strong faith, christians must be in the vanguard of those who care for their fellow-men and who work for greater justice and love in society.[174]

This description of the characteristics of a 'living, mature and lucid faith' is significant, and its rather arresting language – the idea of martyrdom as the image of contrast between naïveté and maturity – serves to emphasize its importance. Interpreting this image of theology in light of the theocentric and Christological attributes of theology, Schillebeeckx is describing the faith that results from the content and structure of revelation: God's essence is visible and present in God's personal involvement within human history and the description of faith must 'function in light of this revelation'. A 'living, mature and lucid faith' is faith consistent with revelation. What is particularly significant in his description, a description that illustrates the nature of faith by using the image of martyrdom, and specifically martyr-dom for justice and love, is the conviction that faith and ethics are clearly connected. If God is the 'meaning' of human life then this meaning of human life is inseparable from the ethical life.[175] The relation between God as the definition of humanity and ethics – humanity's metaphysical and moral significance – is found by Schillebeeckx in eschatology. Essentially, he places eschatology at the very beginning of his theological anthropology. God is the future of humanity.[176] God reveals humanity to itself by revealing him-self as the ultimate human meaning.

[174] Schillebeeckx, 'Christian Faith and Man's Expectation for the Future on Earth', pp. 60; 71. At the heart of Schillebeeckx's critique of the Council is often the idea that the Council did not in the end give clear expression to this mature faith and instead remained naïve in its relation to the world.

[175] The nature of this relationship between the theologal life and the ethical life is devel-oped by Schillebeeckx in greatest depth in his Christology. Two key ideas are most significant there: God's revelation in the personal humanity of Jesus – the emphasis on incarnation and the kenotic relationship of Son to the Father and to the world. For this study, the relation between ethics and the theocentric definition of humanity is picked up again in the chapter on grace and then developed at greater length in the christology chapters.

[176] Schillebeeckx, 'Christian Faith and Man's Expectation for the Future on Earth', p. 86.

This is a good juncture to recall the 'intention' of theological anthropology. For Schillebeeckx, the 'intention' of theological anthropology is to 'discover what God in his grace intends' for humanity:

> It is our intention to discover what God in his grace intends for humanity . . . What does the Word of God say about humanity? *How does God see humanity?* That God sees humanity does not mean simply that he knows what man is making of his life here below. On the contrary, it is the gaze of one who is personally interested, who calls us to salvation and participates with us in a personal, creative and sanctifying way: he is involved in the fortunes of man.[177]

The intention of theological anthropology is to describe the meaning of human existence in light of its relationship to God where this relation itself is described as creative, salvific, sanctifying, participative and personal. Furthermore, this anthropology is not a statement made about the nature of humanity, but it is a description of what humanity is called to be: this is a description of a vocation to a particular relation with God that is definitive of what it means to be human. It is a vocation to a particular relationship with God that defines the nature of humanity itself. This is what Schillebeeckx means when he says, 'In the constitutive relationship to God who is a mystery, I am a mystery. The whole crux of my definition is precisely the mystery of God'.[178]

The intention of theological anthropology is determined by the mystery of God: God as creator – cause, transcendence and difference – and God as redeemer – personal and immanent. As Schillebeeckx describes it: theological anthropology is determined by the God who 'is personally interested, who calls us to salvation and participates with us in a personal, creative and sanctifying way'. Logically therefore, a description of human life that is coherent with the nature of God and reflects the creative, salvific, sanctifying, participative and personal nature of humanity's relation to God must be one that reflects both God's transcendence and difference and God's personal immanence. For Schillebeeckx these two aspects are best held together in an eschatological anthropology. The God who is immanent and personally involved in human history transcends it as its ultimate meaning. An eschatology that holds together God's immanence and transcendence best reflects the nature of God as God for humanity. God transcends human history in a manner that redeems this history: God is the future of humanity and precisely as its future secures the ultimate meaning and not the negation of the human.[179] This is the insight Schillebeeckx brings to the treatise on

---

[177] Schillebeeckx, 'Dialogue with God and Christian Secularity', p. 214.
[178] Ibid. p. 215.
[179] Schillebeeckx, 'Christian Faith and Man's Expectation for the Future on Earth', p. 86.

God: God is the absolute future of humanity. For this claim to work, it must be consistent with Schillebeeckx's interpretation of the treatise on God that holds together the God of creation with the God of the covenant – it must reflect the relation between *theologia* and *oikonomia*.

Eschatology comes at the beginning of theological anthropology for Schillebeeckx precisely because of his interpretation of the mystery of God: God is the meaning of humanity as the future of humanity. Therefore there is a particular relation for Schillebeeckx between the following two statements: 'Humanity exists first for God' and 'what is necessary is not a naïve faith, but a living, mature and lucid faith which is strong enough for martyrdom'. In other words, there is a particular relation between humanity's metaphysical and moral significance. The relation between these two truths is found in the nature of God as the future of humanity. Humanity exists first for the God who is its future:

> All that the christian knows in the light of revelation is that this expectation of the future on earth is included and secure in the absolute, gratuitous and forgiving proximity of God's grace. This is why this dimension of the future has a central position in contemporary theology. Speculation about the relationship between 'nature' and the 'supernatural', which preoccupied theologians in the past, has been transformed, in modern theology, into the problem of the relationship between man's expectation for the future here on earth and the eschatological kingdom. Theology has become eschatology in confrontation with the building of the 'city of man'. The light that the theologian has here has remained the same – man is 'of God', he is included in the mystery of God that was manifested in the life and death of Jesus who was brought to life by God.[180]

For Schillebeeckx to describe the nature of God as the future of humanity is coherent with the fundamental insight that humanity is defined in relation to God where this relation is non-dualistic, non-reductive and non-competitive. Just as it is possible to describe God as cause in a manner that establishes the meaning of the finite, and just as it is possible to describe God as the Lord of history without negating the temporal, so too it is possible to describe God as the future of humanity that does not negate the meaning of human being in the present. In other words, 'the light that the theologian has here is the same' – the infinite is revealed in the finite without destroying it. God is ultimately constitutive of humanity as the absolute future of humanity.

Human action – humanity's moral significance – is 'included in the absolute, gratuitous and forgiving proximity of God's grace'. Included in the

---

[180] Ibid. p. 82.

relation that is constitutive of human meaning, human action is established, not negated. This is the insight he attributes to the post–World War II theologians of the *ressourcement* and *nouvelle théologie*, among them Chenu, whose commitment to a pastoral and socially active theology was a formative influence on Schillebeeckx while he was himself a student of theology.[181] With the Council,

> [S]ome of the basic ideas which have been elaborated by theologians since the second world war [*sic*] have become officially the common property of the church. These ideas themselves come from the post-war theologians' attempt to interpret, in light of the christian revelation, the new existential experience of mankind. The watchword is no longer flight from the world, but flight with the world towards the future, a taking of the world itself with us in our christian expectation of the future which is already transforming the earth here and now. It is precisely because the christian hopes for a 'new heaven and a new earth' that he can never reconcile himself to an 'established order' in the world, since this would be, by definition, a forsaking of his eschatological hope.[182]

This assessment of the work of the *nouvelle théologie* clearly reflects Schillebeeckx's own theology, which is at the same time speculative and pastoral; more particularly, it is consistent with his theological anthropology that holds together humanity's 'metaphysical and moral significance'.

There are several insights here – the 'common property' of Vatican II theology – that are especially important for this theological anthropology: the doctrine of revelation and the theological definition of humanity need to coincide in a coherent manner; this results in an anthropology that is both temporal and eschatological and is defined as a task or vocation and hence the description of human meaning is inseparable from a description of human action.

The first of these insights, that the doctrine of revelation and the theological definition of humanity must cohere, means that just as revelation is historical so too is theological anthropology. That is, theological anthropology is 'the attempt to interpret, in light of the Christian revelation, the new

---

[181] Schillebeeckx underlines especially the work of the Dominican school of Le Saulchoir and the Jesuit school of La Fouvière. *Theologisch testament*, p. 42. 'Soms wordt gezegd dat de theologie in de Rooms-Katholieke kerk vernieuwd werd door het Tweede Vaticaans Concilie. Dit is onjuist. Vaticanum II was (althans in theologisch opzicht) veeleer zelf een bevestiging van de vernieuwende tendensen in de Westeuropese theologie die zich na de anti-modernistische crisis tot op de vooravond van het nieuwe concilie had gevormd.' *Theologisch testament*, p. 40.

[182] Schillebeeckx, 'Christian Faith and Man's Expectation for the Future on Earth', p. 71.

existential experience' of humanity. There is no contradiction between a temporal and hence dynamic anthropology and a theocentric anthropology that defines the meaning of human life in its relation to God. The lack of contradiction here follows from the nature of God in whom there is no contradiction between transcendence and immanence, difference and relation. Schillebeeckx underlines the specifically theological coherence of a dynamic anthropology in light of revelation: 'The light that the theologian has here has [*sic*] remained the same – man is "of God", he is included in the mystery of God that was manifested in the life and death of Jesus who was brought to life by God'.[183] And precisely because of this particular theocentric interpretation of the meaning of human life, one which holds together divine transcendence with divine personal immanence within history, Schillebeeckx can say at the same time, 'The task of revelation continues to acquire constantly new forms in light of man's increasing understanding of himself'.[184]

The result of this coherence between a historical and therefore dynamic understanding of human life, and the transcendent yet immanent nature of God – the interpretation of the existential experience of humanity in light of revelation – is an anthropology that is both temporal and eschatological: 'a taking of the world itself with us in our christian expectation of the future which is already transforming the earth here and now'.[185] Because God who is our meaning both transcends creation and yet is immanent within creation, an anthropology that is coherent with the nature of God necessarily holds together the meaning of humanity that transcends history – 'the Christian expectation of the future' – with the meaning of humanity that is immanent within history – 'which is already transforming the earth here and now'.[186] This is the theocentric and Christological significance of an anthropology in light of revelation: because God is transcendence God is the meaning of humanity as its ultimate future that transcends history; because God is immanent God is the meaning of humanity as its future already present in a personal and salvific manner within history.

Implicit in this theocentric anthropology that is both temporal and eschatological is the understanding that anthropology in light of revelation is a description of the meaning of human life that involves an understanding of what constitutes meaningful human action. To separate the definition of the meaning of human life from an understanding of meaningful human action would be, in Schillebeeckx's terms, a 'forsaking of our eschatological hope': 'It is precisely because the christian hopes for a "new heaven and a new earth" that he can never reconcile himself to an "established order" in the world, since this would be, by definition, a forsaking of his eschatological

---

[183] Ibid. p. 82.
[184] Ibid. p. 80.
[185] Ibid. p. 71.
[186] Ibid. p. 71.

hope.'[187] Because our eschatological hope – God who is our future – is the meaning of human life, to forsake this eschatological hope would be to forsake the definition of what it means ultimately to be human. It follows that the meaning of human life cannot be found in an established order but is rather found in meaningful human action: active participation in 'transforming the earth here and now'. Therefore, in the light of revelation, of its theocentric and Christological nature, humanity's metaphysical significance – the meaning of human being – and our moral significance – meaningful human action – is inseparable.

Schillebeeckx's description of a mature and lucid faith – 'a living, mature and lucid faith which is strong enough for martyrdom'[188] – and hence also of a correspondingly mature theology – 'all that the christian knows in the light of revelation is that the expectation of the future on earth is included and secure in the absolute, gratuitous and forgiving proximity of God's grace'[189] – is found in an essay, which is his commentary on one of the most important of the documents of Vatican II, 'The Pastoral Constitution on the Church in the World Today'(*Gaudium et spes*).[190] This commentary is interesting in several respects. Certainly one of these is that it illustrates quite vividly the extent to which Schillebeeckx's theology prior to the Council had reached a maturity, both generally in its pastoral and intellectual commitments and quite specifically in its theological anthropology; furthermore, it underlines the significance he attaches to the eschatological theology vis-à-vis theological anthropology. For these reasons it is a fitting place to end this chapter.

Schillebeeckx's reflections on *Gaudium et spes*, written in the immediate aftermath of the Council, are interesting and apposite at present as theologians look back over more than forty years since the approbation of the final text, and they are important for an interpretation of his own theology, which had clearly come to maturity prior to the Council. Moreover, here, his reflections on *Gaudium et spes* are of particular importance because they highlight the fundamentally eschatological nature of his theological anthropology. Essentially, his commentary on *Gaudium et spes* and his analysis of its strengths and weaknesses is a critique of its theological anthropology, and this critique revolves around the question of eschatology: 'What is the connection between humanity's expectation for the future on earth and the christian hope of eschatological completion? What is the relationship

---

[187] Ibid. p. 71.
[188] Ibid. p. 60.
[189] Ibid. p. 82.
[190] Tanner, ed., *Decrees of the Ecumenical Councils, II*, pp. 1069–1135. For Schillebeeckx's commentary see 'Christian Faith and Man's Expectation for the Future on Earth', pp. 51–89.

between humanisation and the kingdom of God?'[191] For Schillebeeckx the eschatological aspect of anthropology contributes substantively to the non-dualistic, non-reductive and non-competitive characteristic of a theology of human action: 'competition between God and man's process of humanisation is senseless'.[192] His summary of the anthropology of *Gaudium et spes* serves equally as a description of his own: 'No christian anthropology; rather God is close to man in grace'.[193]

Placing eschatology at the heart of his interpretation of the merits of *Gaudium et spes* makes sense for Schillebeeckx both as a pastoral theologian and as a speculative theologian. Pastorally, one of the great strengths of Vatican II and of *Gaudium et spes* is the recognition of the historical and therefore dynamic characteristic of human self-understanding and, in the face of this truth about human life, an openness to respond to the contemporary human situation. One of the strengths of *Gaudium et spes* is its recognition that humanity itself is 'becoming more and more the subject of history'. Humanity 'makes history' – and the goal of this history-making is to create a 'future on earth in which it is good to live'.[194] In its modern self-understanding, humanity has become conscious of itself as the subject of history.[195] In light of this contemporary situation of humanity, Schillebeeckx's critique of *Gaudium et spes* is at one level a pastoral reflection. Commenting on the attempt of an early schema of *Gaudium et spes* to present an adequate theological anthropology – a 'christian anthropology in outline' – Schillebeeckx makes the following observation:

[I]t presented a very dualistic picture of the church and the world and it did not seem to be sufficiently aware of the fact that christian believers did not regard the world as something outside themselves, but as

---

[191] Schillebeeckx, 'Christian Faith and Man's Expectation for the Future on Earth', p. 63.
[192] Ibid. p. 64.
[193] Ibid. p. 72.
[194] Ibid. p. 63.
[195] Schillebeeckx describes this new self-consciousness of humanity in relation to a new world-view: the understanding that humanity controls nature and hence controls its own future. 'Christian Faith and Man's Expectation for the Future on Earth', p. 81: 'In the past, nature was directly experienced as God's creation. Now, however, it is regarded as the rough building material from which man creates his human world. Nature is no longer the subject – it has become the object of man's control. This change in man's view of the world has brought about a change in his view of man. Man now experiences himself as a being who makes history. Humanising nature, he humanises himself. . . . The new image of man and the world is directed toward the future. This new image, unlike the earlier image of man and the world, is basically a project for the future. Man's aim is to build a new world. Paradise, the "golden age", is no longer in the past. It lies ahead, in the future, and nature is the raw material with which man is to build this new world for the benefit of all.'

their own lives . . . [I]t also failed because the view of man expressed by the document remained static and firmly individualistic, with the result that man's social and historical dimensions and his relationship with nature did not emerge sufficiently clearly from the background. Above all, however, the document threw no light whatever on the relationship between man's expectations for the future on earth and the christian expectation for the future.[196]

Following from this observation, Schillebeeckx goes on to remark that his own analysis of *Gaudium et spes* – there were already many commentaries on this document – will focus on one perspective: 'the relationship between humanity's expectations for the future on earth and the christian expectation'.[197]

Schillebeeckx has clearly identified one question as the most pressing: although many aspects are important for a theological anthropology, including the social, temporal, and contingent: the relation between meaningful human action and the divine fulfilment of human life is the pivotal question. There are clear echoes here of Schillebeeckx's understanding of the 'intention' of the theological discourse on human life: theological anthropology is the reflection on what God intends for human life – it belongs within the discourse on divine Providence. The interpretation of God's providence and the interpretation of eschatology are coherent, and together they provide Schillebeeckx with a theocentric anthropology that is consistent with his doctrine of God. It is an anthropology that defines humanity in terms of its creative, salvific, sanctifying, participative and personal nature in relation to God. At the centre of this definition is Schillebeeckx's fundamental conviction that theology must be consistent with the truth that *theologia* – the *Sacra Doctrina de Trinitate* – cannot be separated from, or worse, contrasted with, *oikonomia* – the theology of the mystery of Christ.[198] 'The creator and the bringer of salvation cannot be played off against each other'.[199]

These echoes become even more pronounced when considering the more speculatively theological reasons for placing the question of eschatology at the beginning of a critique of the theological anthropology of *Gaudium et spes*. Clearly there is a pastoral reason for this: the acknowledgement that the Council must address the contemporary situation of humanity.

---

[196] Schillebeeckx, 'Christian Faith and Man's Expectation for the Future on Earth', p. 52.
[197] Ibid. p. 53. Schillebeeckx acknowledges that a large number of commentaries had already been written on *Gaudium et spes;* however, in his opinion, many of these have 'forgotten to make clear what the constitution really has to say to us.' In other words, in neglecting to evaluate the eschatological question other commentaries had not provided a sufficiently robust theological analysis of the text.
[198] Schillebeeckx, 'What is Theology?', p. 98.
[199] Schillebeeckx, 'Christian Faith and Man's Expectation for the Future on Earth', p. 64.

For theological anthropology this meant addressing humanity's understanding of itself as the maker of history and as the creator of its own future on earth. Yet for Schillebeeckx, the pastoral nature of *Gaudium et spes* flows from its theology: its pastoral commitment to humanity's historical and hence developing self-understanding is the result of a theology of revelation and a doctrine of God. This theology of revelation – 'God reveals humanity to itself precisely by revealing himself as love to humanity' – and of the nature of God – 'the *same* God who is the creator is the redeemer' – Schillebeeckx describes as the two 'fundamental insights of the pastoral constitution, in light of which many of the other statements in the constitution become clear'.[200] And here it becomes clear just to what extent he thought that the theology of Vatican II was the affirmation of the theology which he had made his own in the two decades prior to the Council.

The pivotal ideas which govern Schillebeeckx's own theology are found in his description of the two fundamental insights in light of which he argues *Gaudium et spes* is to be interpreted. The first insight is a statement of the theocentric and Christological nature of revelation which for Schillebeeckx has clear anthropological consequences:

> God gives man an insight into his own conditions, God reveals man to himself precisely by revealing himself as love to man. This insight is basic to the theological foundations of the constitution. Every theological statement, that is, everything that is said about God, is at the same time a statement about man. The consequence of this, which, although it is not explicitly formulated, is clearly felt in the constitution, is that man's new experiences also have something to say to us about God's intentions with us.[201]

The anthropological consequence is that God reveals humanity to itself: God gives humanity insight into what it means to be human. Divine revelation discloses the truth of what it means to be human in itself – in its own condition. At the heart of this insight is an interpretation of the doctrine of

---

[200] Ibid. p. 54. These two 'fundamental insights' are contained in one article of the Constitution that serves as a summary for Schillebeeckx of the entire document: 'Contemporary humanity is in process of developing its personality and of increasingly identifying and claiming its rights. Since the church has been entrusted with making manifest the mystery of God, who is our ultimate goal, at the same time it discloses to us the meaning of our existence, or the intimate truth about ourselves. . . . Only God, who created us in the divine image and redeemed us from sin, can give a complete answer to these questions; and God does this through his revelation in the Son who became human. Whoever follows Christ, the perfect human being, becomes more of a human being'. *Gaudium et spes* art. 41. See Tanner, ed., *Decrees of the Ecumenical Councils, II*, p. 1094.

[201] Schillebeeckx, 'Christian Faith and Man's Expectation for the Future on Earth', p. 54.

revelation in which the 'infinite is disclosed within the finite without destroying it'.[202] What is most interesting here is the interpretation of divine revelation that describes the relation of infinite to finite specifically in terms of God's self-revelation. In other words, for Schillebeeckx, the full significance of the meaning of revelation is disclosed only when these two truths are interpreted together: 'The infinite is disclosed in the finite without destroying it', and 'God reveals humanity to itself precisely by revealing himself as love to humanity'.

By holding these two insights together Schillebeeckx is underscoring a fundamental assumption expressed in his Christology. Not only does the relationship of the divine to the human constitute the meaning of human life, the divine also presupposes the human in order to be meaning for humanity.

Based on God's universal will to save and of the central fact of Christ's death and resurrection for all, grace is concealed but active in the whole of human life, in everything that we call human. It is evident from the fact that the Son of God was truly man, that Jesus' personal humanity was the revelation of grace. In him the deepest meaning of our being man was made manifest to us. Personal humanity is therefore always a possibility of revelation, the sphere in which revelation and grace are accomplished. What is human is thus the material through which the revelation of God's grace is expressed.[203]

The extent to which a theological discourse on humanity must be non-dualistic is quite clear from Schillebeeckx's Christology. At the heart of this Christology is a particular interpretation of incarnation: 'It is evident from the fact that the Son of God was truly man, that Jesus' personal humanity was the revelation of grace'.[204] The emphasis on the personal nature of the humanity of Jesus that is characteristic of Schillebeeckx's interpretation of incarnation – and a characteristically Dominican interpretation – is of decisive importance for his theological anthropology.

Although this topic of Christology and incarnation begins to encroach on the following chapter on grace and also anticipates the analysis of Christology in the second half of the thesis, it is worth introducing here because it is also an important feature of the relation between revelation and the theological discourse on humanity. For Schillebeeckx to say that humanity is revealed to itself in God's self-revelation as love to humanity means that God's self-revelation presupposes humanity. This is the 'deepest meaning of being human' as it is revealed in Christ: 'What is human is the material through which the revelation of God's grace is expressed'.[205] This is the relation between the theologal life and ethics that Schillebeeckx describes as 'the demand of revelation': the structure of revelation itself demands of humanity

---

[202] Schillebeeckx, 'What is Theology?', p. 109.
[203] Schillebeeckx, 'Christian Faith and Man's Expectation for the Future on Earth', p. 75.
[204] Ibid.
[205] Ibid.

a 'radical love of our fellow human beings which is the gift of God's absolute and forgiving love'.[206] The relationship with God is not something added, it is constitutive of humanity's 'metaphysical and moral significance'.[207]

For Schillebeeckx this insight into the content and structure of divine revelation, and hence into the revealed nature of humanity, is entirely dependent upon another fundamental insight: the nature of God. The God who is creator – cause, transcendence and difference – is the God who is redeemer – immanent and personal. In fact, there is perhaps no more accurate description of Schillebeeckx's theology than to say that it is an extended commentary on the following:

> [T]he *same* God who is the creator is also the redeemer; the *same* God is also the Lord both of the history of man and of the history of salvation. Creation and covenant – these form one divine structure and this is also seen in its historical consequences.[208]

In this 'divine structure' humanity is revealed as an absolute dependence which is at the same time a situated freedom. The ground for humanity's definition as dependence and freedom is divine transcendence: the God who is creator and the Lord of history is the ultimate meaning of human being.

In this chapter the extent to which the content and structure of revelation – *theologia* and *oikonomia* – determines theology has emerged. The consequence of this for a theological anthropology is the definition of humanity as a vocation to intimacy with God, which is coherent with the content and structure of revelation itself. Such an anthropology is defined by the nature of the human–divine relation: creative, salvific, sanctifying, participative and personal. In God's self-revelation, humanity is revealed to itself in a specific providential relationship to the divine where God is the meaning of humanity. The topic for the following chapter is Schillebeeckx's theology of grace that builds on this relation between revelation and theological anthropology. In particular, the implications of his treatise on the mystery God for an interpretation of humanity's historicity – situated freedom – are developed more fully. God is the future for humanity in a relationship of grace, and this means that just as the divine is constitutive of the human so too is humanity's future constitutive of its present. Humanity's vocation to intimacy with God is the vocation to intimacy with God as our future where this in no way negates human historical existence. Ultimately, the relation of human–divine intimacy is sacramental.

---

[206] Ibid. p. 80; 61. Schillebeeckx's kenotic Christology is the ground for a kenotic interpretation of the meaning of human life: 'Humanity comes to itself in giving itself to the other'.

[207] Schillebeeckx, 'Dialogue with God and Christian Secularity', p. 215.

[208] Schillebeeckx, 'Christian Faith and Man's Expectation for the Future on Earth', p. 54.

2

GRACE AND HUMAN BEING

Introduction

Edward Schillebeeckx has never written a theological treatise on the nature of human being. In fact from some of his own remarks it would seem he has quite deliberately not written a theological anthropology. Of the Vatican II document that most closely resembles a theological anthropology, *Gaudium et spes*, Schillebeeckx says with approval: 'No christian anthropology; rather God is close to man in grace' – *'Geen "christelijke" antropologie, slechts: God is de mens genadig nabij'*.[1] For a study of his theological anthropology this is a rather arresting statement and provides the subject for this chapter: what does it mean to say that there is no Christian anthropology, rather God is close to humanity in grace?

Schillebeeckx's reflection on the meaning of grace is given a particular focus by the time and context in which he is writing. Not only does he say 'no treatise on Christian anthropology', but he goes further and suggests the 'old' treatise on grace itself no longer works: 'Speculation about the relationship between "nature" and the "supernatural", which preoccupied theologians in the past, has been transformed in modern theology, into the problem of the relationship between man's expectation for the future here on earth and the eschatological kingdom'.[2] The tension between a historical consciousness and belief in the eschatological fulfilment of human life gives a new context for a theology of grace. In fact, in Schillebeeckx's own work and in the writing of many other theologians in the mid-twentieth century, this context provided the catalyst for a wholly renewed theology of grace. Thus the topic for this chapter becomes slightly more specific: what does it

---

[1] Schillebeeckx, 'Christian Faith and Man's Expectation for the Future on Earth', in *The Mission of the Church*, p. 73; 'Christelijk geloof en aardse toekomstverwachting', in *De zending van de kerk*, p. 61.

[2] Schillebeeckx, 'Christian Faith and Man's Expectation for the Future on Earth', p. 82.

mean to say that God is close to humanity in grace when the nature of grace itself is eschatological? The answer to this question picks up the theme of the previous chapter and provides the structure for this chapter on grace: revelation itself does not 'provide us with a christian anthropology ... Christianity knows no more about human anthropology than this – whatever man is, this is included in the mystery of God, in other words, the mystery that is man is in the deepest sense the mystery of God'.[3]

For Schillebeeckx understanding what 'grace' means infers the interpretation of God as a value in himself because it is in this manner that God is the value, and hence the meaning, of human life.[4] Grace describes the relationship between God and humanity to which Schillebeeckx is pointing when he says: theologically everything said about God is at the same time said of humanity. In short, God is the future of humanity. This truth gives decisive shape and content to the theological treatise on grace. This is consistent with Schillebeeckx's understanding of the overarching task of theology. The task of theology is 'letting God be God'; and it is the 'priority of grace' that lets God be God for humanity.[5] Grace is the theological discourse on God as the ultimate value of human life. The priority of grace means theology can never be concerned with *either* God *or* humanity but must always address God *and* humanity.

Schillebeeckx's theology of grace attempts what he describes as 'the breakthrough of a new appreciation of God, of God as a value in and of himself worthy of love – the heart and the centre of all values'.[6] What this actually means for Schillebeeckx is a theological *ressourcement* in light of the pressing pastoral questions posed by modern humanity's deepening historical consciousness, and in particular as it takes the forms of secularism and atheism. How does the theologian respond as humanity becomes more and more conscious of itself as the maker of its own history, as the bearer of its own future? Can the theologian maintain in any coherent fashion a theological discourse on the meaning of human life and the value of human action? How is it possible to say, on the one hand, 'I am really myself in and of this world, becoming myself more and more therein', and on the other hand say, 'I am really myself completely of God, from whom I borrow myself and by whom I am given to myself'?[7]

---

[3] Ibid. pp. 78–79.

[4] Schillebeeckx, 'What is Theology?', in *Revelation and Theology, I: Revelation, Tradition and Theological Reflection*, 2nd ed. (London: Sheed and Ward, 1987), pp. 138–139.

[5] Schillebeeckx, 'Thomas Aquinas: Passion for Truth and Loving Service to Men and Women', in *For the Sake of the Gospel*, p. 125; *God is New Each Moment: in Conversation with Huub Oosterhuis and Piet Hoogeven*, trans. David Smith (Edinburgh: T&T Clark, 1983)., p. 9.

[6] Schillebeeckx, 'Life in God and Life in the World', in *God and Man*, trans. Edward Fitzgerald and Peter Tomlinson (London: Sheed and Ward, 1969), p. 95.

[7] Edward Schillebeeckx, 'Dialogue with God and Christian Secularity', in *God and Man*, trans. Edward Fitzgerald and Peter Tomlinson (London: Sheed and Ward, 1969), p. 215.

In Schillebeeckx's estimation Thomas Aquinas does just this, and it represents the crowning achievement of his theology. For Thomas the treatise on God reveals God as constitutive of the meaning of human being.[8] The insight upon which this is founded is that the one and the same God is creator and redeemer. The true subject of theology is the living God: the *Deus sub ratione Deitatis* who is the *Deus salutaris*'.[9] Theology is the reflection upon the nature of God in light of God's self-revelation in history as salvation. The implication for theological anthropology follows therefore that 'the definition of humanity will only be seen clearly when we consider humanity in light of the dogma of creation and salvation'. For Schillebeeckx this means theological speculation on the meaning of human life takes place from within, it presupposes, the entire historical existence and experience of humanity.[10] When he turns to interpreting the relationship between nature and grace it follows logically that he understands grace is both constitutive of, and presupposes, nature.

To say God is the 'value' of human existence means there can be no natural end to this existence apart from this value, that is to say, apart from God. God, creator and redeemer, is the beginning and end of humanity, and in this God is the value of humanity. This is what Schillebeeckx means when he says God is the future of humanity – there is no human existence apart from grace:

> Human existence is something granted, it is a grace: an overwhelming grace. I am given the chance to be a human being . . . [this] reminds us of the biblical idea of our fortunes being dependent upon God's grace: 'Towards you was I cast from my birth' (Ps. 22. 10).[11]

Human existence is of its very nature, grace. In its beginning and in its end humanity is dependent upon God as creator and as redeemer. God is

---

[8] Schillebeeckx, 'Theologia or Oikonomia?', in *Revelation and Theology, II: The Concept of Truth and Theological Renewal*, trans. N. D. Smith (New York: Sheed and Ward, 1968), pp. 83–84: 'While conceptual thought in all its forms is not pernicious, not every form of such thinking can be approved . . . there is in other words a rationalising kind of conceptualism which attempts to enclose the inexpressible in conceptual terms, and there is, on the other hand, a kind of conceptual thought which leaves the mystery *as a mystery* and tries somehow to express it precisely as a saving mystery, with the result that the concepts of faith radiate a value for life. . . . Aquinas' crowning achievement in the sphere of theology may well be that he built the value of dogma for life on the basis of its meaning and value as truth, at the same time remaining fully aware of the value of truth for human life.'

[9] Schillebeeckx, 'What is Theology?', pp. 138–139.

[10] Schillebeeckx, 'Dialogue with God and Christian Secularity', p. 215.

[11] Ibid. p. 210.

close to humanity in grace as the ultimate meaning of human existence: this is the theology of grace that is coherent with the mystery of God and with the structure of revelation. For Schillebeeckx the treatise on grace means that God is the value of human life, and in light of revelation itself this is both an eschatological truth and a historical reality; this truth that God is the value of human life is dependent upon 'an appreciation of God, of God as a value in and of himself worthy of love – the heart and centre of all other values'. The theological treatise on grace must be coherent with the nature of God. The influence of Thomas in this context is very apparent.

One of the ways theology has responded meaningfully to the contemporary human questions of historical consciousness is by recovering from within the tradition a true and faithful interpretation of Thomas' treatise on grace. This *ressourcement* is a very fruitful and creative source within twentieth century theology because it has recovered an interpretation of the meaning of grace that is not predicated on a dualistic relation of grace to nature.[12] This transforms the relationship of church to world and of eschatology to history. The ultimate expression of a non-dualistic interpretation of grace is one that binds together human historical reality with eschatology: 'No longer flight from the world, but flight with the world towards the future, a taking of the world with us in our christian expectation of the future which is already transforming the earth here and now'.[13] The ground for this particular eschatology, one in which the Christian expectation of the future is already at work in the present is the historical nature of God's personal presence to humanity: 'all that the christian knows in light of revelation is that this expectation of the future on earth

---

[12] See Fergus Kerr, 'French Theology: Yves Congar and Henri de Lubac', in ed., David Ford, *The Modern Theologians* 2nd ed. (Blackwell, 1997), pp. 105–117 (p. 114): it is the insight of the ressourcement theologians, expounded most thoroughly by Henri de Lubac, 'that in the whole Catholic tradition until the sixteenth century the idea of humanity as the image of God had prevailed. Neither in patristic nor in medieval theology, and certainly not in Thomas Aquinas, was the hypothesis entertained of a purely natural destiny for human beings, something less than the supernatural and eschatological vision of God. There is only this world, the world in which nature has been created for a supernatural destiny. Historically there never was a graceless nature, or a world outside the christian dispensation. . . . Aquinas recognises only one destiny, a supernatural one, for the human being. With the whole patristic and earlier medieval tradition, he is looking at the one and only world in which nature and grace, though totally different, are yet intimately related, in the sense that nature exists for the sake of grace, is subordinate to it, and has its ultimate destiny in it. For Aquinas there is no ultimate happiness for the human soul that brackets out an eschatological vision of God.'

[13] Schillebeeckx, 'Christian Faith and Man's Expectation for the Future on Earth', p. 71.

is included and secure in the absolute, gratuitous and forgiving proximity of God's grace'.[14]

In Schillebeeckx's understanding, 'no christian anthropology; rather God is close to humanity in grace' means that the definition of humanity is given as the vocation to intimacy with God who is the beginning and the future of humanity. Theological anthropology is not a 'definitive statement' or a 'theory' about humanity, it is description of an active hope that best describes the eschatological relation of grace between the mystery of humanity and the mystery of God:

> Precisely because the christian believes in the absolute future, the future which is God himself for man, he cannot describe the precise shape of this future meaningfully . . . and he can never confuse or iden- tify the result of man's historical striving on earth with the promised 'new world'. After all, if God is the intangible, incomprehensible mys- tery and man is embraced by this mystery, then man's being is, by definition, also a mystery. . . . But christian hope in God who is man's future, is not a theory, but an active hope, which only becomes a real- ity in man's working for a better future on earth. . . . This radical commitment to our fellow-men is an incomprehensible love and this love, because it is incomprehensible, makes the commitment com- pletely radical. . . . Our commitment as christians to our fellow-men is completely radical because it is the other side of the coin of God's personal love for man. . . . It is of its very nature, a hoping in God as the future of man.[15]

It is this 'veiled' but nevertheless 'real' relationship between human tempo- rality and contingency and the eschatological future, between the future on earth and God who is the future of humanity, which leads Schillebeeckx to describe theological anthropology itself as a treatise on grace. It is an eschatological interpretation of grace that establishes the value of the historical by holding the historical in a non-reductive, non-dualistic and non-competitive relation with its eschatological future. The nature of human action finds ultimate meaning rather than negation in this relationship.

Theology is always an activity of 'conversion': 'Theology must allow itself to be corrected by the reality of revelation'.[16] For the theologian the most 'profound conversion can sometimes be the recognition of old truths', and in Schillebeeckx's estimation, theology's recovery of a properly Thomist non-dualistic treatise on grace, grounded in the intrinsic relation between the historical and the eschatological, is one of the most significant gains of

---

[14] Ibid. p. 82.
[15] Ibid. pp. 86–87.
[16] Schillebeeckx, 'What is Theology?', p. 132.

mid-twentieth century theology.[17] This chapter has three sections as it analyses the treatise on grace central to Schillebeeckx's theological anthropology. It continues to develop the ideas central to his interpretation of revelation and builds upon these by expanding upon the nature of humanity's vocation to intimacy with God and the nature of humanity's vocation to this intimacy in the world. The first section of the chapter is on grace and revelation; the second section is on intimacy between God and humanity as 'graced nature'; and the third section is on being incarnate in the world in grace. This final section turns more consciously from the theocentric aspects of theological anthropology to begin the discussion of its Christological structure – although of course these are inseparable for Schillebeeckx. In this section, Schillebeeckx's *ressourcement* recovers a patristic kenotic Christology, and this forms the basis for his description of the human vocation to be in the world as radical love: 'I only come to myself in giving myself to the other'.[18]

There is a subtopic that runs alongside the subject of grace in this chapter, that is, the relation between positive and speculative theology in Schillebeeckx's work: positive, or historical theology, is theology itself. Some of the most significant contributions that Schillebeeckx makes to theology in the first half of his career are found in his analyses of the theological tradition and in his abilities as a *ressourcement* theologian. One of the strengths of this work is that it is not divorced from speculative theology: his reading of the tradition is in itself the *locus* for much of his own originality as a theologian, and this follows from the fact that historical theology itself is never practised in abstraction from contemporary pastoral questions. In response to the human questions that theology must address, and in dialogue with fresh insights of contemporary philosophy and theology, Schillebeeckx retrieves from the tradition strands that have been forgotten – his kenotic Christology is one example – or strands that have been distorted – the treatise on grace. In light of the relation between speculative and positive theology in Schillebeeckx's writings, and in part because he offers a valuable insight into the development of theology itself, this chapter focuses on Schillebeeckx's analysis of modern theology just prior to Vatican II.

Grace and Revelation

What Schillebeeckx means when he states, 'no christian anthropology; rather God is close to humanity in grace' becomes clear in light of his theology of

---

[17] Schillebeeckx, 'Life in God and Life in the World', p. 95.
[18] Schillebeeckx, 'Christian Faith and Man's Expectations for the Future on Earth', p. 61.

revelation: in divine revelation the 'infinite is disclosed in the finite without destroying it'.[19] This is a statement concerning the ultimate value of the human and the historical. Human knowledge of the God who is creator – cause, transcendence and utter difference – presupposes creaturely concepts; and human knowledge of this same God as the Lord of salvation history – personally immanent – presupposes the historical. In other words the human relation to the divine reveals and establishes the ultimate value of the human. Divine revelation is sacramental: it takes a human and historical form. Schillebeeckx's theology is a constant reflection on the following:

> The same God who is the creator is also the redeemer; the same God is also the Lord both of the history of man and of the history of salvation. Creation and covenant – these form one divine structure and this is also seen in its historical consequences.[20]

The pivotal concept here is that the divine structure of revelation, and consequently the nature of the relation between God and humanity, has historical consequences. For Schillebeeckx this means that revelation is received in history – revelation in word – and revelation makes history – revelation in reality.[21] The implication for a theological interpretation of human freedom is significant, especially for a modern theology that addresses the tension between humanity's expectation for the future, which women and men build on earth and the future expectation of the eschatological kingdom. God does not 'bypass' human freedom to intervene in history. Just the opposite: our freedom to bring about events in this world is the revelation of God's action . . . this revelation is a charge imposed on our free will'.[22]

One of the essential features of Schillebeeckx's anthropology is the concept that the value of the human is established and not negated by the transcendent. It is simply not the case that 'for every step forward man takes, God has to take a step backwards'.[23] The ultimate value of the human does not depend on the denial of the transcendent; rather it depends on a correct understanding of the God's nature as transcendence and, for that matter, as immanence. This is so much the case for him that he is prepared to hold

[19] Schillebeeckx, 'What is Theology?', p. 109.
[20] Schillebeeckx, 'Christian Faith and Man's Expectations for the Future on Earth', p. 54.
[21] Schillebeeckx, 'Revelation-in-reality and revelation-in-word', in, *Revelation and Theology*, I, pp. 36–62. 'Werkelijkheidsopenbaring en woordopenbaring', in *Openbaring en Theologie*, pp. 33–49. First published in *Lumière et Vie* 46 (1960), 25–45.
[22] Schillebeeckx, 'God in Dry Dock', in *God and Man*, p. 10.
[23] Ibid. p. 4.

theologians themselves, and theological misconceptions of God's nature, to blame for the 'death of God':

> For our part we must ask ourselves whether it wasn't the believers themselves who brought atheism into being – not in their beliefs, of course, but by their distorted interpretations of those beliefs. And there we have it: it was through their erroneous ideas about God that believers gave atheism its real chance. However, we should not over-look the implication of this: that atheism is nothing other than a rejection of those erroneous ideas about God and a condemnation of a Christianity which is not being systematically lived and experienced. In short the real atheists are probably not where we think we have encountered them. Because of all this it has frequently been pointed out that perhaps present-day atheism is, after all a merciful dispensa-tion, a new chance of salvation offered us by God, a chance to purify our beliefs of all the human dross and all the selfish distortions inevitably involved in any attempt to ensure ourselves a quiet life.[24]

Here the link between theology's pastoral responsibility to the present and speculative theology's responsibility to offer a critique of the tradition is clear. The theologian acts as a 'catalyst' not only with respect to contempo-rary developments in theology but with respect to interpretations of past tradition. Theology, 'submits the present with its own possibilities to comparison with the dangerous recollections of certain events and legacies from the past'.[25] Here quite specifically, Schillebeeckx calls speculative theology to its properly pastoral responsibility: there can be no disjunction between humanity's 'metaphysical' and 'moral' significance, and hence descriptions of the nature of God and of meaningful human action must be non-contradictory.[26]

For Schillebeeckx the ultimate value of the human does not depend on the denial of the transcendent rather, it depends on a specific understanding of the transcendent. This is the importance of his appropriation and interpreta-tion of Thomas' treatise on God. There are two key features to this for Schillebeeckx. First, in the tripartite distinction – God as cause, transcend-ence and difference – the identity of *de Deo Uno* is constitutive of human being. In God's absolute transcendence and difference, God is constitutive of humanity and is therefore utterly immediate to human being: God is the

---

[24] Ibid. pp. 8; 9: 'The fact believers put their trust in God is not what brings grist to the atheist mill, but that in the meantime they neglect their secular duty and worldly tasks'.
[25] Schillebeeckx, 'Dominican Spirituality', in *God among Us: The Gospel Proclaimed*, trans. John Bowden (London: SCM, 1983), p. 240.
[26] Schillebeeckx, 'Dialogue with God and Christian Secularity', p. 215.

most immediate relation and humanity exists 'first for God'.[27] The key anthropological interpretation here for Schillebeeckx is the truth that in this most immediate relationship to absolute transcendence humanity receives its personal nature – humanity comes from the hand of God as 'person', as a 'situated freedom'.[28]

The second feature of Thomas' treatise on God, as Schillebeeckx receives it and worth noting again, is the insight that the same God who is creator is also redeemer:

> How splendid and illuminating a treatise on de Deo Uno could be if it were a theological reflection on the experience of the people of Israel with their God in the history which provides the clearest intimation of God's innermost being.[29]

Just as God's transcendence and difference establishes and presupposes the finite, so too does God's immanence. God immanent in history and person-ally active in history does not negate the historical. On the contrary, this establishes its ultimate meaning without destroying it: 'The history that is made by men becomes itself the material through which God makes saving history and through which he accomplishes his revelation'. Furthermore, God immanent in history presupposes the historical: 'God's saving activity is revealed by becoming history, and it becomes history by being revealed'.[30]

This is the treatise on God – God's transcendence that establishes the human in its personal contingent and temporal identity – from which Schillebeeckx derives his theology of grace. Therefore when Schillebeeckx states, 'no christian anthropology; rather God is close to man in grace', he is arguing against any dualistic or reductionist understandings of the relation between the infinite and finite, between the human and divine, between church and world, and between faith and ethics. It follows logically from the premise that 'whatever is said of God is at the same time something which is said of humanity', that a false understanding of God's transcendence – or immanence – leads inevitably to a false understanding of what it means to be human:

> Perhaps the prompt retreat of God each time man makes a step for-ward in his history really shows us that it is only a pseudo-God which fades away, and not a living God under whose protection man has just

---

[27] Ibid.
[28] Ibid.
[29] Schillebeeckx, 'Theologia or Oikonomia?', p. 96.
[30] Ibid. p. 103.

made a step forward. Again and again he walks one step further with us; and together, God and ourselves, we dislodge the pseudo-God.[31]

Here the importance of the relation between *theologia* and *oikonomia* for theological anthropology asserts itself: if 'creation and covenant' are 'one structure' it follows that any theological anthropology that posits 'competition between God and man's process of humanisation' would be 'senseless'.[32]

This idea that 'creation' – the plan for humanity of the God who is transcendence and difference – and covenant – the intention of God who is personally immanent as salvation – is reflected in Schillebeeckx's understanding of the content and structure of theology itself: the subject of theology is the living God and hence theology is theocentric with a Christological structure. This understanding of theology secures the human definitively:

On the basis of God's universal will to save and of the central fact of Christ's death and resurrection for all men, grace is concealed but active in the whole of human life, in everything that we call human. It is evident from the fact that the Son of God was truly man, that Jesus' personal humanity was the revelation of grace. In him the deepest meaning of our being man was made manifest to us. Personal humanity is therefore always a possibility of revelation, the sphere in which revelation and grace are accomplished. What is human is thus the material through which the revelation of God's grace is expressed.[33]

For Schillebeeckx then, a theological anthropology that is coherent with the nature of God is a theocentric anthropology which has a Christological structure: 'revelation tells us no more than this' about what it means to be human in the relation to God that is constitutive of our being in this world.[34]

---

[31] Schillebeeckx, 'God in Dry Dock', p. 11; 'Christian Faith and Man's Expectation for the Future on Earth', p. 58.

[32] Schillebeeckx, 'Christian Faith and Man's Expectation for the Future on Earth', p. 64.

[33] Ibid. p. 75.

[34] Schillebeeckx, 'Christian Faith and Man's Expectation for the Future on Earth', p. 78: 'Revelation is concerned with God's love for the world. The bible does not provide us with an anthropology or a cosmology. All that it tells us is that man in the world is divinely loved by God. Precisely what man in the world is has to become apparent from human experience and therefore from human history. Revelation does not tell us what man appears to be in the course of history. It only tells us that whatever man appears to be in the course of history is sustained by the love of God, who does not

If there is one term that describes for Schillebeeckx the relation between God and humanity it is 'grace'. This is clear from his understanding of revelation: humanity is revealed to itself in God's self-revelation. In God's gracious relationship to humanity, the 'infinite is disclosed in the finite, without destroying it'. By binding the question of human identity to the question of God's self-revelation, Schillebeeckx indicates humanity is given to itself by God, and God gives humanity to itself in a specific manner: 'Human existence is something granted, it is a grace: an overwhelming grace. . . . "Towards you was I cast from my birth"'.[35] In other words, humanity is dependent upon the mystery of God both as creator and as redeemer. God's self-revelation is effected as salvation history. Therefore the questions, 'what is humanity?' and 'what is meaningful human existence?', are bound ineluctably to the questions: 'Who is God?' and 'How has God acted for humanity in history?'

If the question of human being and the question of God are bound together by God's self-revelation then it follows for Schillebeeckx that the structure of any theological anthropology must reflect the structure of revelation. In this manner theology can never be *either* theocentric *or* anthropocentric, it is always both. This has some clear consequences for his own theological anthropology, several of which come into focus with a careful consideration of what he means by the term 'grace' and what he understands to be the relation of nature to grace. It is the task of this chapter to offer a reading of Schillebeeckx's understanding of grace and the relation of grace to nature and, in light of this relation, to identify the specifically theological descriptions of human freedom and agency. From Schillebeeckx's theology of grace, it emerges that at the heart of his anthropology is a particular commitment to metaphysics – a metaphysical realism. This follows from his understanding of revelation, the relation of *theologia* and *oikonomia*, and the structure this interpretation of revelation gives to his theology, and in turn, points towards the manner in which Christology provides the structure for his theological anthropology.

Two distinct yet related issues are brought into focus when exploring Schillebeeckx's understanding of grace in its relation to nature, and the interplay between these has some bearing on the dynamic of this chapter itself. The first of these is of course the material question of the theological

regret the gift of his love. Revelation tells us no more than this about man in the world. That is borne out in the appearance of the man Jesus on earth. This absolute love of God to the very end appeared in him . . . And it becomes clear in the human life of Jesus that the only adequate human response to this love of God is *radical* love for our fellow-men, a love that is so radical and absolute that it is inwardly an absolute witness to God, in other words, that it only becomes intelligible in its radical character in light of the gift of God's love for us. This is really the whole of revelation'.

[35] Schillebeeckx, 'Dialogue with God and Christian Secularity', p. 210.

content of the treatise on grace itself. The second of these is the formal question of method. These two issues, the content of the Christian understanding of any particular 'dogmatic' question and the question of method are never separate questions for Schillebeeckx.

In all of Schillebeeckx's writings there is a constant and deliberate interplay between doctrinal questions and questions of method. These are not distinct realms of inquiry for him. This interplay is focused quite sharply in his understanding of the nature–grace relation. Indeed it is precisely because of his understanding of this relation that there is such an interplay between material and formal questions throughout his work. Consistently the formal questions of method are determined by the material questions of the content of Christian faith. In this chapter, Schillebeeckx's theology of grace is discussed as it comes to light through his own assessment of the strengths and weaknesses of modern twentieth century theology. This acknowledges Schillebeeckx's contribution both to speculative theology and positive theology. Much of Schillebeeckx's analysis of this period of theology focuses on the exchange – good and bad – between theology and contemporary philosophies. From his assessment of this exchange, it becomes clear the treatise on grace establishes the value of human historicity precisely by refusing to abandon the treatise on God as both transcendent and immanent, as utter difference and involvement in human history. Here it is evident that Schillebeeckx's treatise on grace is coherent with his theology of human being: it is the metaphysical and moral significance of humanity to exist first for God in the world – as absolute dependence and as situated freedom:

I am really myself in and of this world, becoming myself more and more therein, and yet at the same time created, even to the most delicate fibres of my being: completely of God, from whom I borrow myself and by whom I am continually given to myself. I am myself in dependence on God: the more I am God's the more I am become myself.[36]

The treatise on grace continues the description of the constitutive nature of the relation between the human and the divine, the finite and the infinite, the historical and the eschatological. It describes the nature of humanity's vocation to intimacy with God.

In the following section, the material question of the content of the treatise on grace and the formal questions of theological method are treated under the following rubrics: the notion of 'graced nature as communion' in the divine life; the motif of 'address and response' and corresponding implications for human freedom and agency; the necessary commitment of theology to metaphysics and its relation to contemporary philosophy; and the

[36] Ibid. p. 215.

81

question of the knowability of God and the relation between conceptual and non-conceptual knowledge.

Grace: The Human Vocation to Intimacy with God

There can be no doubt that one of the strengths of Schillebeeckx's theology is its engagement with those questions that most press upon meaningful human existence. Such engagement is marked by courage and academic rigour, fuelled by genuine pastoral interest and a restless intellectual energy. Far from being a theology without norms or criteria, this pastoral theology is shaped by a particular obligation that lies at the very core of Schillebeeckx's theological commitments. 'We have learnt', he wrote during the heady if fractious time immediately following Vatican II, 'that a dialogue without obligations, in the long run, itself becomes frozen'.[37] For the theologian, the obligation is to reflect continually upon the absolute primacy of God's grace as this is revealed by God in God's dealings with humanity. The graciousness of God's activity secures human dignity and identity. At the same time it determines what may be known about God. In other words, everything we claim theologically depends entirely upon the understanding of grace.

Nothing stands outside of God's grace. This, on Schillebeeckx's account, determines everything else because it prevents theology from slipping into dualistic descriptions of the relation between the divine and the human. In securing a non-dualistic foundation for theology, the understanding of grace and its relation to nature cut into the heart of the theological task. The nature–grace relation, if properly understood, allows for the development of a theology which – as Schillebeeckx would say – is not 'squint-eyed', that is, a theology that is not preoccupied with a series of pseudo-problems:

If there is anywhere in theology where we have an accumulation of psuedo-problems it is in the case of twin concepts like humanity and Christianity, human freedom and grace, evolution and creation, and even self-liberation and justification by grace alone. Often, such opposed concepts, which in fact have some support in reality are projected *as such* on to reality, where they then become two opposing realities which have to be dialectically reconciled! That is of course, a hopeless task, as is evident from the dispute over grace which has

---

[37] Schillebeeckx, 'Woord vooraf' in Mark Schoof, *Aggiornamento: De doorbraak van een nieuwe katholieke theologie* (Baarn: Wereldvenster, 1968), p. 11: '[M]en heeft ook lessen getrokken uit een vrijblivende dialoog die op den duur dialoog zelf bevriest'. *Breakthrough: Beginnings of the New Catholic Theology* (Dublin: Gill and Macmillan, 1970).

taken place in the Roman Catholic Church. In such cases we find ourselves up a blind alley.[38]

The pseudo-problems which beset theology once it becomes trapped in a dualistic description of the human–divine relation are derived not from acknowledging the difference between the human and divine – there is after all an intrinsic similitude which is also a dissimilitude – rather, the problems arise from the manner in which that difference is described and the way in which theology seeks to overcome it. The difficulty is not 'difference', it is the description of the relation.[39]

Theology gets into difficulty when it sets the human and divine in a relation of opposition. The distinction for Schillebeeckx between a theology that is, and is not, 'squint-eyed', lies between a theology that acknowledges there is 'some support in reality' for conceiving of the difference between the divine and human as 'opposition', and a theology that 'projects' a relation of opposition 'as such onto reality'. Theology assigns to itself a hopeless task if it seeks to describe the relation between the divine and human as a series of twin concepts or opposing realities that must be dialectically reconciled. Schillebeeckx's own theology attests to the recognition of difference between divine and human.

Schillebeeckx's insistence on placing grace at the centre of the theological task, his characteristically Dominican attentiveness to the questions of the knowability of God while acknowledging mystery and the place of negative theology, his constant grappling with the anguish of history and the eschatological promise for human history, all suggest that he is well prepared to address the issue of difference between the divine and human. Furthermore, the stark contrast between human suffering, the freedom and the real possibility to choose our own perdition, and God's active desire for human well-being and salvation suggest that the difference between divine and human is sometimes the difference of opposition. Yet theology is never *either* theocentric *or* anthropocentric, it is both. As we have seen, this is well described by Schillebeeckx in his understanding of revelation: God reveals himself to humanity by revealing humanity to itself. It is further underlined by the examples he selects to describe the accumulation of pseudo-problems

---

[38] Schillebeeckx, 'Christian Identity and Human Integrity' in *The Language of Faith: Essays on Jesus, Theology and the Church*, ed. Robert Schreiter (London: SCM, 1995), pp. 185–197 (pp. 185–186); also in *God among Us: the Gospel Proclaimed* (London: SCM, 1983), pp. 154–163. 'Christelijke identiteit en menselijke integriteit', *Concilium* 18 (1982), 34–42; also in *Evangelie Verhalen* (Baarn: Nelissen, 1982).

[39] Schillebeeckx, 'The Non-conceptual Intellectual Dimension in Our Knowledge of God according to Aquinas', in *Revelation and Theology, II*, p. 163: 'We know God as cause and by his transcendence and by his utter difference . . . a *similitude* which is naturally accompanied by a basic *dissimilitude*: in the effect is found something by means of which it differs from its cause'.

within theology: the anthropological questions of freedom, evolution and self-liberation, are not set in opposition to the theological understandings of grace, creation and justification. Nowhere is this more the case than in a theological anthropology.

The task of theological anthropology is to discover what God intends for humanity. The description of this intention provides the description of the divine–human relation and therefore of humanity itself. In light of Schillebeeckx's description of the relation between God and humanity – creative, salvific, sanctifying, participative and personal – any dualistic or competitive account of 'difference' within the human–divine relation is incoherent:

> It is our intention to discover what God in his grace intends for man by considering the living reality of divine Providence. What does the Word of God say about man? *How does God see man?* That God sees man does not mean simply that he knows what man is making of his life here below. On the contrary, it is the gaze of one who is personally interested, who calls us to salvation and participates with us in a personal, creative and sanctifying way.[40]

The intention of theological anthropology rules out from the outset the problematic of God or humanity. In Schillebeeckx's analysis, the hopelessness of overcoming a relation of opposition between the mystery of God and the mystery of humanity is nowhere more clearly in evidence than in the disputes over grace, which gradually, over several centuries, led Roman Catholic theology 'up a blind alley'.

The primacy of God's grace revealed in the utter graciousness of God's relationship with humanity is the horizon within which theology must function. When this horizon becomes distorted theology too becomes distorted, as certainly occurred in Roman Catholic circles beginning in the sixteenth century when a dualistic account of nature and grace – nature and supernature – crept in. What began as a development – and later flourished as a dispute – among Thomists, held immense consequences for Roman Catholic theology on the whole, leaving no area of doctrine untouched; Schillebeeckx provides a rich and insightful account of this very significant piece of intellectual history. His analysis of the mid-twentieth century nature–grace debates is interesting in two respects. First, he brings to his reading of this 'history' a critical analysis of the relative merits and strengths of the various players in the debates.[41] Second, his interventions in these Thomistic debates are also

---

[40] Schillebeeckx, 'Dialogue with God and Christian Secularity', p. 215.

[41] In this regard his interpretation of Max Seckler is interesting. See Schillebeeckx, 'The Non-conceptual Intellectual Element in the Act of Faith: a Reaction', in *Revelation and Theology, II*, pp. 30–75. 'Het niet-begrippelijk kenmoment in de geloofsdaad: probleemstelling', in *Openbaring en theologie*, pp. 233–261. First published in *Tijdschrift voor*

a vehicle for his own constructive theology. The several essays in which he published his interpretation of the development of the *nouvelle théologie* and contributed to the current discussions of Aquinas, contribute substantially to an understanding of his own development of the nature–grace relation. As such these essays provide clear indicators of the direction in which his theology will develop.[42] Within any reading of his theology, these writings stand as a corrective to some of the later interpretations of his work.

One of the pivotal moments within the 'dispute over grace which has taken place in the Roman Catholic Church' was certainly the publication, by the Jesuit *ressourcement* theologian, Henri de Lubac, of *Surnaturel*.[43] Undeniably, de Lubac's greatest achievement was the retrieval of a non-dualistic understanding of the nature–grace relation. Rather than asserting a dualism between grace and nature, Aquinas – and indeed the tradition behind him – held to an understanding of 'graced nature'.[44] The importance of this for the development of theology cannot be overestimated, in large part because it leaves no area of theology untouched; and the significance of this insight for the history of theology is clearly acknowledged by Schillebeeckx in his own account of the 'New Trends in Present Day Dogmatic Theology'.[45] His

Theologie 3 (1963), 167–194. His interpretation of De Petter belongs to this period. See Schillebeeckx, 'The Concept of "Truth"'.

[42] See especially Schillebeeckx, 'The Concept of "Truth"'; 'The Non-Conceptual Intellectual Element in the Act of Faith: a Reaction'; 'The Non-Conceptual Intellectual Dimension in Our Knowledge of God According to Aquinas', in *Revelation and Theology, II: The Concept of Truth and Theological Renewal*, pp. 5–29; pp. 30–75; pp. 157–206.

[43] Henri de Lubac, *Surnaturel. Etudes Historiques* (Paris: Aubier, 1946). This was revised and expanded and republished in 1965 as two volumes: *Le mystère du surnaturel* (Paris: Aubier, 1965); *Augustinisme et théologie moderne* (Paris: Aubier, 1965). *Surnaturel* analyses the developments within the tradition which lead to a post-Thomas dualistic distortion of the nature–grace relation. De Lubac anticipates a new theology founded on the retrieval of a correct reading of Thomas and the culmination of this can be seen in the theology which shapes the documents of Vatican II. Schillebeeckx's approbation for de Lubac's work on grace is clear in his comments about the *ressourcement* theologians vis-à-vis the Council. See Schillebeeckx, 'Christian Faith and Man's Expectations for the Future on Earth', p. 71. Schillebeeckx specifically mentions the contributions made to this theology by the Jesuit school of theology in Lyons, La Fourvière where de Lubac was so influential. See Schillebeeckx, *Theologisch testament*, p. 42.

[44] Kerr, 'French Theology: Yves Congar and Henri de Lubac', in *The Modern Theologians*, ed. David Ford, 2nd ed (Oxford: Blackwell, 1997), p. 114: 'Neither in the patristic period nor in medieval theology, and certainly not in Thomas Aquinas, was the hypothesis entertained of a purely natural destiny for human beings, something less than the eschatological vision of God . . . Aquinas recognises only one destiny, a supernatural one, for the human being'.

[45] Schillebeeckx, 'The New Trends in Present-day Dogmatic Theology', in *Revelation and Theology, II*, pp. 106–154. 'De nieuwe wending in de huidige dogmatiek' in *Openbaring en Theologie*, pp. 282–312. Originally published in *Tijdschrift voor Theologie* 1 (1961), 17–46.

assessment of this period in the history of theology – both its strengths and weaknesses – is structured around the ability of theology to give expression to a non-competitive relation between nature and grace, between the finite and the infinite, between the human and the divine. In fact, the essays in which Schillebeeckx offers his own analysis of the history and the task of theology are tremendously important because in them he develops the foundations of his own theology. It is not oversimplifying his work to say that his theology is a never-ceasing attempt to describe the nature–grace relation as one which holds together both the mystery of God and the dignity of humanity. As becomes clear in his historical sketch of theology it is the primacy of grace, the transcendence of God, which secures the identity and destiny of humanity and does so by establishing a relation of communion, not one of competition, between the divine and the human.

The traditional relationship between the infinite and the finite to which Thomas held is described in one of the most familiar Thomistic axioms: grace does not destroy nature but perfects it.[46] This axiom, expressive for Aquinas of the non-competitive relationship between the divine and human, is taken up by Schillebeeckx: 'The infinite is disclosed in the finite without destroying it'.[47] With de Lubac, Schillebeeckx has no doubt that 'the elements of truth that had been acquired in the traditional theology were not sacrificed by Aquinas',[48] and he quite deliberately wades into the debate against neo-Thomism.[49] For Schillebeeckx, so many of the 'psuedo-problems' that plague theology can be dismissed by a properly interpreted understanding of the relation between nature and grace. Grace is not something extra added onto nature as if nature had an end in itself apart from the supernatural end for which it was created and to which it is called by God:

> Human existence is something granted, it is a grace: an overwhelming grace. I am given the chance to be a human being . . . [this] reminds us of the biblical idea of our fortunes being dependent upon God's grace: 'Towards you was I cast from my birth' (Ps. 22. 10).[50]

---

[46] See Kerr, *After Aquinas: Versions of Thomism* (Oxford: Blackwell, 2002), p. 138. This axiom is not unique to Thomas and in fact pre-dates him.

[47] Schillebeeckx, 'What is Theology?', p. 109.

[48] Schillebeeckx, 'The New Trends in Present-day Dogmatic Theology', p. 107.

[49] Schillebeeckx, 'The Concept of "Truth"': Epistemology, the question of the knowability of God and the relation between conceptual and non-conceptual knowledge, is the principal arena in which Schillebeeckx engages in debate with neo-Thomism. For an analysis of these epistemological debates see Kennedy, *Deus Humanissimus*, pp. 79–142. Kennedy identifies Schillebeeckx's understanding of the nature–grace relation as a relational ontology and argues convincingly that this is the core of both Schillebeeckx's epistemology (philosophy) and his theology. See esp. p. 80; pp. 105–107. In what follows it becomes clear that this relational ontology is described by Schillebeeckx as a 'communion of love' which reflects his understanding that we are drawn into the Triune life.

[50] Schillebeeckx, 'Dialogue with God and Christian Secularity', p. 210.

Schillebeeckx affirms Aquinas' fidelity to the biblical–patristic heritage of early medieval theology and sees no incompatibility between this faithfulness to tradition and the innovations Aquinas brought to theology:

> The meeting between new experiences, clarified by reflection, and the older insights into the faith has not only produced new problems in theology but has at the same time led to a fresh theological synthesis. For the new problems and insights have not simply been added onto the earlier theological findings in an external way, like an appendix. These older theological gains are themselves renewed by the modern problems and insights. This process has taken place frequently throughout the history of the Church. It is strikingly evident for example, in Aquinas' time. The older insights of the official theology of the church that were current at that period – that is, Augustinian theology – were brought to life in a completely new way by Aquinas, who not only had a distinct feeling for the new Aristotelian, Arabian and Jewish philosophy that was coming to light in those days, but also went back to ancient scriptural and patristic sources.[51]

Schillebeeckx underlines Aquinas' strength as a positive theologian, his care interpreting the older insights of the tradition. Furthermore, he underlines his openness to reflect on these traditional insights critically in light of newer ones. Aquinas brought to life traditional insights in a completely new way. There are echoes here of the Dominican *présence à Dieu et présence au monde*.[52]

Theology, in some respects, has changed little in the time between Aquinas and Schillebeeckx:

> Very much the same thing is happening today. A complete renewal of dogmatic theology has been brought about in the thinking of the Church by the new perspectives opened up by modern thought, by a return to original sources, and especially to scriptural sources, and also by Catholic contact with Anglican, Protestant and Orthodox theology.[53]

---

[51] Schillebeeckx, 'The New Trends in Present-day Dogmatic Theology', pp. 106–107. Nicholas Lash, in his study of doctrinal change and continuity, considers the relation between theology and historical development: the recovery of history. He considers one of the strengths of Schillebeeckx's work in this area to be the 'standpoint from which he approaches' the issue of development within tradition. Lash identifies this 'standpoint' as 'the broad hermeneutical framework' which was familiar to Schillebeeckx from his own formation in contemporary philosophy. While this is no doubt true it is a significant omission not to focus in this discussion on the nature–grace relation in Schillebeeckx's work and its clear implications for Schillebeeckx's theology of revelation and the relation between revelation and history. See Lash, *Change in Focus. A Study of Doctrinal Change and Continuity* (London: Sheed and Ward, 1973), p. 134.

[52] Schillebeeckx, 'Dominican Spirituality', p. 240.

[53] Schillebeeckx, 'The New Trends in Present-day Dogmatic Theology', p. 107.

Theology continues to proceed by a *ressourcement*, being attentive to the sources of its tradition where 'tradition' is taken in its fullest ecumenical sense.[54] We are not confronted by a 'different theology' but by the 'ancient theology of the Church'. The point of continuity is not the specific practices of theology but the subject of theology: the reality of faith. Thus, '[i]t is not a different theology that confronts us today, but the ancient theology of the Church that has come to possess the reality of the faith more firmly'.[55]

It is the phrase 'reality of faith' – '*geloofswerkelijkheid*' – that is the pivotal one for understanding Schillebeeckx's analysis of the history and development of theology, and for appreciating what he is attempting with his own. For Schillebeeckx the 'reality of faith' with which theology must be concerned is conditioned by the phrase: 'the harmony' – '*harmonie*' – 'between nature and supernature'. The 'reality of faith', conditioned by the 'harmony between nature and supernature', points to a certain metaphysical realism that grounds anything that might be said of the nature–grace relation. The treatise on grace – the relation between 'nature' and 'supernature' – cannot be abstracted from historical revelation. Just as the *theologia* cannot be abstracted from the *oikonomia*, grace has an intrinsic *oikonomia* in relation to nature. Insofar as theology is attentive to this reality and the harmony between nature and supernature to which it attests, theology, even as it renews itself, will continue to be an opportunity for grace. Hence Schillebeeckx's appreciation of the so-called new theology is neither anxious nor naïve, and his own theology, not burdened by either 'bewilderment or suspicion', has a sense of energy and measured hope:[56]

> This renewal of theology is above all an opportunity for grace. At the same time, however, it can now as at all times, also lead to the possibility of error. The harmony between 'nature' and supernature' is not, so to speak, automatically brought about in the incarnation of faith which has to be continuously renewed in human thought any more than it is automatically brought about in practical, active life. By definition this harmony can only be reached in detachment and constant self-criticism.[57]

Theology now, as for Aquinas, is not 'purely a phenomenon of fashion' but the continued 'fumbling' to bring to expression the 'reality of faith'.[58]

---

[54] The return to original sources – in scripture and Christian practice – and painstaking historical research in the context of theology – as undertaken by de Lubac in *Surnaturel* – as well as an attentiveness to contemporary philosophy are the 'new perspectives opened up by modern thought' which characterise the 'new theology'. See 'The New Trends in Present-day Dogmatic Theology', p. 108.

[55] Schillebeeckx, 'The New Trends in Present-day Dogmatic Theology', p. 107.

[56] Ibid.

[57] Ibid. p. 108.

[58] Ibid. pp. 107–108.

The 'reality' with which theology is constantly preoccupied is the mystery of God revealed as the meaning of humanity. Hence theology's 'reality' is the relation of the infinite to the finite, of the divine to the human, of grace to freedom and of history to eschatology. Theology is the continuous reflection upon God's self-revelation given in God's saving activity in human history.[59] This means the reality with which theology is concerned is both the mystery God and the mystery of humanity where both are interpreted and understood by the terms creative, salvific, sanctifying, participative and personal. One characteristic way in which the tradition has attempted to give expression to this situation, Schillebeeckx suggests, is to speak of nature as having (*hebben*) sanctifying grace. But the reality (*werkelijkheid*) is far more than this:

> [W]e are taken up into a living communion with God, we live, have our being and move in the rhythm of the divine life. We dwell in God, as in our own house. Quite individual, personal relationships exist between God and ourselves. [60]

Here, as in so much of his theology, Schillebeeckx's description of the human is predicated upon a description of divine action and thus, by way of God's self-revelation, of the nature of God. The vocation to intimacy with God is the intimacy of the relation of grace: it is a living communion that is constitutive of the mystery of humanity – constitutive of what it means to be human as person.

For Schillebeeckx, it is divine action or initiative that grounds human being in a living communion with God. Hence grace – God's gracious initiative – establishes the definition of humanity as participation in the divine life. This participation in the divine life is what Schillebeeckx calls the 'ontological implication of the reciprocity in grace between God and ourselves'.[61] This 'ontological implication of reciprocity' does away with the divisions between 'sanctifying' and 'created' grace classic to the 'old' treatise on grace. In its place it sets a description of grace as a reciprocity between divine and human that is personal and hence non-reductive. The most fitting description for this reciprocity, one that holds both the nature of the divine and the nature of the human in this non-reductive relation, is 'participation' as 'communion'. Furthermore, by identifying an 'ontological implication' from this reciprocity, Schillebeeckx draws clear attention to the fact that this is both a historical reality – not bypassing humanity's

---

[59] Schillebeeckx uses the terms 'reality of salvation', 'reality of revelation' and 'reality of faith' interchangeably.

[60] Schillebeeckx, 'The New Trends in Present-day Dogmatic Theology', p. 109.

[61] Ibid. p. 109 n 1.

incarnate historical existence – and an eschatological reality: 'We dwell in God as in our own house'.[62]

The relation of nature to grace is one of communion in which the initiative is God's act (we are taken into) and this initiative or divine act is constitutive of human life (we live, have our being and move). The dichotomy or relation of opposition between divine and human is dispelled (we dwell in God, as in our own house) and yet the aspect of difference is not collapsed (quite individual, personal relationships exist between God and ourselves). The relation between nature and supernature is constitutive of nature, not by collapsing the difference between the divine and the human but in a certain sense by heightening that difference: we are *taken into* a living communion with God. Furthermore, this communion is constitutive of nature in a very particular manner, that is, according to the rhythm of the divine life. If what we can say about the divine – here the rhythm of divine life – is given to us in God's self-revelation in human history – and Schillebeeckx holds to this throughout his theology – then it follows that the rhythm of divine life into which we have been taken is at one and the same time creative and salvific. The same God who is creator has revealed himself to be redeemer. This raises the theologically anthropological question: what does it mean to say that humanity has both its being and its end in God? In other words, the question that arises from Schillebeeckx's description of the relation between nature and grace as a living communion with God in which we are taken up into the divine life is: what is the nature of our participation in the divine life? How does he describe this relation in which the finite finds its fulfilment in the infinite without being destroyed? In essence, Schillebeeckx describes this relation as a personal relation that follows from divine initiative as invitation – the invitation to salvation – which leaves human freedom intact – we can only respond in the midst of human history in which this invitation is extended.

Schillebeeckx does not have a sustained or speculative theology of the Trinity. Therefore his Trinitarian references here in the context of a discussion of the divine life and our communion with this life are rather startling and need to be noticed. It is clearly not an exercise in speculative Trinitarian thought but instead it attests to the metaphysical realism, rooted in God's self-revelation – God's being-God in history as salvation – which undergirds his theology:

Drawn by this divine offer of love, which we can only accept in faith, and hoping and trusting that this initiative in love will, in the future take personal care of our lives, we too, by virtue of the divine love that is given to us in Christ in the boundless infusion of his Holy Spirit, step

[62] Ibid. p. 109.

90

outside ourselves into this communion of love. [I]n its essence, then, the content of faith, or revelation, is an invitation to salvation made by God to living mankind, a giving of himself on God's part. The word of revelation is directed, through the medium of the history of salvation, to the whole of mankind, and inwardly to the heart of every man. It is also addressed to us.[63]

Here the personal nature of human intimacy with God is quite explicit: addressed to us in the history of salvation it is both a statement of the reality of humanity and, because of the very nature of this address, directed to the whole of humanity and to the heart of every person, it is constitutive of each person in their own individuality and identity. Human freedom and subjectivity in relation to God are here an ontological reality – an invitation to salvation made by God to living humanity; and it is the reality of personal and hence individual identity – it is addressed to the heart of each person. The vocation to intimacy with God is the vocation to personal identity. This is heightened by the nature of this intimacy: Schillebeeckx describes the communion between God and humanity as one of call and response. This recalls the importance of the relation between humanity's 'metaphysical and moral significance'.

Just as Schillebeeckx is not given to speculation about the inner Triune life, he is not given to speculative description of the participation of human nature in this life. His description of the living communion with God into which we are drawn is conditioned by his description of God's self-giving in revelation. One of Schillebeeckx's favourite motifs for describing this communion is that of address and response. It is this motif that perhaps best illustrates the nature of humanity as the vocation to intimacy with God:[64]

[O]ur faith in God never utters the first word in theological reflection. Religion and faith are a response – a reply – and therefore the second word. The first word is spoken by God himself. The whole basis of our concrete religion is revelation, and revelation is that extremely personal divine gesture through which the living God as it were steps outside himself and approaches us with the offer of his love – the offer of 'communion with him,' of a love which is fulfilled only when we return it.[65]

Here humanity's metaphysical significance, precisely because it is an invitation – 'the offer of communion with God' – is bound completely to humanity's moral significance – the offer of a communion with God, of a

[63] Schillebeeckx, 'The New Trends in Present-day Dogmatic Theology', p. 109.
[64] Schillebeeckx, 'Dialogue with God and Christian Secularity', pp. 216–217.
[65] Schillebeeckx, 'The New Trends in Present-day Dogmatic Theology', p. 108.

love that is only fulfilled when we return it. God's gracious initiative – the exercise of divine freedom – establishes human freedom, and in doing so, it establishes the moral significance of human life. Grace, far from a magical intervention in human history that absolves humanity of responsibility, is constitutive of human responsibility for history: 'Our belief in the existence of God should be a conviction, a divine certainty that our free, responsible and resolute behaviour in this world is secure in him who is life.'[66]

The motif of address and response has endured from beginning to end of Schillebeeckx's writings precisely because it serves so well to heighten the priority of God's grace and the graciousness of God's activity in human history while describing this activity as constitutive of humanity's personal freedom: 'Without exception, there is an absolute priority of God's grace on all that human beings think, do, feel and say. To speak as human beings is always a response'.[67] Rather than a speculative description of the communion between humanity and God, Schillebeeckx's description tends in the direction of a practical one.[68] This follows from the intrinsic relation that holds between humanity's metaphysical and moral significance. It also underlines the importance of the conceptual aspect of human knowledge of God and hence of a realist metaphysics. Of the mystery of God, Schillebeeckx says repeatedly that we need to understand at least enough of this mystery – which ultimately remains impenetrable – in order to live from it.[69]

---

[66] Schillebeeckx, 'God in Dry Dock', p. 10.

[67] Schillebeeckx, 'Prologue', in *The Praxis of the Reign of God*, ed by Mary Catherine Hilkert and Robert Schreiter (New York: Fordham University Press, 2002), pp. ix–xviii (p. xiii).

[68] The word 'practical' is used here simply to describe Schillebeeckx's theology as being non-dualistic. Christian life, and hence theology, is not concerned with *either* mysticism *or* ethics but with both. He is somewhat nervous that an excessively speculative theology lends itself to an interpretation of the Christian life in which too great an emphasis is placed on interiority and individual spirituality. His tendency to a 'practical' theology is clearly in evidence in his discussions of the relation between salvation and ethics. Schillebeeckx, *Christ: the Christian Experience in the Modern World*, trans. John Bowden (London: SCM, 1980), p. 61: 'We do not find salvation primarily by means of a correct interpretation of reality, but by acting in accordance with the demands of that reality.' *Gerechtigheid en liefde. Genade en bevrijding* (Bloemendaal: Nelissen, 1977).

[69] Schillebeeckx, 'Religion and the World: Renewing the Face of the Earth', in *World and Church*, trans. N. D. Smith (New York: Sheed and Ward, 1971), p. 1: 'It is doubtful whether man, despite his seeking, will ever penetrate fully to the heart of this reality for the simple reason that he is here confronted with a problem, the two terms of which merge into the mystery, on the one hand, of man's existence as spirit in the world and, on the other, of God's being-God, the deeper mystery into which we have been allowed to enter through the mystery of Christ. Although it is, of course, impenetrable, a mystery does always have a nucleus of openness, of intelligibility – it always

This is a point of profound continuity in Schillebeeckx's work. His theology, in its relation to ethics, indicates the seriousness of his commitment to a metaphysics of reality. In other words, the truths that define the transcendence and difference of God as constitutive of human meaning are revealed and encountered as historical reality and hence are constitutive of human historical existence: 'The real mystery of God lies in the fact that with his world man lives *in* God – in a godly or ungodly fashion'.[70]

Recalling Schillebeeckx's description of theology as theocentric in its content and Christological in its structure, it is not surprising that his fullest descriptions of human participation in the divine life – the life of grace – are developed within his Christology.[71] Here the motif of call and response – the communion of love – which describes human–divine intimacy in its creative, savific, sanctifying, participative and personal manner finds it ultimate expression. Humanity's vocation to intimacy with God is a vocation to 'faithfulness'. In its ultimate expression, the life of grace is the invitation to a faithfulness that finds its very ground in the invitation itself. In Christ God reveals and establishes the 'entirety of mankind's vocation to faithfulness'.[72] For Schillebeeckx, Christ is the sacrament of the human vocation to intimacy with God, which is the call to life in the world lived as faithfulness to the nature of this intimacy – human, and therefore within history, salvation.

In Schillebeeckx's later Christology the descriptive words that point towards our communion with God are very much in keeping with the motif of address and response and the relation between a metaphysical and moral

---

presents itself to man's experience and reflection via conceptual, recognisable ideas which at least provide us with some perspective. In this way, we are able, within the mystery, to become sufficiently conscious of its content, at least sufficiently conscious to be able to live from it'.

[70] Schillebeeckx, 'God in Dry Dock', p. 10.

[71] Schillebeeckx, *Christ the Sacrament of the Encounter with God* (London: Sheed and Ward, 1963), p. 16 n 14.

[72] Ibid. p. 13: 'God's ultimate purpose was to call a faithful people into life. Broadly speaking, there would be continual failure, until God himself raised up a man in whom was concentrated the entirety of mankind's vocation to faithfulness, and who would himself keep faith with the Covenant in the perfection of his fidelity. This man was Jesus. In him there was a visible realisation of both sides of faith in the Covenant. In the dialogue between God and man, so often breaking down, there was found at last a perfect human respondent; in the same person there was achieved the perfection both of the divine invitation and of the human response in faith from the man who by his resurrection is the Christ. The Covenant, sealed in his blood, found definitive success in his person. In him grace became fully visible; he is the embodiment of the grace of final victory, who appeared in person to the Apostles. Christ himself is the Church, an invisible communion in grace with the living God manifested in visible human form. For this is what he is as the "first-born" and Head of all creation. Consequently the whole of humanity is already " assembled" into communion with God'.

significance: *metanoia*, obedience, discipleship, trust and hope.[73] This echoes his earlier essays where this motif of address and response is expressed in the fullness of Christ's commitment to the relation with the Father:

> What Christ showed us above all was what a *man* is like who has declared himself to be fully committed to God, the invisible Father. He showed us the practical form of religious worship, the face of the truly religious man. And so . . . he also showed us what God is. His witness to God is a visible support for us. His visible living relationship to the invisible God reveals the mystery of the true God to us . . . in this man Jesus we can see how a dialogue relationship is possible between God and man, and that this prayer represents the profoundest meaning of life.[74]

For Schillebeeckx the description of the relationship between Jesus and the Father is an especially critical *locus* for the description of Christian life.

Schillebeeckx describes the divine gesture in which God extends the offer of communion – the call to intimacy – with reference to the relationship between Father and Son:

> The whole basis of our concrete religion is revelation, and revelation is that extremely personal divine gesture through which the living God as it were steps outside himself and approaches us with the offer of his love – the offer of 'communion with him,' of a love which is fulfilled only when we return it. It is through this personal relationship with the Father, the relationship of a son who, in Christ, grows to the full stature of a mature man – that we come to live in the grace that makes us holy.[75]

Our communion with God – the life of grace – is understood by Schillebeeckx in terms of God's self-communication that is revelatory. God's self-revelation causes something to happen: revelation in word is inseparable from

---

[73] Schillebeeckx, *Jesus: an Experiment in Christology* (London: Collins, 1979).

[74] Schillebeeckx, 'God in Dry Dock', pp. 12–13. This is not a 'spiritualized' account that divorces worship from ethics. Schillebeeckx elaborates on the 'practical form of religious worship' that Christ reveals: 'Through him we know that the Father is with him *in all things*, even in loneliness and worldly oppression – and in that loneliness which can now be the expression of an unobtrusive presence. From him we learn that regardless of the extent to which the world is governed by natural and historical laws and the free will of men, all its events are in the hands of God . . . the world in which we live and the tasks our freedom in it imposes on us thus become a dialogue with the living God, an invitation challenging us to face the world in a freedom secure by its unity in him.'

[75] Schillebeeckx, 'The New Trends in Present-day Dogmatic Theology', p. 108.

revelation in reality. In this manner revelation, as God's self-giving, theocentric in subject and christological in structure, forms the basis of a description of our participation in the divine life.

There are at least two ideas that need to be picked up again at this point. The idea being developed here is that Schillebeeckx holds to a relation between grace and nature that is non-dualistic, non-reductive and hence non-competitive. It is a relation he describes as one of 'harmony' or 'communion'. Grace is the relationship in which the human and the divine 'coincide' in a creative, salvific, sanctifying, participative and personal relation. Thus grace is the relation of human intimacy with God. Schillebeeckx holds to this relation because he holds to the absolute graciousness and transcendence of God that establishes a relationship between the divine and human in which the dignity and freedom of humanity are assured.

In Schillebeeckx's theology of grace, finitude is not something which must be overcome as if it were a threat to our participation in the life of grace. Quite the opposite. The infinite, far from destroying the finite, is revealed through it, and in this the relation between nature and grace is established. A description of the life of grace is not served by sidestepping human nature. This cuts to the heart of theology *in toto*. All of theology is quite rightly concerned with the 'implications of man's communion of grace with God', and this includes of course the '*theological* treatise on man in the context of creation'.[76] Humanity is defined as 'absolute dependence' precisely in its situated freedom. This is the meaning of 'I am really myself in and of this world, becoming myself more and more therein, and yet at the same time created, even to the most delicate fibres of my being'.[77]

Here we come back to the ideas which must be picked up: the dynamic nature of our living communion with God and a fuller exploration of Schillebeeckx's discussion of this communion as the existence of 'quite individual and personal' relationships. These aspects of the nature–grace relation lead into two related issues raised within Schillebeeckx's theology. The first is his metaphysical realism: how is metaphysics to be understood if it is to be appropriate to theology, if it is appropriate at all? The second is the question of contemporary philosophy in relation to theology,

---

[76] Ibid. p. 138. These comments are found in his reflection on eschatology: 'We have come with greater justification to accept the idea, on the one hand, that the historical, non-mythical character of the end of the world cannot be denied, but on the other, that the *eschata* will be nothing but the implications of man's communion of grace with God in the mode of completion.' Schillebeeckx provides a very brisk exploration of how the 'distinctive character of the human condition influences theology' by describing very briefly the implications for Christology, Mariology, ecclesiology and sacramental theology, and eschatology. See 'The New Trends in Present-day Dogmatic Theology', pp. 121–140.

[77] Schillebeeckx, 'Dialogue with God and Christian Secularity', p. 215.

specifically, how are current philosophies of phenomenology and existentialism to function within theology, if at all? If there is to be a viable theological anthropology, that is to say, an anthropology descriptive of human nature as it is 'taken up into the rhythm of the divine life' then both these questions must be raised.

The life of grace is not static. For this reason it is not circumscribed by concepts or propositions as is evident in Schillebeeckx's discussions of the relation between conceptual and non-conceptual knowledge and the life of faith. Against the neo-Thomists he argues for the 'reality of faith' that is never fully graspable. God, and hence our communion with God, is quite simply not a truth to be grasped.[78] It is a relation between persons, between Father and Son, between human and divine, between temporal and eschatological, and therefore it is dynamic not static, 'real' not abstract. Schillebeeckx's description of the dynamism of the life of grace – an offer fulfilled in its return – echoes Aquinas' description of all reality as an *exitus reditus*.[79] In other words, Schillebeeckx's conception of reality is grounded in the belief that all things come from God and return to God. The initiative is divine, and it is gracious: the living God as it were steps outside himself and approaches us with the offer of his love. Furthermore, this initiative is purposive, it is inseparable from the end for which it is made: the offer of 'communion with him'. It is an offer of a love that is fulfilled only when we return it. The dignity and meaning of human nature is realized in its coming from and returning to God. Ultimately this is realized in God's nature as the future for humanity. Grace as communion between God and humanity is eschatological.

In this *exitus reditus* movement, questions both of the transcendence or sovereignty of God and of the freedom and agency of human nature are raised. The description of the dynamic character of the nature–grace relation suggests clearly that these are not two concepts that are to be set opposite one another and then in some dialectical fashion, reconciled. On Schillebeeckx's account human freedom and dignity are secured precisely by God's sovereign and gracious activity. In a footnote in which he expands upon the notion of sanctifying grace – 'our fumbling expression' of human

---

[78] This analysis was begun in the preceding chapter in relation to Schillebeeckx's assessment of De Petter in the discussion of the notion of truth in relation to faith and the understanding of the relation between conceptual and non-conceptual knowledge. At issue is the relation between the subjective and objective aspects of the life of faith. It is picked up again here in this chapter in Schillebeeckx's analysis of contemporary strands of theology and is at the centre of his critique of existential theologies.

[79] Schillebeeckx's motif of address and response by which he configures the relation between God and humanity is a translation of Aquinas' *exitus reditus*. It is a motif that conveys both the subjective and objective freight of Aquinas' description of reality.

participation in the life of grace – it is the transcendence of God – *creatio ex nihilo* – that establishes the communion of grace:

> The *religious* relationship between God and man on the basis of sanctifying grace can therefore not be expressed in terms of relationships of 'cause and effect'. It transcends such relationships. On the other hand, however, this living communion with God does not fall outside God's universal causality, because even God's action 'outside himself' is divine – it is an absolute activity and thus 'creates from nothing.' This explains the necessity of the *gratia creata*, created grace, as an ontological implication of the reciprocity in grace between God and ourselves. The mere 'phenomenology' of the 'encounter' cannot account for this.[80]

For Schillebeeckx's part, this is an extremely compressed bit of writing, and there are several things going on that become more recognizable when this is set within its context. He has two arenas in mind here. The first is the quite specific discussion internal to theology concerning the notion of grace. The second is the broader and equally contentious issue of the relation between the 'new theology' and contemporary philosophy and the place, if any, that metaphysics might have.

First then, in its very specific context as a commentary on how sanctifying grace 'works' in the relationship between God and humanity, this footnote indicates the transcendent and gracious nature of God's activity, captured in the description of divine action as absolute, *creatio ex nihilo*. Absolute dependence on God is the expression of the ultimate immediacy of the relation between God and humanity: humanity exists first for God. This ultimate immediacy, described by Schillebeeckx as the 'ontological implication of the reciprocity in grace' overturns the 'old' distinction between 'sanctifying' and 'created' grace. Grace is not something 'added to' humanity; nor is it something 'done to' humanity – it is quite simply constitutive of humanity. It is both its beginning – its possibility – and its end – its fulfilment. This is secured for Schillebeeckx by the description of the personal nature of God and hence the personal, intersubjective and reciprocal nature of the human–divine relation. This is, in essence, the whole treatise on grace.

The essentially personal nature of God's relation to humanity is secured in the divine nature as personal. There is, as it were, not a disparity between God's inner Triune life and God's activity 'outside himself': the *Deus sub ratione Deitatis* is the *Deus salutaris*. The transcendent God who creates out of nothing is the personal Triune God revealed in his saving activity in human history. By implication here the personal, intersubjective quality of

---

[80] Schillebeeckx, 'The New Trends in Present-day Dogmatic Theology', p. 109 n 1.

the life of grace is secured. It would be inconsistent to describe the humanity with which God has established a personal relation as a 'thing', an 'object' of the relation. Rather humanity is a subject of a relation that is properly intersubjective and hence not amenable to a mechanistic description of 'cause and effect'. Put another way, humanity is 'effect', *gratia creata*, only in relation to the specific manner in which God is 'cause'. Created grace – a term which in Catholic dogmatic theology of this period normally indicates the effect of grace or the work of the Holy Spirit upon nature – is the onto-logical implication for Schillebeeckx of a certain metaphysical realism, the reciprocity in grace between God and ourselves in which we are taken up into the rhythm of the divine life.[81] In the phrase, 'the necessity of *gratia creata*' the word 'necessity' is telling: it is the ultimate affirmation of the identity of created nature as a value in itself. The 'necessity of the *gratia creata*' in the specific context of the relation of cause and effect appropriate to the relation of creature to creator – cause, transcendence, difference – means simply that grace presupposes nature. Grace is constitutive of nature in that it presupposes nature.[82]

The first point then is that divine transcendence and difference establish a 'reciprocity in grace', which has an 'ontological implication'. This 'ontologi-cal implication' might best be summarized as: human being is 'graced nature', not a nature to which grace is 'added'. Grace works *in* nature rather than *upon* nature. Secondly, in its broader context of an analysis of 'the new trends in theology', this 'reciprocity in grace' signals that Schillebeeckx is committed to a place for metaphysics within theology. However, he is at the same time specifying the type of metaphysics that is proper to theology. The subject of theology – our living communion with God – does not fall outside of metaphysics – God's universal causality – yet this metaphysics is not

---

[81] The phrase 'the reciprocity in grace' is a translation of '*de genadevolle wederkerig-heid*'. A literal translation of this would be 'the grace-filled reciprocity'. Although 'reciprocity in grace' is a tidier translation there is need for emphasis on the word '*in*' to capture the full sense of the grace-filled reciprocity as one constituted by grace.

[82] The idea of 'identity' is underlined by the concepts of similitude and dissimilitude that Schillebeeckx holds in his theology of creation. Schillebeeckx, 'the Non-conceptual Intellectual Dimension in Our Knowledge of God According to Aquinas', p. 163: 'We know God . . . as cause and by his transcendence and by his utter difference. These are three inseparable aspects of causality in which the effect as such is participative the act of the cause itself. *Participatio obiectiva* and *participatio causalis* are thus always essentially connected in Aquinas. The participational character of the effect in respect of its cause consequently implies a similitude, which is naturally accompanied by a basic dissimilitude: in the effect is found something by means of which it is assimilated to its cause and something by means of which it differs from its cause.' The nature of 'participation' – relation – is determined by the nature of the particular cause and its effect. The necessity of *gratia creata* is the relation – constitutive – which is particular to the participation of the effect (creation) in relation to its cause (God).

expressed as the relation between cause and effect. It transcends this to speak of the relation between Creator and creature – *creatio ex nihilo*.

It has already become clear that the place which Schillebeeckx gives to metaphysics within his theology and his understanding of the type of metaphysics appropriate to theology are of considerable importance. These are questions of keen interest for him and they form the crux of his analysis of the 'new theology'. They also form the crux of his theology:

> If we accept, correctly with Aquinas that the true subject of theology is the living God, the *Deus salutaris* or the *Deus sub ratione Deitatis* – that is, the saving God, God as seen under the aspect of his Godhead – (for it is precisely as such that he is our salvation), then it is clear that we shall only be able to reach this living God where he revealed himself as such – in Christ Jesus, who is the public manifestation of God.[83]

The God who 'steps outside himself' and offers to us the possibility of communion with him does so precisely as the Triune God, as God as he is in himself. God is not salvation for us in some other way or under some other guise: the *Deus salutaris* is the *Deus sub ratione Deitatis*.

Schillebeeckx's metaphysical realism is grounded here; hence his consistent and repeated descriptions of theology as theocentric and christological, his insistence that *theologia* and *oikonomia* not be separated and his systemic interest in the relation between historical experience and revelation. Theology must work as it does because of the pattern of God's self-revelation: the infinite has been revealed in the finite without destroying it.

This earthly structure of our personal communion with God determines the method employed by dogmatic theology. The content of faith that is, in its distinctive quality, really inexpressible here on earth, is expressed in concepts that are rooted in a certain experience – our experience of the history of salvation.[84]

Thus, at the heart of Schillebeeckx's theology is a commitment to a non-dualistic and therefore non-competitive account of the relation between God and humanity, between nature and grace. It follows he will neither advocate the 'essentialist' theology of the past nor the complete abandonment of metaphysics. Rather, he holds to what he describes as the renewal of metaphysics on an anthropological basis, or, in other words, he holds to the 'inevitably earthly form of theological thought'.[85] This needs some further explanation.

---

[83] Schillebeeckx, 'What is Theology?', p. 138.
[84] Schillebeeckx, 'The New Trends in Present-day Dogmatic Theology', p. 117.
[85] Ibid. p. 121.

Schillebeeckx identifies a threefold tension within theology between those theologies that hold to a cosmologically orientated metaphysics, or the abandonment of metaphysics entirely, or the renewal of metaphysics on an anthropological basis. Working through this tension is, in his estimation, critical:

> I am of the opinion that a state of balance has by no means as yet been achieved in the eager recourse to phenomenological analyses, however necessary these be in theological renewal. It is here, I believe, that the critical point of the new theology can be found – the point at which theology will either go on to make a new, authentic flight or else be fatally grounded in a complete emptying of content of the Catholic faith.[86]

Lying behind this sense almost of urgency is his characteristic concern to do two things at once: to be alive to current pastoral concerns and to be alert to the theological implications of any pastoral response. The 'new theology' is confronted by the secular concerns of what Schillebeeckx describes as the 'first generation' who can imagine the 'dismissal' of metaphysics altogether. Secularism, atheism and more recently the depth of human suffering, are both pastoral and theological preoccupations for Schillebeeckx, as becomes quite clear in his lengthy critique of one particular attempt to address the current pastoral situation, that of John Robinson's *Honest to God*.[87]

Tellingly, although Schillebeeckx has no quarrel with Robinson's pastoral concerns, he does have substantive difficulty with Robinson's failure to see the theological implications of his pastoral approach, namely his inability to sustain a coherent metaphysics within his theology. Remarking on *Honest to God*, he indicates that without a certain metaphysical realism, theology runs a significant risk of losing sight of its obligation.

> [The] pastoral approach to our present age has essential theological implications, and these must be judged theologically within the perspective of the word of God to which we are bound. But in this respect care must be taken not to fall into a 'magic' of the *word* which is not so very different from what was formerly experienced as the 'magic' of the sacrament.[88]

Here Schillebeeckx is suggesting that Robinson abandons metaphysics and in doing so has lost the capacity to describe a non-reductive, non-competitive

---

[86] Ibid. p. 121.
[87] Schillebeeckx, 'Life in God and Life in the World' .
[88] Ibid. p. 98.

relation between God and humanity. The relation-in-difference (the relation of similitude and dissimilitude) is lost.[89]

In Schillebeeckx's estimation, Robinson is a textbook example of a certain forgetfulness of metaphysics to which modern theology falls prey:

> These modern theologians seem to forget that any phenomenological elucidation of faith will be quite inadequate if it fails to penetrate to the metaphysical implications of the life of faith and if it neglects the distinctively divine manner of, for example, the reciprocal relationship between God and man. Furthermore, they also seem to forget, in fact, though not in theory, that conceptual theological knowledge is really the expression *par excellence* in this world of the content of man's experience of faith.[90]

The tension that theology must manage to hold in balance is one between 'conceptual knowledge' and the 'distinctively divine manner of the reciprocal relationship between God and man'. Metaphysical realism here cannot be reduced to a magical 'cause and effect' explanation of the relation between nature and grace. Nor can theology rely entirely on a mere phenomenology of encounter, as noted above, to describe the grace-filled reciprocity, which is the relation between divine and human. Instead, within the threefold debate between those theologies that hold to a cosmologically orientated metaphysics, the abandonment of metaphysics entirely and the renewal of metaphysics on an anthropological basis, Schillebeeckx aligns himself with the renewal of metaphysics.

Two examples taken from Schillebeeckx's theology bear this out: the theology of creation and sacramental theology. It is clear, however, he has a particular understanding of how metaphysics is to be renewed if it is to serve theology, and this is laid out in his analysis of what he calls 'the distinctive character of the human condition: its good and bad influences on dogmatic theology'. Furthermore, his own epistemological construction of the relation between non-conceptual and conceptual knowledge with the attendant turn to the notion of experience contributes to understanding the metaphysical

---

[89] In summary, Schillebeeckx's critique of Robinson follows these lines: because Robinson conflates all metaphysics with a metaphysics bound to concepts – an essentialist metaphysics – he fails to see the resources offered by a realist metaphysics to theology. This is not unrelated to the fatal omission of an eschatology in Robinson's text. In his existentialist theology, metaphysics becomes reduced to a 'depth psychology'. Robinson is correct to argue that God cannot be graspable by concepts. This however does not lead inevitably to the rejection of metaphysics. By abandoning any capacity to speak of the transcendent – God as transcendence and difference – in a 'real' relation to history, Schillebeeckx suggests Robinson can take theology 'just about anywhere'.

[90] Schillebeeckx, 'The New Trends in Present-day Dogmatic Theology', p. 120.

realism that lies at the heart of his theology. Each of these areas deserves comment, beginning with his theology of creation.

One of the areas in theology in which the question of metaphysics is raised most acutely is the doctrine of creation or, more precisely, it is the manner in which the doctrine of creation functions within theology that is significant.[91] The manner in which Schillebeeckx treats of the Christian belief in creation is of central importance for all of his theology.[92] However here, as part of a discussion of his metaphysical realism, it is interesting to explore just briefly Schillebeeckx's description of what the Christian belief in creation is *not*.

First, the Christian belief in creation is not a cosmology. Creation is not an explanation of how things work, or even of how things began:

> The Jewish–Christian belief in creation, which does not seek to be an explanation of our world and our humanity, makes us ask quite different questions from those involved in the presuppositions that this belief in creation is a kind of alternative explanation of human-kind and the world to the explanations given by the natural sciences and anthropology. . . . [B]elief in creation does not claim to give an explanation of the origin of the world.[93]

---

[91] The word 'doctrine' is used here simply to denote what Schillebeeckx specifies as the Christian belief in creation, which is the understanding of creation specific to theology, as distinct from the understanding of creation proper to science or anthropology.

[92] Schillebeeckx's understanding of creation is instrumental in his description of human freedom as 'situated freedom'. Consistently, he maintains that the finite is not destroyed by the infinite and hence the infinite is not something which must be overcome in order to secure human freedom. This non-reductive, non-competitive, constitutive relation between finite and infinite holds the theological discourse on human meaning in an intrinsic relation to human action and ethics. The purposive nature of human action and the responsibility to act are affirmed in this interpretation of God's tran-scendence. Schillebeeckx, 'God in Dry Dock', p. 10: 'The real mystery of God lies in the fact that with his world man lives *in* God – in a godly or an ungodly fashion ... our freedom to bring about events in this world is the revelation of God's action, and his revelation is a charge imposed upon our free will'.

[93] Schillebeeckx, *Church. The Human Story of God*, trans. John Bowden (London: SCM, 1990), p. 229. Schillebeeckx is not suggesting here that the explanations given by the natural sciences or anthropology are to be set in a dialectic relation of opposition with what he describes as 'creation faith'. That would in fact be an example of the twinning of concepts, which in his estimation has led to so many pseudo-problems in theology. He is careful here to underline that the explanations of natural science and anthropol-ogy are themselves acceptable to believers. His theological concern is simply to elucidate a creation faith that is not 'falsified' or 'turned into a misplaced explanation'. The job that must be performed by creation faith or the Christian belief in creation is one of elaboration upon God's self-revelation in human history as both creator and saviour and hence the locus for a theology of creation is the *reality* of the relation between the divine and the created.

Nor is the Christian belief in creation an explanation of how things will end:

> If God is said to be the *explanation* of the fact that things and events are what they are, then any attempt to change these things and situations (for better or for worse) is in fact blasphemous, or on the other hand, it turns human beings and our whole world into a puppet-show in which God alone holds the strings in his hands behind the screen: human history as a large-scale muppet show! In that case one's duty is simply to fit oneself into the universe which was determined from the beginning. In that case, moreover, God is the power and guarantee of the established order – not *Salvator*, Saviour, as Christians call him, but *Conservator*, as the Roman Hellenistic religions called him. The consequences of this is that if anything has gone wrong, the only meaningful transformation of the world and society is in a restoration of things to their ideal order.[94]

The Christian theology of creation seeks not to say something about how the world works, rather it strives to describe the relation between God and humanity.

In 1961 while assessing the 'new theology', Schillebeeckx was at pains to speak of God's universal causality in such a manner that the relation between nature and grace jeopardises neither divine transcendence nor human freedom; in 1989 – as is clear from the above quotation taken from *Church* – he is still preoccupied with theology's attempts to describe this relation, although the more classical language of the tradition, the nature of sanctifying grace, has been replaced by the slightly more colourful reference to the 'muppet show'. References to the 'muppets' aside, Schillebeeckx is clearly not grounding his metaphysical realism in a cosmology but in God's self-revelation within history. This revelation is sacramental: the divine revealed in human and historical form.

Recalling that theology is theocentric in its content – the true subject of theology is the living God, who is both the *Deus salutaris* and the *Deus sub ratione Deitatis* – and Christological in method – we shall only be able to reach this living God where he revealed himself as such, in Christ Jesus, who is the public manifestation of God – it becomes quite clear that a metaphysical realism must find its ground in the 'rhythm of divine life' and in the 'distinctively divine manner' of the reciprocity in grace between the human and divine. Schillebeeckx is clearly distancing himself from the mechanistic or essentialist metaphysics of scholastic theology. The relation between the human and the divine transcends the relation between cause and effect

---

[94] Schillebeeckx, *The Human Story of God*, pp. 229–230.

because this is not the relation which describes the pattern of divine life. Creation, if it is to describe divine activity, is *creatio ex nihilo* because even God's action 'outside himself' is divine – it is an absolute activity and thus 'creates from nothing'.

Schillebeeckx has never written a substantive monograph on the doctrine of creation yet the same cannot be said of sacramental theology. His doctoral thesis, developed in part as the result his own teaching requirements in dogmatic theology at Louvain, was a lengthy study of sacramental theology. Like de Lubac's *Surnaturel*, Schillebeeckx's *De sacramentele heilseconomie* is a massive recovery project that goes back to the tradition and via historical study recovers for sacramental theology a non-mechanistic or non-cosmological metaphysics.[95] Here his understanding of 'reality' as Aquinas' *exitus reditus*, transposed in his own work as 'address' and 'response', relocates sacramental theology within the *oikonomia* and hence grounds sacramental theology in Christology. The metaphysics of cause and effect – the relation between substance and accidents in the eucharist – is replaced by a realist metaphysics which reflects the distinctively divine manner of the reciprocity in grace between God and humanity.

The overarching concern of *De sacramentele heilseconomie* is to retrieve from within the tradition itself a sacramental theology which is non-dualistic. By establishing the sacramental nature of salvation history itself – the relation between *theologia* and *oikonomia* which he understands from the structure of revelation itself – the *concursus* between human and divine action is not built upon a dichotomy between nature and grace but upon an acceptance of the notion of graced nature.[96] The importance of this study for Roman Catholic sacramental theology cannot be overestimated.[97] Nor can

---

[95] *De sacramentele heilseconomie. Theologische bezinning op S. Thomas' sacramentenleer in het licht van de traditie en van de hedendaagse sacramentsproblematiek* (Bilthoven: Nelissen, 1952). Never translated in its entirety into English the essence of the christological structure of sacramental theology is represented in *Christ the Sacrament of the Encounter with God*. This is built upon an interpretation of incarnation and kenosis – the topic of the final two chapters of this book.

[96] *De sacramentele heilseconomie* is the first volume of what was intended to be a two-volume work. The second volume was never published, but the first volume is subtitled *Objectieve Structuur en Subjectieve Beleving* indicating a non-dualistic metaphysics.

[97] See Mark Schoof, *Breakthrough*, p. 138: '*De sacramentele heilseconomie* was an event in the Catholic theology of Dutch-speaking countries. Almost seven hundred pages in length, it was in fact only the first, more historical part of a much longer work. But this freshly conceived approach to the sacramental element in the Church as a dynamic reality undeniably had all the characteristics of a new beginning. Even more impressive than the unbelievably magnificent knowledge of the whole tradition of the Church which Schillebeeckx displayed in the book, from scripture down to recent times, were his presentation and interpretation of this tradition and the part played by modern anthropological and personalistic thought in this. As though they had been set out in ordered lines by an invisible magnet, the many tendencies and counter tendencies in

its importance for appreciating the character of Schillebeeckx's own work be overestimated. As the first book which he published it is a classic example of his rigorous attention to the tradition and his pastoral concern to address questions of meaning and practice which shape Christian life. In fact, apart from Christology, Schillebeeckx has published more on sacramental theology than on any other topic.[98] Thus, Schillebeeckx's critique of how sacramental theology has been interpreted within the 'new theology' must be considered as more than a glancing blow.

As Schillebeeckx himself has incorporated aspects of contemporary philosophy, namely phenomenology and existentialism, within his primarily Thomistic account of sacraments, his comments concerning the strengths and weaknesses of other like-minded sacramental theologies are telling:

> The playing with concepts which characterised later scholasticism has nowadays frequently been replaced by a kind of literary playing with phenomenological ideas on the part of those theologians who claim that they are orientated towards phenomenology. And this tendency constantly brings the authentic theological renewal into disrepute. Confronted with such phenomenological attempts to reach an understanding of the dogma of Transubstantiation, we are forced to admit that these studies provide an excellent *introduction* to the theology of the Transubstantiation. But they do not come anywhere near the real problem of the dogma. In the belief that they are interpreting the dogma in a modern theological way, all that these theologians have in fact succeeded in doing is unwittingly to coat the dogma with

the tradition of the Church were related in this book to the burning question of man's personal encounter with the God who has shown himself in Christ as someone who also plays a part in our world.'

[98] Schillebeeckx has most recently been engaged in writing a book (not surprisingly of some length) on sacramental theology. It remains unfinished, but it will presumably be the last major piece of work, bringing his career full circle. It is a return both to the tradition – hence not a radical departure from *Christ the Sacrament* – and an appropriation of current studies of ritual action – thus an attempt to re-present the tradition. It is intended as a pastoral and theological response to the current situation in which liturgy has ceased to have a meaningful place in daily life. See Schillebeeckx, 'Naar een herontdekking van de christelijke sacramenten. Ritualisering van religieuze momenten in het alledaagse leven', *Tijdschrift voor Theologie* **40** (2000), pp. 164–187. The other books on sacraments are: *Eucharist* (London: Sheed and Ward, 1968). *Christus' tegenwoordigheid in de eucharistie* (Bilthoven: Nelissen, 1967); *Marriage: Secular Reality and Saving Mystery* (London: Sheed and Ward, 1965). *Het huwelijk, aardse werkelijheid en heilsmysterie* (Bilthoven: Nelissen, 1963). As with *De sacramentele heilseconomie, Marriage* is the first of a projected two-volume affair. The first volume is primarily an historical study; the second volume was never published. *Ministry. A Case for Change* (London: SCM, 1981); *Kerkelijk ambt. Voorgangers in de gemeente van Jezus Christus* (Bloemendaal: Nelissen, 1980).

phenomenology. In reacting – rightly – against a form of metaphysics that was cosmologically orientated, their mistake has been to abandon metaphysics entirely in their phenomenological analyses and to forget that it is possible to renew metaphysics on an anthropological basis.[99]

Clearly, as indicated well in his own work, Schillebeeckx is not suggesting a return to a systematized theology that is closed to the world of contemporary thought.

Most important, in light of his sacramental theology and a theology of grace, Schillebeeckx is not arguing for a mechanistic metaphysics that might explain how things work:

> On the other hand, scholastic reactions to phenomenological analyses of this kind manifest such a physical approach and such a lack of understanding of phenomenology that even these speculations about Transubstantiation fail to satisfy us.[100]

Rather, as demonstrated both in his doctrine of creation and in his sacramental theology, he has a particular understanding of the balance that must be achieved between the temptation to abandon metaphysics altogether – 'the phenomenological essentialist tendency of recent dogmatic reflection' – and the appeal to a 'cosmology' – 'the essentialist theology of the past'.[101] This balance is found, he is persuaded, in what he understands to be the anthropological renewal of metaphysics.

Although Schillebeeckx is alert to the contributions contemporary philosophy makes to theology, he has a certain sense of both the advantages and the limits that existentialism and phenomenology bring to the theological task. Therefore, although he quite deliberately describes the nature of our relationship with God as 'individual', 'personal', and 'reciprocal' (hence intersubjective) he recognizes the inability of a 'mere phenomenology of encounter' to describe what is an ontological reality: the communion in grace between God and ourselves.

Christian immortality is seen to be quite different from immortality in the philosophical sense, although the latter forms the necessary preamble to the former. Philosophical immortality is an *implication of the human state of being a person*, whereas Christian immortality is *an implication of our communion of grace* with the living God in Christ.[102]

The relation between philosophy and theology described here is significant, and quite possibly, when taken out of the wider context of his concern

---

[99] Schillebeeckx, 'The New Trends in Present-day Dogmatic Theology', p. 120.
[100] Ibid.
[101] Ibid. p. 119.
[102] Ibid. p. 142.

to articulate a non-dualistic relation between nature and grace, is open to misinterpretation. Schillebeeckx is not particularly invested in establishing philosophical foundations from which theology can then proceed. It is not in this sense that philosophy 'forms the necessary preamble' to theology. Philosophical immortality forms the necessary preamble to Christian immortality simply because in God's self-revelation throughout salvation history, the divine does not negate the human but fulfils it.[103] There is not for Schillebeeckx a human nature as such that is independent of human nature created for communion with God. A clear example of this is his brief treatment of the classic anthropological category of contingency, which then leads into his discussion of the appeal to human existential experience and its repercussions for dogmatic theology.

The relation between the contingent and the absolute comes to the fore in Schillebeeckx's discussion of the perspectival character of human knowing. Although this discussion is largely of interest to him because of his preoccupation with the epistemological question of the knowability of God and the relation between conceptual and non-conceptual knowledge, it also serves to underscore the pivotal role that a non-dualistic account of the nature–grace relation plays for him. As with finitude, contingency – what Schillebeeckx often describes as human situatedness – is not a problem to be overcome. Just as the finite does not need to be destroyed for the infinite to be revealed, so too the absolute does not destroy the contingent. Human nature, precisely in its finitude and contingency, is the subject of the communion in grace with the divine.

However absolute and unchangeable the saving value may be, it nonetheless shares, as something that is known by us in faith, in those characteristics that are distinctively human – in the imperfection, the relativity and the growth or historical nature of every human possession of truth. We must

---

[103] Schillebeeckx, 'Theologia *or* Oikonomia?', p. 103: 'Even in theology which is orientated towards the history of salvation, metaphysics can and must have an irreplaceable function to perform, although this is bound to be subordinate. Philosophy seeks intelligibility of the datum of experience, and in this sense it is not dethroned by faith and theology. Revelation itself does not provide us with any supra-metaphysical truths, but only with explications along the lines of salvation history. As a consequence, metaphysics always has some contribution to make in any case in which we have to do with the intelligibility of reality, even when it is a saving reality. Although in metaphysics, God is not considered as God, but only as fundamental being, the divine being is nonetheless also a being and as such intelligible. It is certainly not a question of the mystery of God being situated at a deeper level than the mystery of being. It is one and the same mystery, reached metaphysically in and through the created world and theologically in and through the economy of salvation. Both views of God are complementary and throw light on each other. The existential unity between the order of creation and the order of salvation is therefore the basis for the application of philosophy in theology.'

always distinguish, in the implicit totality of faith, between the reality of salvation and our consciousness of this reality in explicit faith at any given moment. It is a consequence of our physical nature and our situation in this world, without which the life of faith is not possible, that our awareness of faith is always a vision of the reality of salvation, seen in a certain perspective.[104]

The extent to which the human is not negated by the divine in this relationship of grace, the life of faith, is clear for Schillebeeckx. The life of faith is 'not possible' as an abstraction from the physical nature, which situates human being in this world.

Although the perspectival characteristic of our knowledge of the saving reality is a 'consequence' of our situatedness, this human contingency does not have to be destroyed for the reality of salvation to be realized. The life of faith is 'not possible' without our 'physical nature and our situation in this world'. Schillebeeckx will appeal neither to a description of human nature as a body–soul duality nor to an otherworldly spirituality that simply sidesteps our situation in this world, as if to be situated were an obstacle to faith. The full force of his argument is captured in a passing eschatological reference.

We are never able to make any definitive and all-round statements concerning faith. Our faith, which is manifested in an earthly and human form, provides us, from a finite, limited and historical standpoint, with a view in perspective of the absolute reality of salvation that we, because of our very nature, never have in our power – not even in the beatific vision of God.[105]

The non-competitive relation between the divine and human and the difference between them is both a reality in history and an eschatological reality. Human nature is not divinized, taking on the power of the divine. Rather, it is in 'our very nature' that we come face to face with God.

Schillebeeckx's analysis of the significance of the 'new philosophies' of phenomenology and existentialism for dogmatic theology is a valuable contribution to the intellectual history of one of the most fruitful periods of Roman Catholic theology; and his insights into the gains and losses for theology in its relation to philosophy are acute. He will neither allow theology to practise in isolation from other intellectual disciplines, indeed he will argue that theology, if rooted in its own tradition has nothing to fear from other conversation partners, nor will he concede to these partners the ground rules by which theology is to operate. The truths by which theology must be guided are given in God's salvific and self-revealing activity in human history. That is to say, theology, to be coherent, must hold to the truth that the infinite is revealed in the finite without destroying it. Theology, on this account, is theocentric in its subject and Christological in its method, and

---

[104] Schillebeeckx, 'The New Trends in Present-day Dogmatic Theology', p. 110.
[105] Ibid. p. 111.

the extent to which theology will gain from, or be impoverished by, the 'new philosophies' is measured against this understanding of theology itself.

In this section of the chapter on grace as the human vocation to intimacy with God, two related but distinct ideas have been developed. The first is that grace, described as communion and reciprocity between the human and the divine expresses humanity's relation to God in a non-dualistic, non-reductive and hence non-competitive manner. Humanity's metaphysical and moral significance are established and bound together in a theology of grace that interprets the mystery of God to be the future of humanity. Human historicity and freedom function from within the relation to God which is creative, salvific, sanctifying, participative and personal.

The second idea – a subsidiary one – has developed from the context in which Schillebeeckx's theology of grace is articulated, and that is his analysis of the strengths and weakness of contemporary theology and the contributions, good and bad, of contemporary philosophy. Here the idea of a realist metaphysics comes to the surface with the understanding that being and hence truth are present in and as historical realities. For theology this means that this is the metaphysics appropriate to a description of the being of God revealed as God's being-God within history as salvation. *Theologia* and *oikonomia* are bound together in God's self-revelation. Theology is always therefore both a speculative and a practical discipline. For theological anthropology this means humanity's metaphysical and moral significance are intrinsically related: 'I am myself in absolute dependence upon God'; and 'I am myself as a situated freedom'.

Turning now to the third section of this chapter, Schillebeeckx's analysis of this realist metaphysics ('the renewal of metaphysics along anthropocentric lines') identifies the incarnational reality of human being as its most substantive contribution to theology. This is the turning point in this study in which the focus shifts from the emphasis on transcendence and difference to the emphasis on immanence and personal – although these are of course inseparable. In other words, the Christological structure of Schillebeeckx's theological anthropology comes more into the foreground and here the idea of incarnation – both as a Christological truth and as a human reality – is pivotal.

Grace: Incarnation as Human Intimacy with God

The decisions Schillebeeckx takes in his assessment of those developments within philosophy which, in his estimation, could contribute most productively to the renewal of theology, have been outlined above in his description of these developments as the 'anthropological renewal of metaphysics.' He is neither interested in an 'essentialist phenomenology' that abandons metaphysics nor is he interested in the 'essentialist metaphysics' that transforms theology into cosmology and reduces descriptions of the divine–human relation into an explanation of 'how things work'. This is precisely the achievement of his sacramental theology: *De sacramentele heilseconomie* establishes the sacramental nature of salvation history and hence the sacramental nature of human life and locates a theology of 'the sacraments' there.

From contemporary phenomenology Schillebeeckx is most interested in what he describes as 'the anthropological idea of incarnation' with its 'recognition of the distinctive character of the "human condition"'.[106] It is because of this development – the anthropological idea of incarnation – that phenomenology is of real importance to theology.

Probably the most important advance made by the philosophy of modern phenomenology is its recognition of the distinctive character of the human condition and its resolute abandonment of physicism, according to which man, like the things of nature, was seen as something that is 'determined by nature'.[107]

Here he is true to his theology of creation: personal human identity and uniqueness are given in the creative activity of God. Therefore human nature cannot be conceived of apart from the end for which it is intended.

Theologically Schillebeeckx develops this distinctive character of the human condition by describing human nature as graced nature, a case that he demonstrates christologically. He is true to his own intellectual formation, which was characterized by an openness that embraces both the past, the classic texts of the tradition and here especially Thomas, and the contemporary insights of philosophy. This intellectual openness was a decisive feature of his theological formation in which he was encouraged to read both the classic texts of the tradition and at the same time to study contemporary philosophy. At the time of his theological education this was remarkable and came at no small cost. Quite apart, therefore, from his own critical interpretations of the 'new philosophies', Schillebeeckx's appeal to contemporary philosophy in itself is of note because it situates him within this very fruitful yet turbulent period of theology.

Schillebeeckx analyses the gains that modern phenomenology has won for anthropology and hence for theology. His reading of these developments hinges upon the success with which philosophy overcomes a series of dualisms: body–spirit, contingency–freedom, nature–action.

> The distinctive anthropological character of man, whose mode of being and mode of being one is to be found in an essential correlation between the spirit that communicates itself to the body and the physical nature that participates in this spirit, is nowadays becoming clear. This insight could be called the affirmation of man's essential incarnation, in which is also seen as a fundamental freedom, and as a 'possibility'.[108]

[106] Ibid. p.121.
[107] Ibid.
[108] Ibid. pp. 121–122.

Schillebeeckx wants to secure two positions from philosophical anthropology here: the first is that humanity is essentially incarnate, that is to say, human nature is contingent, relational and bodily, and these qualities are not incidental but essential; the second is that human freedom is grounded in humanity's incarnate nature, which is to say, that human freedom is contingent, relational and bodily and therefore, in Schillebeeckx's terms 'situated'.

The term 'freedom' is qualified for Schillebeeckx by the term 'possibility', which in his work suggests both the reality of human historical agency – human beings do make history – and the ultimate ambiguity of history – the relation between human history and the eschatological character of salvation or human well-being. Ultimately history remains open. Both of these claims – that human nature is essentially incarnate and also a freedom experienced as possibility – depend for Schillebeeckx on a non-dualistic understanding of the body–spirit relation, a relation he describes as an essential correlation. The uniqueness of human nature and of human identity is found here: 'We are confronted by a complete break with the dualistic conception of man'.[109]

Whether or not the assertion that philosophy has at last made a 'complete break' with dualistic anthropology can ultimately be sustained, the importance of this description of philosophical anthropology is nevertheless significant. With respect to Schillebeeckx's own anthropology, it highlights the key ideas which undergird his description of human being as a 'situated freedom'. The anthropological renewal of metaphysics is captured for him in the insight that he describes as the 'affirmation of man's essential incarnation'. Crucially, this affirmation of humanity's essential incarnation is the ground from which to speak of human being as a 'fundamental freedom' and as a 'possibility'. This is the crux of the argument: 'It is only in this world that man comes to himself'.[110]

Contingency, finitude, situatedness and bodiliness are not incidental to human freedom but essential to freedom. This of course suggests for Schillebeeckx human freedom is essentially the freedom to act: 'I am really myself in and of this world, becoming myself more and more therein'.[111] Human being and becoming are inseparable and so Schillebeeckx's treatment of the concept of freedom is frequently qualified by the ideas of responsibility and task, and there are clear echoes here of the theological concept of vocation. Humanity is defined as a vocation:

A synthesis between the consistent acceptance of personalism and the recognition of the essential incarnation of the human person is gradually

---

[109] Ibid. p. 122.
[110] Ibid.
[111] Schillebeeckx, 'Dialogue with God and Christian Secularity', p. 215.

111

coming about. This has enabled us to see more clearly than in the past that the specifically human character of man is not something that is given, a datum, but a task, something that has to be realized (and therefore also something that can be neglected).[112]

This understanding of the 'essential incarnation' of humanity places emphasis on the relation between being and becoming – the specifically human character of humanity is given as a task to be realized or neglected – and hence it focuses on the dynamic qualities of human freedom and responsibility. This implies that human consciousness itself is essentially incarnate. This is the basic insight that underpins the understanding of human nature as essentially incarnate: human consciousness is an incarnate consciousness. This insight has significant implications for Christology. For Schillebeeckx it 'permits a purer dogmatic light to be thrown on the implicit riches of Christ's "true humanity".

Certainly the most obvious place from which to explore Schillebeeckx's Christology in the first half of his career is his book, *Christ the Sacrament of the Encounter with God*, and this exploration is the topic for the next two chapters of this study. However, in the essay on 'The New Trends in Dogmatic Theology', there is a very brief but significant reflection on Christology vis-à-vis the 'more finely shaded insights of modern anthropology' that contribute to the theological recovery of 'the implicit riches of Christ's "true humanity"'.[113] Schillebeeckx sets out what he describes as a 'few guidelines' for Christology, a 'Christological outline', which, however 'concise and schematic', is an excellent introduction to his Christology and especially helpful as an introduction to Christology as the 'structure' for a theological anthropology.[114]

Specifically, in this Christological outline, and in light of the gains made for contemporary theology in its dialogue with the anthropological renewal of metaphysics, Schillebeeckx is engaged in yet another piece of *ressourcement* theology: the 'renewal' of theology, he suggests, is in fact the 'throwing of new light on what was previously latent and unexpressed' within the tradition yet which was 'nonetheless implicitly accepted'.[115] In the previous section of this chapter Schillebeeckx's retrieval of Thomas' understanding of the relation between nature and grace was the centrepiece of his description of a non-dualistic, non-reductive and non-competitive relation between the finite and the infinite. Nature has no 'natural' end apart from that for which it was created, that is to say, because the relation of nature to grace is

---

[112] Schillebeeckx, 'The New Trends in Present-day Dogmatic Theology', p. 122.
[113] Ibid. p. 123.
[114] Ibid.
[115] Schillebeeckx, 'The New Trends in Present-day Dogmatic Theology', p. 127.

constitutive, there is not a relation of nature *and* grace, rather there is graced nature: 'Human existence is something granted, it is a grace: an overwhelming grace . . . "towards you was I cast from my birth"'.[116] God is the future of humanity in a creative, salvific, sanctifying, participative and personal relation.

Turning here to this brief 'Christological outline' the relation of human to divine comes to its ultimate expression in incarnation. The incarnation reveals the meaning of human life as intimacy with God:

> What Christ showed us above all was what a *man* is like who has declared himself to be fully committed to God, the invisible Father. . . . His visible living relationship to the invisible God reveals the mystery of the true God to us . . . in this man Jesus we can see how a dialogue relationship is possible between God and man, and that this prayer represents the profoundest meaning of life.'[117]

For Schillebeeckx, the *locus* of this human–divine relation of intimacy, and hence constitutive of the vocation of humanity itself are the 'implicit riches of Christ's "true humanity". This time Schillebeeckx's *ressourcement* takes him back to the patristic tradition of a kenotic Christology that gave full expression to the personal meaning of Jesus' human nature.[118]

Schillebeeckx's reading of the history of theology is always quite particularly marked by a concern to retrieve 'neglected aspects of the Christian tradition' and to re-evaluate strands that at one time might have been lost through misunderstanding or through inadequate reading.[119] An example of such re-evaluation is the Christology of Theodore of Mopsuestia, quoted by Schillebeeckx as an example of the Christology of the Antiochian school that struggled to represent adequately the humanity of Christ and was, as a consequence, suspected of denying his full divinity. Gains in philosophical

---

[116] Schillebeeckx, 'Dialogue with God and Christian Secularity', p. 210.

[117] Schillebeeckx, 'God in Dry Dock', pp. 12–13.

[118] Schillebeeckx, 'The New Trends in Present-day Dogmatic Theology', p. 123.

[119] John Galvin, 'The Story of Jesus as the Story of God' in Mary Catherine Hilkert and Robert Schreiter, eds *The Praxis of the Reign of God* (New York: Fordham University Press, 2002), p. 88. Galvin remarks that Schillebeeckx's interest in retrieving 'neglected aspects of the Christian tradition is an important element of his overall theological programme'. The remark is used by Galvin to explain Schillebeeckx's interpretation of the crucifixion – in *Jesus: An Experiment in Christology* – in which Schillebeeckx draws attention to interpretations of Jesus' death that do not isolate his death from his life. Thus he discusses the crucifixion as the death of a 'prophet-martyr or 'righteous sufferer', rather than drawing on models of atonement, to retrieve interpretations 'largely bypassed in the history of theology'.

anthropology serve well for Schillebeeckx as the impetus to delve back into the tradition and to read its history with new insight:

> It is perhaps characteristic that the whole of this speculative 'renewal' due to anthropological insights is accompanied by a differently orientated historical judgment of, for example, the christology of Theodore of Mopsuestia, which, in the past was always regarded as suspect. In spite of some awkward formulations, this teaching now appears to those who support the new historical research as orthodox and Catholic. These parallel influences can, in my opinion, be explained by the fact that the content and meaning of the past – of the Bible and of patristic theology, for example – become constantly clearer according to the light in which these writings come to stand in the continuously renewed spiritual situation of mankind.[120]

Even when it is most speculative, theology remains a historical discipline because of our relation to the past: 'The past is never completely dead' for humanity but stands in a critical and creative relation to the present.[121]

In his christological outline the neglected piece of the tradition to which Schillebeeckx turns is kenotic Christology – the emphasis placed by some biblical and patristic Christology on the kenotic nature of the incarnation: the self-emptying of the Son as the incarnate, human Jesus. The biblical texts which underpin this retrieval for Schillebeeckx are the christological hymn from Philippians and the description from Romans of our sharing in the life of Christ through adoption. These scriptural references are not the subject of the extended exegesis which so marks his later Christology yet they are nevertheless essential to it and hence, by implication, they are pivotal to an understanding of his theological anthropology:

> The nature of intimacy with God, which is the primary task of human life, can be seen in detail by considering the man Jesus. In and through Christ, God the Father has also become, in the force of the 'Spirit of sonship,' truly *our* Father, so that we are taken up into the special

---

[120] Schillebeeckx, 'The New Trends in Present-day Dogmatic Theology', p. 127.

[121] Ibid. p. 128. Tellingly, as early as this 1961 essay, Schillebeeckx extends his reflection on theology as an historical discipline to include biblical study: 'The content of the Bible speaks to us even now, not only in the light of the word of revelation, but also in light of our present-day awareness, perspectives and insights. For this reason, we are correct to refer to biblical theology as a part of dogmatic theology, a biblical theology in which the light of faith includes within itself the light of the intellect, that is, the light of human experience that reflects upon itself. We therefore recognize that in each period of history, man approaches Scripture differently and thereby discovers aspects which escaped the attention of those who studied the same Scripture in previous periods.'

providential relationship which exists between God the Father and the incarnate Son . . . That we are children of God is the deepest significance of our being made in his image and it is also the fundamental definition of man: a definition that is ultimately still in the making and which is accomplished through truly intimate intercourse with the living God.[122]

The context for Schillebeeckx of a theological anthropology is the providential relationship between God and humanity: the creative, salvific, sanctifying, participative and personal relation between the human and the divine which defines humanity as a vocation to intimacy with God. This definition finds its fundamental expression in the unique 'providential relationship which exists between God the Father and the incarnate Son'. This relation between the Father and the incarnate Son has a kenotic structure and it is this which is the ground for our adoption into the relation of intimacy between Father and Son: 'we are taken up into' this relation; and 'that we are children of God is the fundamental definition of humanity'. In his Christology Schillebeeckx acknowledges clearly and consistently the gains for theology that are achieved in the increasing attentiveness to the biblical text and especially in the biblical account of redemption. It is in a biblical, patristic Christology that Schillebeeckx finds the 'kenotic structure' for his theology of grace and hence for his theological anthropology.

Both Schillebeeckx's interest in the theology of grace, which follows the *ressourcement* lead of de Lubac and of the *nouvelle théologie*, and his interest in the contemporary philosophies of phenomenology are driven by one conviction: the need to overcome dualistic descriptions of the relation between human and divine and dualistic descriptions of what it means to be human itself, body and spirit. In his 'Christological outline' both the nature–grace debates within theology and the phenomenological 'recognition of the human condition', the anthropological renewal of metaphysics within philosophy, pay dividends:

> The Son himself is personally man, and the man Jesus is personally God the Son. A human act on Jesus' part is therefore a personal act of God appearing in human form. The entire concrete existence of this man is thus a grace, because this man's state of being a person for this humanity, which does not belong to itself but to the divine Son, is pure grace.[123]

It is clear from this text that it is the fully personal nature of Christ's humanity that is the 'implicit richness' of 'Christ's true humanity. This is the heart

---

[122] Schillebeeckx, 'Dialogue with God and Christian Secularity', pp. 220–221.
[123] Schillebeeckx, 'The New Trends in Present-day Dogmatic Theology', pp. 123–124.

of Schillebeeckx's interpretation of the doctrine of incarnation.[124] Here
Schillebeeckx draws both on the efforts of philosophy to overcome the sense
of humanity's 'alienation' within the world – 'the person is no longer regarded
as extrinsic to nature, but nature as the content of the person' – and on the
efforts of theology to describe the nature–grace relation as 'reciprocity' in
which grace is not extrinsic to nature but nature is seen rather as 'graced
nature'.[125]

Schillebeeckx's sketch of the renewal of Christology focuses on the growing recognition of the 'implicit riches of Christ's true humanity' and the
concurrent overcoming of the 'antitheses between the Alexandrian and the
Antiochian Christologies', a polarization that he underlines by placing stress
on its persistent character, colouring 'the entire history of the Church.[126] He
describes the overcoming of the antitheses thus:

> The affirmation that Christ is not a human person *besides* being a
> divine person has undoubtedly been preserved (although sufficient jus-
> tice has not always been done to this affirmation in certain circles). On
> the other hand, the humanity of Christ has not been 'depersonalised' –
> a thing that occurred quite frequently in some theological manuals,
> which referred in so many words to the 'impersonal human nature' of
> Jesus. Jesus' humanity is regarded, in a more consistent way as the
> basis, not indeed of his state of being a person, but of his state of being
> a person in a human manner. The Son himself is personally man, and
> the man Jesus is personally God the Son.[127]

In this description – 'the Son himself is personally man, and the man Jesus is
personally God the Son' – Schillebeeckx is offering a particular interpretation of the incarnation. Specifically, he is developing a Christology in which
the fully personal nature of Christ's humanity is recognized. At the same
time he is alert to the Christological issues this raises, most critically the
nature of the incarnate Christ's self-consciousness and the relation this suggests between the personal nature of the incarnate Christ and the divine
person, the pre-existent Son.

Schillebeeckx is clearly aware of the Christological implications of the
description of Christ's human nature as 'person': Christ's humanity is understood as the basis, 'not indeed of his state of being a person', that is to say,
not as the basis of his divine nature as Son but as the basis of 'his state of

---

[124] Schillebeeckx, *Christ the Sacrament*, p. 14 n 10. This interpretation of incarnation is
the pivotal concept for the christological structure of Schillebeeckx's theological
anthropology. This is discussed in Chapters 3 and 4 of this study.
[125] Schillebeeckx, 'The New Trends in Present-day Dogmatic Theology', pp. 126–127.
[126] Ibid. p. 123.
[127] Ibid.

being a person in a human manner'. Yet he is also concerned to describe the fullness if Christ's humanity in the incarnation. The positive influence of philosophical anthropology upon theology is apparent here in the enriched concept of human nature: 'nature' is qualified by the notion of 'person'. Attention is drawn to Christ's humanity in this particular manner which acknowledges the 'essential incarnation' of human being. The personal nature of human being is always an incarnate consciousness. In Schillebeeckx's carefully constructed Christological statement, he secures both the transcendence or divinity of God – the pre-existence of the divine Son as person – and at the same time, because of the reference to the 'personal' – the fully personal nature of Christ's humanity – he establishes the possibility for the intersubjective relation between humanity and God.

At the very heart of Schillebeeckx's theology is his interpretation of the doctrine of the incarnation. Specifically, for Schillebeeckx the incarnation reveals the fully personal nature of Christ' humanity. It is this understanding of the incarnation that allows Schillebeeckx to describe Christology as the structure for his theological anthropology: it is the structure for theological anthropology because it expresses the 'ontological implications of the reciprocity in grace between the human and the divine'. In the doctrine of the incarnation Schillebeeckx's theology of grace finds its fullest expression:

> It is evident from the fact that the Son of God was truly man, that Jesus' personal humanity was the revelation of grace. In him the deepest meaning of our being man was made manifest to us. Personal humanity is therefore always a possibility of revelation, the sphere in which revelation and grace are accomplished. What is human is thus the material through which the revelation of God's grace is expressed.[128]

In other words, Christ's incarnation becomes the 'structure' for humanity's intimacy with God, and hence the description of the fully personal nature of Christ's humanity is pivotal for theological anthropology.

Schillebeeckx develops the idea that Christ's incarnation is constitutive of humanity's vocation to intimacy with God – the Christological structure of his theology – by indicating three key developments in contemporary Christology: the first is the understanding of humanity's essential incarnation – the intrinsic and non-dualistic relation between incarnate nature and consciousness, and the influence this has had on Christology; the second is the renewal of kenotic Christology; and the third is the emphasis placed on resurrection in the event of redemption. A brief outline of these three developments concludes this chapter and sets up the discussion of the following two chapters.

---

[128] Schillebeeckx, 'Christian Faith and Man's Expectation for the Future on Earth', p. 75.

First then, the personal nature of Christ's humanity or the personal character of the incarnation: Schillebeeckx's discussion of the personal nature of Christ's humanity revolves around a reflection on consciousness. In Christology, the manner in which the question of Christ's self-consciousness is treated is indicative of how seriously a Christology is committed to the fully personal nature of Christ's humanity. This follows from an anthropology that does not adhere to a dualistic relation between body and spirit: human self-consciousness is always incarnational. Furthermore, human self-communication, human speaking, is always incarnational. For Schillebeeckx, Christ's incarnate and therefore fully human 'self-consciousness' is one of the 'implicit riches of Christ's true humanity' – it is an expression of the fullness of the personal nature of Christ's humanity.

If true humanity is, then, impossible without consciousness of self, this means that Jesus' human consciousness, which, like his humanity, is of its very nature a *grace*, implies an intuitive human experience of his divine self, insofar as this self is conscious of itself in a *human* consciousness.[129] This particular description of the self-consciousness of the incarnate Son, and hence this description of the relation of the pre-existent Son to the incarnate Christ underlines the fully personal nature that Schillebeeckx attributes to Christ's humanity.

Schillebeeckx's development of this idea reflects his essentially sacramental theology of revelation and hence a sacramental Christology. Christ's human consciousness is the human and historical incarnation of divine self-consciousness:

> The consequence of this consciousness of himself on the part of the man Jesus because of his essential relationship with the Father is that the Father is the centre of Christ's human consciousness. And if all speaking on the part of one man to his fellow man is a revelation of himself, this means, as far as Christ is concerned, that all his human speaking and all of his human activity is, by definition, a revelation of the Father and a pouring out of the Pneuma.[130]

Christ's human self-consciousness is the incarnation of the relation between Father and Son. This description of Jesus' personal humanity is entirely consistent with Schillebeeckx's treatise on God in which the *Deus sub ratione Deitatis* is the *Deus salutaris*: the Father is the centre of Christ' human consciousness. It also entirely consistent with a sacramental theology of revelation: Christ's speaking 'is by definition, a revelation of the Father and a pouring out of the Pneuma'.

---

[129] Schillebeeckx, 'The New Trends in Present-day Dogmatic Theology', p. 124.
[130] Ibid.

The personal nature of Christ's humanity is revealed in his self-consciousness that is incarnate, and in his self-communication that is incarnate. Schillebeeckx develops this full description of the personal nature of Christ's humanity within the Christological doctrine of incarnation by developing a sacramental Christology. Hence his description of the fully personal nature of Christ's humanity is consistent with his treatise on God and the theology of revelation that determines theological method. Two further ideas follow on from the attempt to take Christ's human consciousness seriously: human self-consciousness 'develops' and hence Christ's incarnation is understood as a *'becoming man*, a growing reality'; second, human consciousness is relational, thus Christ in his theocentric self-consciousness indicates the free and reciprocal nature of the divine–human relation. This brings Schillebeeckx to the description of human intimacy with God as a dialogue and hence the nature of human life as vocation, defined by both its call and its response.

First, the incarnation as becoming: here the incarnation reveals and makes present in human historical form the dialogue of faithfulness with God which is the human vocation. Christ's 'becoming man' was a 'growing reality' in which the 'perfection both of the divine invitation and the human response in faith' was incarnate from birth until glorification:[131]

> Christ's incarnation was a *becoming* man, a growing reality. It was not something that took place at one moment, for example, at the moment of conception in Mary's womb. His incarnation, his becoming man, was a growing reality which continued throughout the whole of Jesus' human life and which found its active point of rest in the closing aspect of the incarnation – Jesus' resurrection, glorification and eschatological pouring out of the Spirit.[132]

In Christ therefore, 'God's ultimate purpose is realized': the incarnation of humanity's 'vocation to faithfulness'.[133]

The second and related idea that follows from 'acceptance of the personal character' of the incarnation is the understanding of the nature of intimacy with God as a vocation that is best described as a 'dialogue' of call and response. The 'personal character' of the incarnation points not only to Christ as the revelation of God's love offered, but also to the acceptance of that offer:

> Acceptance of the personal character of the incarnation has also made us all the more clearly aware of Christ, not only as the revelation to us of God's invitation of love, but also as the person who, as a man,

---

[131] Schillebeeckx, *Christ the Sacrament*, p. 13.
[132] Schillebeeckx, 'The New Trends in Present-day Dogmatic Theology', p. 125.
[133] Schillebeeckx, *Christ the Sacrament*, p. 13.

accepted this offer of love from the Father. For this reason, we are bound to say that divine revelation was accomplished in and through the religious life of the man Jesus. His personal relationship with the Father in confrontation with the world was the source of Jesus' discourse addressed to his fellow men, in which he revealed the concrete form of all true religion to us. Religion itself is the sphere of revelation, which is therefore essentially a dialogue.[134]

The fully personal nature of Christ's incarnation – expressed in the understanding of Christ's humanity 'becoming' – and in Christ's free and complete revelation of the nature of humanity's intimacy with God as a dialogue – a vocation defined by both its invitation and response – leads Schillebeeckx to identify two further developments within contemporary Christology as especially significant: the re-emergence of kenotic Christology and the recognition that the biblical account of redemption culminates in the resurrection.

With the identification of these two developments within Christology we come to the two biblical texts around which Schillebeeckx's Christological outline pivots: Phil. 2. 7 and Rom. 8.15–17. The first of these marks a retrieval of a patristic understanding of the kenotic nature of the incarnation – the self-emptying of the Son in the incarnation: 'According to a phrase in Paul's letter to the Philippians – "he emptied himself" – (Phil. 2. 7) – what the incarnation meant for the human experience of the Person of the Son was a *kenōsis* of self-emptying."[135] This understanding of incarnation had been almost entirely lost within theology, at least in the West, or it had been much reduced and applied only to Christ's suffering and death, thereby losing sight of the role it had played in allowing Christology to speak of both of the fullness of Christ's humanity and the fullness of Christ's divinity without diminishing one or the other of these truths. When the incarnation is understood as kenosis then '*kenōsis* is seen to permeate Jesus' entire situational existence', leading to the 'insight that Jesus, although personally God the Son, could as a man here on earth, only be a conscious being in a human manner'. A kenotic Christology that does not limit the role of self-emptying to the cross but applies this to the whole of the human life of Christ is of central importance to Schillebeeckx's own description of Jesus' human life as a 'situated human freedom, sin excepted'.[136]

It is the strongly kenotic emphasis on the Son emptying himself in the incarnation that allows for a much fuller emphasis on the real human and free life of Christ. It follows therefore that it is possible to give full weight to

---

[134] Schillebeeckx, 'The New Trends in Present-day Dogmatic Theology', p. 125.
[135] Ibid.
[136] Ibid. p. 126.

the human life, seeing the saving significance of the whole life (*mysteria carnis Christi*). This suggests for Schillebeeckx that the full force of the biblical account of redemption that describes the life of Christ in its entirety can be brought to bear upon Christology. It suggests further that the biblical account culminates in the resurrection. And here the second biblical reference, Rom. 8.15–17, comes to the fore.

This particular section of his Christological outline in which Schillebeeckx moves from a kenotic Christology to the centrality of the resurrection in the biblical account of redemption is especially compressed and clumsily written. It makes a number of assertions without much explanation. Crucially there is no explanation made for the claim that the resurrection is the culmination of the biblical account of redemption, just the assertion that this is the case. This permits him to present the renewed emphasis on resurrection as a development within contemporary Christology as a fact which is unproblematic. Furthermore, he moves rather seamlessly between Christological claims and Trinitarian claims, again without explanation. It is the briefest allusion to the biblical notion of 'adoption' that provides the explanation to the paragraph, illustrating the redemptive force of the resurrection, the link between Christology and Trinitarian theology, and the anthropocentric consequences of both.

This biblical insight, according to which there is a reference in the idea of the Fatherhood and the Sonship to the *risen* Christ and to the pouring out of the Holy Spirit (by means of which we come to share in his resurrection, Rom. 8: 15–17), is very closely associated with the modern anthropological view. The biblical doctrine of the redemption has thereby acquired greater dimensions and the resurrection has once again been accorded a central place in this doctrine. In speculative Christology, this has at the same time brought the treatise of the Trinity into a closer touch with the mystery of Christ, and via the Christological mystery, the treatise of the Trinity has also been 'renewed'.[137]

Resurrection is here conditioned by the idea of adoption which is clearly a relational one. First, by conditioning the act of resurrection with Rom. 8. 15–17 the act of resurrection is described as a Trinitarian act. Resurrection points towards the life of the Trinity because of the reference to Rom. 8. Secondly, by describing our participation in the resurrection as adoption something is said about what has been done to human life. The allusion to adoption with reference to resurrection is key because it performs two tasks for Schillebeeckx. It binds together Trinity and Christology, and it describes our participation in the divine life.

Schillebeeckx's juxtaposition of resurrection and adoption works because of the fuller, personal, and hence relational concept of 'nature' with which

[137] Ibid.

he is working. Applied here to the understanding of Trinity as 'divine nature' the divine nature is understood as relation and as a way of relating:

> Moreover, purification of the physicist concept of 'nature' has provided us with a better understanding of the divine nature. We no longer see this as a kind of communal, neutrally divine background to the three divine persons, but as indicating the manner in which these persons are one, as pointing to their community or perichoresis. Greater significance has also been given to the trinitarian character of the incarnation and of the redemption, and the treatise of God (the De Deo uno) has become from the outset a theological treatise on the Trinity.[138]

In his analysis of the strengths that contemporary phenomenology brings to theology, Schillebeeckx has very clearly identified the most important advance made by phenomenology as the recognition of the distinctive character of the 'human condition', a condition he has described as the 'anthropological idea of incarnation'. By this he means the particular way in which human being is understood in itself and in relation to the world. Human being is not a dualism of body and spirit; rather, the distinctively anthropological 'mode of being and mode of being one' is found in an 'essential correlation between the spirit which communicates itself to the body and the physical nature which participates in this spirit'.[139] This description of human being is in turn possible because of a renewed understanding of 'nature' with respect to 'human nature'. Nature here is not determined by physicism but by a synthesis of 'personalism' and the recognition of the 'essential incarnation' of the human person. Humanity, on this account is situated and can only come to itself in the world. Yet at the same time, humanity is a fundamental freedom and is not 'determined' as are the things of nature. Human being is a situated freedom. "In a word," this insight of twentieth century philosophy is "a refinement of the ancient affirmation, *anima est forma corporis.*"[140]

Schillebeeckx's translates '*anima est forma corporis*' to mean that to be human is to be a 'situated freedom'. In other words, human being is personal and incarnate, that is, relational and one, body and spirit. Human nature is marked quite decisively as dynamic, not static, and hence it is given not as a 'datum' but as a 'task'. Human being as 'task' points of course to a fundamental freedom: a task might be realized or equally, might be neglected. Hence Schillebeeckx defines human freedom as 'possibility', a term that points both to the 'essential ambiguity of everything that is human', and to

---

[138] Ibid.
[139] Ibid. p. 122.
[140] Ibid. p. 123.

the eschatological proviso. The theological description of just such an understanding of human nature is one of 'adoption', a term that implies a relation of both reciprocity and freedom. It is this Christological structure of the theology of grace, indebted as it is to philosophical anthropology for a far richer concept of 'nature', that transposes what was once a static or instrumental concept into a relational and ontological one:

> [T]he structure of the treatise on grace is no longer based on the case of the conferment of grace upon immature children, but on the 'encounter' between fully grown man and the living God in Christ. The reciprocal relationship existing between God and ourselves has thus been given a central position in the doctrine of grace. The central truth of sanctifying grace is now seen to be the idea that God allows himself to be personally loved by man. The very essence of grace is to be found in this *unio amoris*, and 'created grace' is only the ontological (but necessary) implication of this.[141]

Several ideas are contained in this description of grace: the nature of God, the nature of humanity, and the nature of the relation between these. Schillebeeckx suggests that the 'structure' of a theology of grace is based on 'the encounter' between humanity and 'God', 'in Christ'. This he identifies as a return to a 'biblical and patristic conception of grace', and even, 'in its essence', a scholastic view; and here he signals a return to an understanding of grace held by Thomas who recognized the importance of the biblical and patristic heritage and thus had not cut nature adrift from grace. From these indications of his sources the several ideas that he has brought together here may be interpreted to give a full account of his theology of grace. The key to this interpretation is the phrase 'in Christ', which must be read in light of Schillebeeckx's appeal to the concepts of kenosis and adoption.

Schillebeeckx describes the structure of theology in general as christological. It is consistent with this to suggest that the term which explains the structure of grace as 'encounter' is christological, 'in Christ'. 'In Christ' qualifies the nature of 'encounter' and further it qualifies the nature of the participants in this encounter, both human and divine. And because of his indication that he is so indebted to biblical and patristic sources, the term 'in Christ' is itself interpreted by the references to Christ's kenotic self-emptying (Phil. 2.7) and the adoption by which we come to share in his resurrection (Rom. 8.15–17). Emphasis on the Son's self-emptying in the incarnation allows Christology both to point towards the inner Trinitarian life of the transcendent God – the divine nature – and to take seriously the full force of the personal relationship of the human Christ to the Father – Christ's human

[141] Ibid. p. 129.

nature as a 'situated freedom'. The divine nature as communion of persons is a *unio amoris* and the nature of the relation between the human and divine, between Christ who reciprocates in freedom the love of the Father, is a *unio amoris*. Furthermore, as a result of the Son's self-emptying in the incarnation humanity has come to share in redemption through adoption. Redemption as adoption both points to redemption as the work of the Triune God and describes a relation of reciprocity between God and humanity. Hence, 'in Christ' points both to the 'distinctively transcendent manner of God's reaction to man' and to the 'truly reciprocal relationship of action and reaction between the divine and the human partner involved' in this encounter.[142] The Christological 'terms' by which he structures this theology of grace are 'kenosis' and 'adoption', both of which are consistent with a theology that is anthropocentric and an anthropology that is theocentric.

Schillebeeckx's theology is one long commentary on the nature of God, and his theological anthropology is a reflection on the nature of humanity in light of humanity's relation to the God who is God *for* us:

> The *same* God who is the creator is also the redeemer; the *same* God is also the Lord both of the history of man and of the history of salvation. Creation and covenant – these form one divine structure and this is also see in its historical consequence.[143]

In the first chapter of this study, Schillebeeckx's theology of revelation emerged as the interpretation of God's self-revelation – of the God who is cause, transcendence and difference as personal immanence in history – as the method itself for theology. The consequence of this for a theological anthropology is the definition of humanity as a vocation to intimacy with God which is coherent with the content and structure of revelation itself. Such an anthropology is defined by the nature of the human divine relation: creative, salvific, sanctifying, participative and personal. In God's self-revelation, humanity is revealed to itself in a specific providential relationship to the divine where God is the meaning of humanity.

Schillebeeckx's theology of grace builds on this, and in particular, in this chapter the implications of his treatise on God for an interpretation of humanity's historicity – situated freedom – have been developed more fully. God is the future for humanity in a relationship of grace, and this means that just as the divine is constitutive of the human so too is humanity's future constitutive of its present. Humanity's vocation to intimacy with God is the vocation to intimacy with God as our future where this in no way

---

[142] Ibid. p. 128.
[143] Schillebeeckx, 'Christian Faith and Man's Expectation for the Future on Earth', p. 54.

negates human historical existence. The relation of human–divine intimacy is sacramental.

God as the future of humanity is constitutive of both humanity's metaphysical and moral existence. For Schillebeeckx this relation of humanity's metaphysical and moral existence as it reflects the nature of human intimacy with God comes to its ultimate expression in Christ. In the fully personal nature of Christ's humanity – Schillebeeckx's interpretation of the incarnation – human meaning is defined as a vocation to faithfulness which is grounded in the fully personal relation of adoption. Here the 'Christological method' of Schillebeeckx's theocentric anthropology comes to the fore and the nature of humanity as absolute dependence upon God and as a situated freedom is defined by its kenotic structure: the ultimate consequence of the incarnation is dependence upon God lived in history as radical love of the other: 'This is the last consequence of the historical character of the Incarnation: the penetration of divine external reality into determined temporal situations'.[144] The following two chapters will now take up the question of the human vocation to intimacy with God as a consequence of this historical character of the Incarnation.

[144] Schillebeeckx, 'Love Comes from God', *Cross and Crown* 16 (1964), 190–204 (195). 'De broederlijke liefde als heilswerkelijheid, *Tijdschrift voor Geestelijk Leven* 8 (1952), 600–619.

3

INCARNATION AND
HUMAN BEING

Introduction

In 1982 Schillebeeckx was awarded the Erasmus Prize.[1] To mark the occasion Hans Küng delivered an address in honour of Schillebeeckx. In this address Küng identified the most important aspect of Schillebeeckx's theology: in its pastoral attentiveness to the needs and hopes of the contemporary world it holds fast to its theological centre. Although marked by wide-ranging interests, and although willing to engage actively with other intellectual disciplines, Schillebeeckx's theology has a single 'source'. Indeed his theology is so alive to a wide range of contemporary questions, both cultural and ecclesial, precisely because of the 'great centrifugal force' or '*christlijke* source' to which his theology holds: God's self-revelation given in and for humanity in Jesus. Put quite simply, Schillebeeckx's theology is driven by his 'doctrine' of God: the 'great centrifugal force' that impels his work is the *Deus humanissimus,* and it is this particular interpretation of the doctrine of God that prompts him to describe his project as theocentric *and* Christological. Such theology clearly functions within an overarching soteriological context; hence it is both theocentric *and* anthropocentric.

Theology as Schillebeeckx understands it, must always be done 'for the sake of God, for the sake of Jesus the Christ and for the sake of humankind'.[2] From his writings on revelation and grace, it has become clear that these terms may never be set in opposition one to the other. The human and the divine are not rivals; nor does God's immanence within human history

---

[1] The Erasmus Prize [Praemium Erasmianum] is Europe's most prestigious award for social, cultural or scientific achievement. Schillebeeckx was the first theologian to receive this honour.

[2] Schillebeeckx, *Church. The Human Story of God,* trans. John Bowden (London: SCM, 1990), p. xix.

threaten God's freedom and sovereignty. In his Christology the extent to which this is true, along with the anthropological consequences, becomes even clearer. For Schillebeeckx the fullness of humanity is given in God's saving self-revelation; in Jesus the Christ humanity encounters God in the midst of the world, and this self-revelation of God itself makes possible the humanization of humanity, *de vermenslijking van de mens*.[3] Theology has to do with the humanization of humanity because grace has to do with the perfecting of nature and not with destroying it; in the redemptive mystery of Christ the full meaning of what it is to be human is given.

At the heart of Schillebeeckx's Christology is his interpretation of the incarnation: an interpretation of the incarnation that reflects the fully personal nature of Christ's humanity. This interpretation of the incarnation is the centre of his sacramental Christology, and this sacramental Christology he describes as the *zijnsgrond* – ground of being – for humanity. Schillebeeckx's theological anthropology has a Christological structure and this structure, in light of his interpretation of the incarnation, establishes the human vocation to intimacy with God in its ultimate reality and possibility – the vocation to faithfulness.

This chapter has three sections to it: the first, on Christology as an *itinerarium mentis*; the second, on incarnation as *zijnsgrond*; and the third, on incarnation and a sacramental Christology. The second section opens with a discussion of Marie-Dominique Chenu's incarnational theology as this is clearly influential for Schillebeeckx. Perhaps even more interestingly, it demonstrates the originality of Schillebeeckx's development of the personal nature of the incarnation.

Incarnation: Christology as itinerarium mentis

What Küng describes as the 'great centrifugal force' of Schillebeeckx's work Schillebeeckx himself describes as its theocentric orientation; this orientation has for him a Christological structure. The relation between the 'subject' of theology – the Triune God – and theology's christoform structure is the *christlijke* source from which Schillebeeckx's theology works and from which it derives its consistency and continuity. Küng, in his tribute to Schillebeeckx, describes the dynamism it creates within Schillebeeckx's

---

[3] Hans Küng, 'Een theologie met een jong gezicht', *Tijdschrift voor Theologie* 22 (1982), 354–359 (p. 357). 'Schillebeeckx heft zich kunnen concentreren op zoveel thema's uit randgebieden, omdat zijn theologie, ondanks de zo grote centrifugale kracht, in de christelijk oorsprong haar centrum bleef houden. In zijn theologie kon zozeer sprake zijn van de vermenselijking van de mens, van de vermenselijking van kerk en ambt en van de maatschappij als zodanig, omdat deze vermenselijking voor hem gefundeerd is in God die zijn menslievendheid in Jesus op onachterhaalbare wijze gemanifesteerd heeft.'

theology as the movement between the past 'tradition' – *'veterum sapientia'* – and the contemporary 'context' – *'juvenum experientia'*. This is the dynamism of a theology, which takes seriously the historical arena in which the redemptive mystery is accomplished.

This constant movement between *veterum sapientia* and *juvenum experientia* signals for Küng the depth of Schillebeeckx's indebtedness to Marie-Dominique Chenu, a debt that Schillebeeckx himself is always quick to acknowledge: Chenu embodied for Schillebeeckx, both in his theology and in his life, the Dominican ideal to which he himself aspired.[4] From Chenu, Schillebeeckx inherited a love of the tradition. He also inherited the insight that reading the tradition is often enhanced if this reading is accompanied by the study of new and contemporary schools of thought. Küng notes Schillebeeckx's interest in Thomas was accompanied by his study of various contemporary philosophies and theologies, namely, the philosophy of Paul Ricoeur, the critical theories of the Frankfurt School, British analytic philosophy and contemporary German Protestant theology.[5] Yet behind each of these interests it is clear that the enduring questions for Schillebeeckx are those that he shares with Chenu.[6] Most significantly, Schillebeeckx learnt from Chenu the craft of a pastoral theology that is engaged with the world, holds to a modest ecclesiology and at the same time adheres to rigorous intellectual activity. Therefore, Küng quite rightly points to Chenu as the inspiration behind the dynamism of Schillebeeckx's theology, the movement between past tradition and the contemporary context. Yet behind this tribute to Chenu's formative influence, there is a sense in which Küng's description of the dynamism he finds in Schillebeeckx's theology is polemical, not least in the use of the phrase *veterum sapientia*, a reference that

---

[4] Küng, 'Een theologie met een jong gezicht', p. 355. '[K]enmerkend voor deze leerling van onze gemeenschappelijke vriend Marie-Dominique Chenu is dat hij niet aan de wijsheid der ouden is blijven vastzitten, maar dat hij de "veterum sapientia" vanaf het begin gefronteerd heft met "juvenum exeperientia", de ervaring van de jongeren.' Küng notes Schillebeeckx's own remarks concerning Chenu's influence on his theology: 'Over Chenu zegt Schillebeeckx: "Hij is wellicht de man die mijn theologisch denkend leven in feite het meest heft geïnspireerd, niet zozeer beïnvloed door wat hij zei, maar door heel zijn bezielende persoonlijkheid"'. Küng, p. 43 n 15. Taken from Huub Oosterhuis en Piet Hoogeveen, *God is ieder ogenblik nieuw: gesprekken met Edward Schillebeeckx*, p. 29.

[5] This is by no means an exhaustive list of Schillebeeckx's philosophical interests, and a more complete list must include references at least to Merleau-Ponty and Heidegger.

[6] Schillebeeckx highlights ideology critique as an enduring feature of Chenu's theology and pastoral practice. Ideology critique and the contrast between Christian hope and utopia feature in Schillebeeckx's theology with regularity, particularly in his work post-Vatican II in which he incorporates some ideas taken from negative theory. However, it is interesting to note that he points to Chenu as his teacher in this regard, and it is clear that Chenu's influence accounts for the great continuity in Schillebeeckx's work.

Schillebeeckx would have recognized and appreciated (as no doubt would Chenu himself): it is a reference to the papal encyclical, *Veterum sapientia*, in which John XXIII defended the use of Latin for the teaching of theology and for the liturgy.[7]

The reference to *veterum sapientia* Küng chose to use in his tribute to Schillebeeckx echoes the tension between 'old' and 'new' endemic to Roman Catholic theology in the years just prior to the Second Vatican Council, and in the theology of the Council itself, a tension still very much apparent forty years later. Schillebeeckx himself has been by no means silent on the subject of this tension.[8] Although he became increasingly worried about the cultural optimism prevalent at the time of the Council, a worry reflected in his critique of secularism, of totalitarian political systems, and above all, in his preoccupation with the excessive suffering of humankind, he has never lost confidence in the essential insights of the Council.[9] Küng, in his Erasmus tribute to Schillebeeckx, remarks upon the tension between *veterum sapientia* and *juvenum experientia* so characteristic of Schillebeeckx's work because this tension illustrates that theology is always a '*theologia semper reformanda*', a characteristic especially fitting for one receiving the Erasmus prize and one equally fitting for a theologian committed to the Second Vatican Council. 'Reformation', both theological and ecclesial, was one of the central inspirations of Vatican II. In this creative and difficult context, the tension between 'old' and 'new', Schillebeeckx learnt from Chenu not

---

[7] On 22 February 1962, John XXIII promulgated his encyclical *Veterum sapientia* just months prior to opening the Council. In it he signalled his conviction that Latin remained the language best suited for both the teaching of theology and for the liturgy. This encyclical is symbolic of the juxtaposition between 'tradition' and 'reformation' that marked the Council so decisively in its preparation, development and outcome.

[8] Schillebeeckx notes the 'sensitive concessions made', during the Council itself, 'to a minority which was powerful in church politics but theologically one-sided (fixated on Trent and Vatican I)', and implies that these concessions have been given increasing credence in recent canonical statements: 'precisely those elements in Vatican II which were 'new' in comparison to the post-Tridentine life of the church and its ecclesiology have not been given any consistent institutional structures by the official church. On the contrary, some church structures prescribed by the new Codex are quite alien to the deepest intentions of Vatican II.' *Church*, p. xiv.

[9] The impact of secularism upon theology and the tension between secularism and the religious life of humanity are the subjects of many essays included in *God and Man*, *World and Church*, *The Mission of the Church*. Schillebeeckx cautions against equating what he describes as 'the sorrow of the experience of God's concealment' with the 'absence of God'. Edward Schillebeeckx, 'The Sorrow of the Experience of God's Concealment', in *World and Church*, pp. 77–95. 'Het leed der ervaring van Gods verborgenheid', in *Wereld en kerk*, pp. 114–127. First published in *Vox Theologica* **36** (1966), 92–104.

only the craft of theology but also the patience required when that theology itself is placed under suspicion.

Chenu holds to an incarnational theology that places emphasis on God's living presence in human history. For Chenu this presence of the living word in the world is the 'implementation of the law of incarnation'.[10] This is an incarnational theology in which the richness of the tradition is appropriated through careful study and always in conversation with both its own historical context, the *'veterum sapientia'*, and with the contemporary world, the *'juvenum experientia'*. In Schillebeeckx's theocentric theology with its Christological structure there are distinct echoes of his debt to Chenu, and there are also some clear differences that indicate the originality of his own work.[11]

Theology for Schillebeeckx is concerned with 'truth'; however, because of the very nature of its subject and because it takes seriously its Christological structure, it is a truth 'on the way'. It is practised 'within the open space of the binding gospel of Jesus Christ'.[12] Herman Häring, who would be Schillebeeckx's successor in Nijmegen, aptly described Schillebeeckx's theology as a theology done 'with' and 'for' people 'on the way'.[13] Küng neatly develops the description of *sapientia* that characterizes Schillebeeckx's theology – truth 'on the way' as a following of Christ – by reference to the Johannine Christ. The Christ of John's gospel is not the Christ of static or abstract truths but the Christ who compels discipleship, both intellectual and ethical. The Christ of the gospel did not claim to be 'the tradition': *'ik ben de traditie'*. John's Christ claimed to be 'the way, the truth and the life: *'ik ben de weg, de waarheid en het leven'*. In Küng's estimation this is the Christ and hence the *sapientia* that grounds Schillebeeckx's theology. Schillebeeckx's theology is not, in the first place, either Thomistic or Dominican, Dutch or Roman Catholic. His theology is before anything else,

---

[10] For Chenu theology is possible only in the presence of the living word, which is incarnate in the historical situation of human experience. This idea will be developed further in this chapter.

[11] Chenu's 'law of incarnation', which structures his theology, is discussed below, and from this it becomes apparent that Schillebeeckx's 'christological structure' owes much to Chenu, yet differs in one fundamental aspect that is significant for his theological anthropology. Schillebeeckx's 'christological structure' is centred in his interpretation of the incarnation and the full personal significance of Christ's humanity. It is the emphasis on the personal nature of incarnation that distinguishes him from Chenu and gives his Christology the 'method' for a theological anthropology.

[12] Schillebeeckx, *Church*, p. xiv.

[13] Herman Häring, 'Met mensen op weg, voor mensen op weg. Over het theologisch denken van Edward Schillebeeckx' in *Mensen maken de Kerk*, ed. Huub ter Haar (Baarn: Nelissen), pp. 27–46.

Christian – *christelijk*.[14] Theology is always an *itinerarium mentis*: it is 'that following of Christ enjoined on us by the gospel'.[15]

For Küng, Schillebeeckx's theology most fully reflects this 'truth on the way' in the later Christology books when Schillebeeckx turns to the work of contemporary biblical exegetes, primarily to the historical critical method of scriptural study and applies this to systematic theology as a *'fides quaerens intellectum historicum'*. Here Christology is quite clearly an *'itinerarium mentis'* in which its task is to 'follow step for step the way of the first disciples of Jesus', and by doing so to come to understand and to confess Jesus as the 'messiah, the Christ, the Son and Word of God for our own time.'[16] Although Küng understandably registers some surprise at Schillebeeckx's willingness to turn to such an exhaustive study of modern biblical criticism and to incorporate this within his theology – Schillebeeckx is unique among Roman Catholic systematic or dogmatic theologians in this regard – Schillebeeckx's later description of Christology as an *'itinerarium mentis'* is well prepared for in his earlier writings on Christology. It comes as no surprise at all that Schillebeeckx's first sustained piece of systematic theology works from a Christology, nor does it come as any surprise that the continuity between the theology represented in *Christ the Sacrament of the Encounter with God*, and the later *Jesus* and *Christ* are profound.[17]

Christ the Sacrament of the Encounter with God was written by Schillebeeckx as a sacramental theology 'in keeping with a sound

---

[14] Küng, 'Een theologie met een jong gezicht', pp. 356–357: 'De theologie van Edward Schillebeeckx weet waarheen zij gaat, omdat zij weet waar ze vandaan komt. Toekmost vanuit herkomst! Deze theologie kan breed uithalen omdat ze diep vertworteld is: vertworteld niet alleen in de wijsheid der ouden, maar in de christelijk oorsprong zelf, in die ene die volgens Johannes niet gezegd heft: "ik ben de traditie", maar: "ik ben de weg, de waarheid en het leven". Reeds in zijn vroege boeken over sacramenten heeft Edward Schillebeeckx naar voren gehaald dat deze Jesus van Nazaret Gods sacrament in de wereld is en dat deze wereld in hem God zelf kan ontmoeten. En in zoverre is zijn theologie niet in de eerste plaats thomistich of dominicaans, ook niet in eerst plaats nederlands of ook rooms-katholiek, maar allereerst en vooral christelijk.'

[15] *Perfectae caritatis* art. 2; Schillebeeckx, 'Dominican Spirituality', in *God among Us: The Gospel Proclaimed*, trans. John Bowden (London: SCM, 1983), p. 233.

[16] 'Voor mij en voor vele anderen was het verrassend en verheugend tegelijk: de voormalige filosoof uit de jaren van zijn jeugd begint, reeds ver in de vijftig, een christologie als "itinerarium mentis", om zo te zeggen vanuit het perspective, van de eerste leerlingen van Jezus, en daarbij kiest hij voor een *historisch consequent verantwoorde methode*: "fides quaerens intellectum historicum". Hij volgt stap voor stap de weg de leerlingen van Jezus, om hem zelf te verstaan en te belijden als de messias, de Christus, de Zoon en het Woord van God, ook voor onze tijd.' Küng, 'Een theologie met een jong gezicht', p. 357.

[17] This is not to deny the real differences between the earlier and later Christology. However the depth of continuity in Schillebeeckx's theology is too often overlooked with respect to his Christology.

Christology'.[18] It attests to the all-pervasive Christological structuring of his theology while holding fast to the subject of theology, which for Schillebeeckx is the *Deus sub ratione Deitatis*. The end product is a theocentric sacramental theology that has a Christological structure, and it signals that his work has reached a well-rounded maturity of expression, both with respect to his interests as a speculative theologian and his abilities as a positive theologian. Significantly, it indicates his fundamental commitment to a pastoral theology that sacrifices nothing of intellectual rigour.[19] In essence, *Christ the Sacrament* is a theology worked out 'on the basis of Saint Thomas, in light of the preceding tradition and of the issues of today'.[20] This is the theological 'vision' that was well established at this stage in his work. It provided his theology with a coherence without becoming a rigid or a closed systematization.[21] This theological vision shaped his understanding of the task and method of theology, the nature of God and of humanity and the world in which humanity is situated and hence in which we encounter God.[22]

---

[18] Edward Schillebeeckx, *Christ the Sacrament of the Encounter with God*, (London: Sheed and Ward, 1963), p. 56.

[19] Schillebeeckx's work on sacramental theology, and hence the work which lies behind this Christology, was taken up in response to the needs of his own work as a teacher of theology. At the time it represented a turning away from some of the more philosophical and epistemological issues that preoccupied him, namely the work of De Petter and the relation between conceptual and non-conceptual knowledge, and the perspectival nature of human knowing.

[20] Erik Borgman, *Edward Schillebeekcx: een theoloog in zijn geschiedenis. Deel I: Een katholieke cultuurtheologie (1914–1965)* (Baarn: Nelissen, 1999), p. 233. Borgman identifies this period in Schillebeeckx's work as his 'Louvain synthesis'. The fourth chapter of his Schillebeeckx book is titled 'op basis van Saint Thomas, in het licht van to voorafgaande traditie en van de hedendaagse problematiek. De Leuvense theologische synthese'.

[21] Erik Borgman, *Edward Schillebeekcx: een theoloog in zijn geschiedenis*, p. 233. 'Toen Edward Schillebeeckx begin 1958 van Leuven naar Nijmegen verhuisde en hij als het ware een nieuw begin maakte als Nederlands theoloog, was zijn theologie een afgerond geheel. Het is overdreven om over een systeem te spreken, maar een synthese was zijn theologie well degelijk, een samenhangende, naar de verschillende deelaspecten uitgewerkte visie.'

[22] See also Häring, 'Met mensen op weg, voor mensen op weg', p. 355. 'Zijn visie op de taak en het functioneren van de theologie, zijn spreken over God, zijn denken over mens en wereld zijn doordacht. Het is coherent, naar de centrale thema's van een eigentijdse theologische systematiek toe uitgeplitst, theologisch historisch verantwoord en nog steeds geïnspireerd door de meest vooruitstrevende theologische stroming van de vijftiger jaren. De continuïteit met de nouvelle théologie is overduidelijk. Binnen het relatiekader van de goddelijk God en de wereldlijke wereld zijn alle verdere vragen, ook de antropologie en de christologie geplaatst en op elkaar betrokken.'

To appropriate the full significance of *Christ the Sacrament,* this text needs to be situated in its relation to Schillebeeckx's own doctoral thesis, *De sacramentele heilseconomie. Christ the Sacrament* is the result of Schillebeeckx's interpretation of all of saving history as sacramental. The *Deus sub ratione Deitatis* is the *Deus salutaris* precisely by entering human history in human and historical form:

> The same God who is the creator is also the redeemer; the same God is also the Lord both of history of man and of the history of salvation. Creation and covenant – these form one divine structure and this is also seen in its historical consequences.[23]

The historical consequence of the one divine structure – creation and covenant – is the essentially sacramental nature of salvation history. Christ as the sacrament of the human encounter with God both establishes and reveals human intimacy with God as creative, salvific, sanctifying, participative and personal. In other words, Schillebeeckx's Christology is sacramental and hence he describes Christ as the 'method' for his theology.[24]

Curiously, at the time of the publication of both *De sacramentele heilseconomie* and *Christ the Sacrament,* little attention was paid to the Christology that structures Schillebeeckx's sacramental theology. Reaction to the publication of *De sacramentele heilseconomie* focused on the reworking of sacramental theology in light of the historical reading of the tradition Schillebeeckx brought to bear upon what had most recently been an exercise in *a*historical and abstract theology. *De sacramentele heilseconomie* is a magisterial treatment of the tradition and established Schillebeeckx as a serious and critical historian of the tradition. It also established him as a constructive theologian, and his work was recognized by liturgical theologians as a major contribution to the burgeoning field of sacramental and liturgical theology that would lead to the substantive renewal of liturgical

---

[23] Schillebeeckx, 'Christian Faith and Man's Expectation for the Future on Earth' in *The Mission of the Church*, p. 54.

[24] Schillebeeckx, 'Theologia *or* Oikonomia?', in *Revelation and Theology, II: The Concept of Truth and Theological Renewal*, trans. N. D. Smith (New York: Sheed and Ward, 1968), p. 97: 'When Aquinas spoke about "Christ who, as man, is for us the way leading to God", he was at the same time stating, *ipso facto*, the theological method, since there can be no cleavage between life and reflection about the content of that life'. Here the fully personal nature of Christ's humanity is key for Schillebeeckx's description of theological method: 'since there can be no cleavage between life and reflection about the content of that life'. Humanity's essential incarnation – consciousness is incarnate – is an important concept for interpreting the sacramental structure of revelation and hence of theological method.

and sacramental life in the church.[25] It is however, also a significant Christology that deserves interpretation in itself.[26]

De sacramentele heilseconomie is then, more than an exercise in historical theology. It signals a maturity of thought and indicates that all of the substantive pieces of Schillebeeckx's speculative theology are now in place.[27] Furthermore, it also suggests that by this time he has already made a series of formal commitments that are to be characteristic of all of his subsequent theology: he is willing, in a critical manner, to engage with contemporary philosophy; he understands theology always to be a situated, historical and not a timeless or abstract discipline; he expects theology to be both a rigorous scholarly activity and a responsible pastoral engagement.

De sacramentele heilseconomie was intended to be the first volume in a two-volume work. As with the later text on marriage, this work on sacramental theology was planned in two parts: a historical treatment of the tradition to be followed by a systematic theology worked out in light of the discoveries made during the historical excavation. Similarly, as with the marriage text, the second volume never appeared. In the case of the sacramental theology what appeared in its stead was the much shorter *Christ the Sacrament*.[28] Reaction to *Christ the Sacrament* focused almost exclusively

---

[25] See J. Gaillard, 'Chronique de liturgie,' *Revue Thomiste*, 57 (1957), 510–551 (pp. 512–513): 'L'étude de la position thomiste sur ces problèmes vient d'être reprise par Schillebeeckx dont la maître livre sur *l'Economie sacramentelles du salut* représente l'apport le plus important fait à la théologie des mystères en dehors Maria-Laach et, croyons-nous, un apport qui décidera de son orientation future. Il a été accueilli avec faveur dans le monde théologique. Il méritait cet accueil, car il unit, avec assaince et maîtrese, une information positive très large, dont les éléments ont été soigneusement vérifiés et situés dans leur milieu de pensée original, à une réflexion speculative très personelle, qui prolonge avec bonheur le soufflé vivant du «thomisme historique».'

[26] This Christology, with its particular interpretation of the incarnation – the fully personal nature of Christ's humanity – is also significant with respect to Schillebeeckx's appropriation of Thomas within his own theology. It indicates the clear extent to which Schillebeeckx is indebted to Thomas. See Guido Vergauwen, 'Edward Schillebeeckx – Lecteur de saint Thomas', in *Ordo sapientiae et amoris: Image et message de saint Thomas d'Aquin à travers les récentes études historiques, herméneutiques et doctrinales*, ed. Carlos-Josaphat Pinto de Oliviera (Fribourg: Éditions Universitaires Fribourg, 1993), p. 673.

[27] See Herman Häring, 'Met mensen op weg, voor mensen op weg', pp. 27–46.

[28] In his foreword to the English translation Cornelius Ernst describes *Christ the Sacrament* as a 'non-technical summary' of *De sacramentele heilseconomie*, p. xiv. This is true to an extent. It is not a technical historical study, yet at the same time it builds systematically upon the results of the rich historical analysis of *De sacramentele heilseconomie*. As a result it is a very technical text, expecting of the reader familiarity not only with the historical background, Thomas in particular and traditions of reading Thomas, but also a fluency in systematic theology and an appreciation for the nuanced manner in which philosophical categories are employed vis-à-vis classical treatments of Trinity, Christology, redemption, grace, and theological anthropology. The Christology is subtle, particularly in the interpretation of the personal nature of Christ's humanity.

on the reworking of sacramental theology in light of contemporary personalist and phenomenological philosophies. The real interest in this text focused on sacramental theology and the category of 'encounter' that Schillebeeckx employed in his attempt to shift sacramental theology from the domain of static and *a*historical concepts. This abstract and *a*historical context in which theology was conducted had resulted for so long in a mechanistic description of sacrament, thereby losing sight entirely of the proper theological locus for sacramental theology. The result of this some-what reductive reception of Schillebeeckx's text – little analysis of his Christology in light of his interpretation of incarnation – has been that the reception of his later *magnum opus*, the Christological trilogy of *Jesus*, *Christ* and *Church*, has almost completely overlooked the lines of continuity between the earlier and later Christology. This has led to some misreadings of Schillebeeckx's later Christology.

Incarnation: Christology as zijnsgrond

It was as a theology student at the Saulchoir that Schillebeeckx discovered the vocation to theology, a discovery shaped most profoundly by Marie-Dominique Chenu. Chenu spent his whole theological career arguing against dualisms, and sorting them out, a mark not only of his Dominican spirituality but of the assimilation of all of his work under the general rubric of incarnation. The law of incarnation – Christ has assumed human nature in its entirety so that human nature might be saved and divinized – was the governing principle of his religious life and his theological work.[29] Chenu took with seriousness the soteriological reality within which the law of incarnation functioned: what has not been assumed has not been saved. This soteriological nexus for incarnation has a long history yet Chenu's own originality lay in the manner in which he explored the implications of incarnation and in the resulting non-dualistic, non-reductive understanding of the human in relation to the transcendent. Utterly characteristic of his work is the concern for the integrity of the

---

[29] The importance of incarnation for Chenu is recognized by his Dominican colleague, Yves Congar who describes incarnation as the general principle of the economy of grace within Chenu's theology. See Yves Congar, 'Le Père Chenu' in *Bilan de la théolo-gie du XXe siècle, II*, ed. Robert Vander Grucht and Herbert Vorgrimler, pp. 772–790 (p. 781): 'Ainsi apparaît le thème et le terme d'*incarnation*, que le P. Chenu n'a pas créés, mais don't il a fait largement usage, non certes comme d'un slogan vague et commode . . . mais comme d'un principe général de l'économie de grâce, qui est une économie d'alliance et de communication.' This idea is developed more fully in the substantive analysis of Chenu's theology by Christophe Potworowski. Potworowski identifies incarnation as the overall structure of Chenu's work. See *Contemplation and Incarnation. The Theology of Marie-Dominique Chenu*.

human and nowhere is this defended more rigorously than in his work on the nature of theology and the relation between faith and reason. This is a particularly apt example to explore here if only briefly because it takes us very quickly to the heart of Chenu's theology, and also because this work was already in place by the time Schillebeeckx arrived at the Saulchoir.[30] His programmatic essay *Une école de théologie: le Saulchoir* was already in publication and it is no stretch of the imagination to think that Schillebeeck was familiar with this text.[31]

Une école de théologie reveals an essentially pastoral theology whose systemic principle is the law of incarnation, the presence and activity of the Word in human history. God's self-revelation is the given, the cardinal point upon which both the dynamism and organization of theology are established, *Le donné theologique est le donné révélé.*[32] This is the context in which Chenu takes up the questions of faith and reason and the nature of theology. Faith, on Chenu's understanding, is assimilation or participation in God's self-knowledge.[33] The object of faith therefore is not the knowledge of propositions but the Word who is present and acts within human history, and the task of theology – *le science croyant* – is to make the Word incarnate in human words. Faith, or knowledge of God, is not a self-generating activity, it is given in this presence: *Dieu me parle.*[34] This is the theological realism that

---

[30] Congar identifies two stages in Chenu's theology which he describes using the subtitles under which Chenu himself grouped a collection of his essays: (1) la Foi dans l'intelligence; (2) l'Évangile dans le temps. See Marie-Dominique Chenu, *La Parole de Dieu* (Paris: Éditions de Cerf, 1964). Congar agrees with Chenu's self-assessment that the continuity and coherence between these two stages of his work is substantive and is given 'sur la loi d'incarnation de la Parole de Dieu'. Congar, 'Le Père M-D Chenu', pp. 775–776.

[31] For a summary of the significant ideas which flourished at the Saulchoir – l'humain; l'intelligence dans la foi; l'histoire; la philosophie; la liberté – see Jean-Pierre Jossua, 'Le Saulchoir revisité: 1937–1983' in Marie- Dominique Chenu, *Une école de théologie*, (Paris: Éditions de Seuil, 1985), pp. 81–90.

[32] Chenu, *Une école de théologie*, p. 136. 'Le donné révélé, le donné théologique n'est pas "scientifique": il est révélé . Et si j'en fais la science – quelle audace! – ce ne sera pas par un renforcement de ses bases historiques ou de sa justification apologétique; ce sera une "science de croyant". Sinon, encore une fois, nous n'aurons qu'un jeu rationnel à la surface d'un donné, théologie sans parole de Dieu. C'est là un point cardinal, dont dépendant simultanément l'organisation et l'esprit de la théologie.'

[33] Hence the description of the theologian's task as one practised '*dans* le mystère où sa foi l'a introduit' Chenu, *Une école de théologie*, p. 136. Emphasis mine.

[34] Chenu, *Une école de théologie*, p. 135. 'Ce réalisme de la foi . . . trouve sa raison psychologique dans la qualité strictement surnaturelle de la lumière intérieure, de la "parole de Dieu" en moi. Connaissance de Dieu en moi, la parole de Dieu est toute grâce, grâce personnelle, me mettant en dialogue et en commerce direct avec Lui, présence mystérieuse à laquelle l' homme nouveau a accès, non parce que sa raison l'y à introduit, mais parce que Dieu se révèle, *sibi ipsi testis.*'

lies behind Chenu's discussion of *la surnaturalité de la foi*.[35] Faith is the gracious activity of *Dieu qui me parle* – a divine activity and therefore something given. It is also a fully human activity. Faith is received in human reason.[36] It is here, in systematically expanding upon the human integrity of the act of faith, that Chenu's own particular contribution to the treatise on faith emerges.[37] Chenu explores the relation of faith to reason by way of the incarnation where incarnation is not simply a parallel structure that is useful for explanation of this relation but rather where faith is to reason what the divine is to the human in the mystery of incarnation in an analogous manner. Faith renders us *contemporains du Christ*.[38] The implications for theology and for anthropology are – in a favourite expression of Chenu's – audacious. Theology, given its 'Chalcedonian statute'[39], is *une science des enfants de Dieu*.[40]

[35] Congar, 'Le Père M-D Chenu', p. 776: 'La foi toute divine: elle existe en nous par un acte *de Dieu* qui pose son témoignage vivant dans notre intelligence . . . La Vérité Première qui fait l'objet et en même temps le motif spécificateur de la Foi n'est pas une idée, elle est "une personne vivante et affectueusement connue, Dieu qui me parle – et non pas un principe abstrait de connaissance". Dans ces conditions, la Foi ne se termine pas, comme à son objet, aux *énoncés* dans lesquels le mystère se formule. Elle nous met en contact et en continuité de vie avec les réalités dont elle témoigne . . . La foi, par la grâce, se termine aux Réalités divines dont elle parle.'

[36] Congar, 'Le Père M-D Chenu', p. 780: 'La théologie procède donc de la Foi, mais en tant que la Foi est reçue et s'exerce – pour ce qui concerne sa valeur de contenu intelligible, car le mystère n'est pas l'absurde ni même l'inintelligible: il est ce qui dépasse toute raison et même toute intelligence créée – en tant disons-nous, que la Foi est reçue et s'exerce dans une intelligence humaine, discursive et capable de progresser pas à pas. Nous sommes ici au coeur de l'idée qui rayonne dans toute l'oeuvre du P. Chenu'.

[37] Potworowski underlines and assesses the originality and importance of this development in Chenu's theology in general and in *Une école de théologie* in particular. It is in his work on the treatise of faith that Chenu specifically introduces the doctrine of incarnation. *Contemplation and Incarnation*, pp. 46–55.

[38] Chenu, *Une école de théologie*, pp. 135–136. 'Transcendante et intérieure, [la foi] n'est solidaire ni d'une prédication ni d'une manifestation; elle n'est pas une assertion historique, elle n'est pas engagée dans le temps, même vis-à-vis du Christ, car la foi est précisément cette opération qui nous rend "contemporains" du Christ, et si l'Évangile nous parvient par la continuité du temps, il n'est pas, sous l'oeil de la foi, un livre d'histoire, mais vraiment la parole de Dieu.'

[39] Potworowski's term. *Contemplation and Incarnation*, p. 49.

[40] Chenu, *Une école de théologie*, p. 150. 'De là, dans la théologie en progrès, cette espèce de désintéressement, cette liberté spirituelle vis-à-vis de ses instruments le plus appropriés, cette asiance désinvolte dans le rencontres les plus engageantes avec les philosophies et les cultures, cette création constante au sein des organismes les plus constitués, cette vie nouvelle dans le vieil homme, cette audace dans l'allégresse rationelle de la lumière de foi. La théologie est audacieuse, parce que, dans le désintéressement de sa contemplation, elle est pure; de fait elle peut avoir toutes les audaces dans la mesure où elle est pure – science des enfants de Dieu.' Theology's audacity follows from an understanding of the activity of the Word incarnate as the recapitulation all of history and of everything human – it is the work of a new humanity.

Chenu understands the entire economy of grace in terms of an incarnational realism. Grace is not something added *to* nature, rather grace becomes incarnate *in* nature. So too faith becomes incarnate *in* reason. Just as the Word is not diminished in becoming flesh so too faith is not contaminated by its incarnation in reason. The relation of faith to reason participates analogically in the Christological mystery in which the divine and the human are one.[41] Chenu's incarnational realism means faith is both a fully divine activity – faith is God's *self*-gift – and it is a fully human activity – it is given *in* human reason. I do not need to be other than human to know God, I need to be human. If I know God at all, I know God humanly.[42] This means too that the human is not a duality of grace and nature, faith and reason, or even body and soul.[43] By teasing out the implications of incarnation for the relation between faith and reason, Chenu is well able to describe the human in non-reductive and non-dualistic terms.

Chenu ascribes to theology an incarnational structure that shares analogously in the divine–human relation revealed in the Christological mystery. Theology understood thus is both theocentric and anthropocentric; it has a theological realism that is at the same time a fully human realism. The relation of the light of faith to reason does not work outside of the structures of human knowing but within these structures: *cognita sunt in cognoscente ad modum cognoscentis*.[44] But Chenu is always especially anxious to preserve the integrity of the human and so he further develops this structure by exploring an idea implicit in the law of incarnation itself, the concept of economy. This dynamism is not incidental to incarnation but integral to it.

---

[41] Chenu, *Une école de théologie*, p. 137. 'Pas plus que la grâce en la nature, la foi n'est une lumière posée à la surface d'une raison: elle vit en elle. Et la foi n'est pas contaminée par cette incarnation, pas plus que le Verbe n'est amoindri pour s'être fait chair. Double mystère théandrique, mieux, unique mystère, qui est le mystère même du Christ, en qui le divin et l'humain sont un: unique Personne, en laquelle la foi me plante, Fils éternel; de Dieu entré dans l'histoire.'

[42] Ibid. 'Si vraiment l'homme connaît Dieu, il le connaîtra humainement.'

[43] Ibid. pp. 136–137. Knowledge of God takes place according to the 'natural laws' of human knowing and hence it takes place in space and time – 'liée aux catégories du temps et de l'espace, engagée dans une histoire.' Chenu is sharply critical of any false mysticism which either denigrates the contingent in order to protect the transcendent or which posits human reality outside of grace: 'exclure Dieu de cette loi naturelle de toute connaissance, sous prétexte qu'il est transcendant ou qu'il se révèle, ce serait céder d'avance au désordre spirituel d'une fausse mysticité.' Furthermore, Chenu's description of faith as *fides ex auditu* underlines its essentially embodied and relational character.

[44] Ibid. pp. 136–137. Chenu is following Thomas here. Potworowski remarks that Chenu is so faithful to Thomas that it is difficult at some points to see in his writings where Thomas ends and Chenu begins. *Contemplation and Incarnation*, pp. 52; 61. This remark might equally apply to the relation between Schillebeeckx and Chenu on the nature of revelation and the nature and task of theology.

Just so is it integral to the human act of knowing God. Chenu called this economy the 'paradox of faith'. The Word present and active in history gives rise to a paradox – revelation is accomplished only in its reception: *fides ex auditu*.[45] Theology is the logical consequence of the incarnation of faith in reason: the Word is given to us *in* human words.[46] This economy of the Word in history is essential to Chenu's incarnational structure of theology. The analogical relationship between the human act of knowing God and the Christological mystery depends on the logic of this economy: *le don de Dieu est don à ce point qu'il devient propriété humaine: la foi est un habitus.*[47] The transcendence of the divine is not negated in this relation: there is an essentially gracious and salvific context within which the analogy functions that Chenu notes by describing theology as the work of the 'new humanity'. Furthermore, theology, as with revelation itself, is never complete. Rather it is the attempt to understand the mystery that lies behind revelation.[48] At the same time the relation respects the integrity of the human in all of its contingency, the paradox of infirmity in which the transcendent becomes incarnate within the limits of human reality.[49] Furthermore, of course, if this incarnational structure is an economy, the human is not purely passive and theology is both an act of receiving and the act of constructing, both receptive and poetic.

Inherent in an understanding of theology which receives its structure from the law of incarnation is a certain dynamism because the law of incarnation is an economy. In other words, a theology which takes as its systemic

---

[45] Ibid. p. 136. 'Paradoxe de la foi, qui, *substantia rerum sperandarum*, ne trouve cependant son objet que dans un enseignement reçu: *fides ex auditu*. La parole de Dieu nous est donnée *dans* des paroles humaines, et la foi surnaturelle sera assentiment à des propositions déterminées.'

[46] Ibid. p. 136. 'La formule dogmatique n'est pas un énoncé juridique extérieur à la révélation qu'elle présente; elle est incarnation dans les concepts de la parole de Dieu. Telle est l'économie de cette parole: elle parle humainement.'

[47] Ibid. p. 144. 'Nous voici à la démarche décisive: le théologien est celui qui ose parler humainement la Parole de Dieu. Le don de Dieu est don à ce point qu'il devient propriété humaine: la foi est un *habitus*. Elle n'est pas un charisma extraordinaire, que sa transcendance tiendrait hors notre mode humain de penser; elle est incarnation de la vérité divine dans le tissu même de notre esprit. Elle n'est pas une confiance pure mais une "vertu" insérée en nous comme une puissance l'est dans une nature. La foi reside *dans* la raison, ainsi habilitée à θεολόγειν. Ce n'est pas que "le vieil homme" sorte de son impuissance devant le mystère de Dieu; mais le théologien est "l'homme nouveau". En élaborant rationnellement, scientifiquement, le contenu de sa foi, il ne cesse pas d'être cet homme nouveau; il l'accomplit au contraire. La foi en engendrant la théologie est dans la logique même de sa perfection.'

[48] Ibid. p. 146. '[E]lle ose, dans sa communion à la science de Dieu, chercher les raisons des oeuvres de Dieu, et obtenir ainsi une intelligence de son mystère. *Fides quaerens intellectum.*'

[49] Ibid. p. 138. 'La parole de Dieu est *dans* la parole humaine: la force de Dieu se révèle dans cette infirmité.'

principle the law of incarnation is both *theologia* and *oikonomia*. This economy provides a structure or an ordering of relations, and it also implies a fecundity.[50] For theology this means that the *donné* assumes a priority – theology proceeds from a given. [51] Therefore theology implies a certain receptive capacity to human reason: reason receives faith. But theology also presumes a creative or poetic capacity to reason: reason acts upon faith. [52] For Chenu the relation within theology between the *donné* and the *construit* is an incarnational economy, and in this sense he can speak of a theology that is dependent upon a given and is at the same time poetic.[53] Ultimately it is a theology of the Word as *la realité théandrique* – the divine Word present, made known, and active in human history – which drives Chenu's entire project.[54] Theology is a paradoxical discipline, *le science croyant*. Both the

---

[50] Potworowski underlines both of these aspects of an incarnational economy in his analysis of Chenu's treatment of the exidus–reditus schema of Thomas' *Summa Theologica*. *Contemplation and Incarnation*, pp. 198–211. He emphasizes that the primacy of the *donné* for Chenu 'is more than a logical primacy; it is one of dignity and fecundity as well', p. 74.

[51] Chenu, *Une école de théologie*, p.135. 'La théologie émane de la foi; elle naît en elle et par elle.'

[52] This relationship both of priority and of creativity is expressed well in the relation between contemplation and theology; contemplation and theology were intrinsically related in Chenu's work and in his religious life. *Une école de théologie*, pp. 131; 149–150. 'C'est la contemplation qui suscite une théologie, non la théologie qui conduirait à la contemplation.' Here Chenu found himself in the company of Thomas and especially at home within his Dominican vocation: 'La contemplation n'est donc pas pour le théologien un sommet, atteint ici ou là, par un sursaut de ferveur, au-delà de son étude, comme en s'échappant de son objet et de sa méthode. C'est son milieu normal, constitutif, où seulement peuvent se tenir en unique fécondité l'organisation scientifiqu et l'invention novatrice . . . St Thomas identifie, dans l'exercice de la vertu théologale de foi, doctrine sacrée et vie contemplative. Il suffit pour cela de ne pas réduire la contemplation à des exercises spirituels, et de ne pas traiter vie spirituelle et théologie comme deux quantités hétérogènes. C'est le statut même de l'Ordre de Saint-Dominique, et l'expression authentique nous en est donée dans la sainteté et la doctrine de saint Thomas d'Aquin.'

[53] Chenu appeals to this economy – *la realité théandrique* – to describe the relation between scripture and tradition, a relation in which both the primacy of revelation and the development of tradition are possible. *Une école de théologie*, p. 141.

[54] Chenu, *Une école de théologie*, p. 145. 'Nous croyons donc avec saint Thomas à la raison théologique, à la science théologique. *Intellectus fidei*, au plus plein sens du mot, des deux mots . . . nous tenons fermes l'homogénéité de la science théologique avec le donné révélé . . . Fondés sur l'unité d'une foi où la transcendance de la parole divine et le réalisme humain sont solidaires, nous repoussons toute rupture entre *mystique* et *théologie*, comme entre *positive* et *spéculative*.' Congar notes une distinction between Chenu's theology of the Word with its incarnational realism – 'le Verbe ne s'est pas fait message de transcendance, *il s'est fait chair*' – and Barth's dialectical theology which 'conservait à ce thème toute l'âpreté de l'opposition dialectique de ses termes'. Congar, 'Le Père M-D Chenu', p. 781.

terms are taken with seriousness because, on Chenu's account, the incarnational structure of the knowledge of God implies a specific economy: theology is the logical consequence of the relation between faith and reason. Theology is both a given and a construction because its economy has both a logical priority – *le donné* has primacy – and an essential fecundity – *le construit* is the natural outcome of the faith-reason relation. In sum, what Chenu called *l'effort dramatique du théologien* is the consequence of two related concepts that together describe the law of incarnation: faith is a divine–human act; and faith in its relation to reason has an economy, which is proper to this relation.[55] Under Chenu's direction the Saulchoir developed its theological programme around these two insights: the human integrity of faith and the economy of this faith in reason.[56] Both of these ideas are implications of incarnation, and it is here in the application of the law of incarnation to the nature of faith and its relation to reason that Chenu's particular contribution to the treatise on faith emerged.

The Saulchoir was *imprégné* with the method, the sources, the questions, the preoccupations and the commitments that shaped Chenu's theology. Steeped in these and influenced deeply by this most important mentor, Schillebeeckx would become, and would remain, a *théologien engagé*. For Chenu theology was not the mere repetition of tradition or a speculative discipline abstracted from tradition.[57] Theology was the constant exploration of tradition in response to the questions and pastoral needs of the contemporary world; tradition itself could not be abstracted from history

---

[55] Ibid. p. 136. 'Le théologien est un croyant; il l'est en excellence, et sa tâche s'accomplit formellement dans la mystère où sa foi l'a introduit, et non dans la projection en paroles humaines de la parole de Dieu. "Doctrine sacrée": c'est l'appellation traditionelle, à prendre au sens proper, sans quoi elle tournerait à n'être qu'une science profane, profanation de la parole de Dieu. C'est précisément l'effort dramatique du théologien de tenir dans la fagilité radicale des propositions où il l'incarne la perception réaliste de la réalité mystérieuse de Dieu: dialectique où sa puissance triomphe de sa débilité – dans la foi. Pas de théologie, sans nouvelle naissance.'

[56] Ibid. p. 135. 'C'est la notion intégrale de la foi et de son économie qui va nous permettre . . . d'établir ce programme avec une sûre sérénité.'

[57] Theology was not *either* historical *or* speculative, it was both. See Chenu's preface in Claude Geffré *Un nouvel âge de la théologie* (Paris: Les Éditions du Cerf, 1987), pp. 7–10 (pp. 7; 8). Chenu identifies with approval the tension between the speculative and historical as a characteristic of late twentieth century theology: 'les ruptures opportune en méthode historique et spéculative'. This approval signals the confidence he places in human reason and this in turn is consistent with his incarnational realism. 'C'est la structure même de la théologie qui est en cause, là où elle est la *raison* en travail, en travail d'engendrement, dans la foi, au moment où la raison mesure les exigences de son autonomie. Si l'Eglise est *dans* le monde, selon le principe constitutionnel énoncé par Vatican II, l'Evangile est *dans* l'histoire; la raison *historique* est le nerf de cette "théologie nouvelle". En voici l'anatomie. Je donne joyeuse complaisance au diagnostic.'

because the subject of tradition, God's self-revelation, was given and accessible only as history.[58] Yet this historical consciousness in no way precluded metaphysics. For Chenu theology was a necessarily paradoxical discipline: it sought to provide intelligible explanation of the transcendent when the transcendent itself had been revealed only in historical and contingent events.[59] Theology sought to understand the transcendent mystery of God revealed in the historical events of God.[60] At the Saulchoir

[58] Chenu's commitment to the importance of an historical consciousness for theology found its ground in a particular understanding of the implications of incarnation for history. The Word incarnate in history accomplishes the recapitulation of history. See Chenu, 'Preface' in *Un nouvel âge de la théologie*, p. 9: 'Histoire: passé, présent, futur. Voici récupérées toutes les dimensions de la Parole de Dieu. La plus notable peut-être, la plus grosse de problèmes, est la présence: Dieu parle aujourd'hui . . . Théologie engagée. Le monde est le lieu de la Parole de Dieu, sans détriment pour sa transcendance ni sa gratuité. Le théologien, homme parmi les hommes, doit assumer, avec sa fonction scientifique, une fonction prophétique.' History in Chenu's theology of the Word becomes the space of meaningful human action, an idea which is expressed in the continuity between dogmatic theology, moral theology, and pastoral practice. It is the premise behind his *Spiritualité du travail* (Paris: Éditions du Temps Présent, 1941) and the articles included in *Pour une théologie du travail* (Paris: Éditions de Seuil, 1955).

[59] Chenu embodied theology's paradoxical nature: 'Il n'y a pas deux "Chenu"; le Chenu historien et le Chenu théologien. Il n'y a qu'un Chenu et c'est toujours le *théologien de l'incarnation*.' Claude Geffré, 'Le réalisme de l'incarnation dans la théologie du Père M-D Chenu', *Revue sc ph th* **69** (1985), 389–399 (pp. 389; 392). For Geffré it is Chenu's recognition of theology's essential contingency and historicity which is the most important consequence of this incarnational realism: 'Si j'ai commencé par souligner l'historicité de la théologie comme incarnation de la foi dans le tissu même de l'esprit humain, c'est parce que la théologie, selon sa contingence historique, conditionne nécessairement les formules dogmatiques. Le Père Chenu distingue évidemment l'historicité de la théologie et l' historicité des formules dogmatiques. Mais ni l'une, ni l'autre ne troublent sa sérénité, car elles renvoient toutes les deux au mystère théandrique de la Parole de Dieu comme incarnation du Verbe de Dieu dans les mots humains.' The paradoxical nature of Chenu's theology is grounded in the twofold acknowledgement of the 'primauté' and the 'historicité' of the Word.

[60] Chenu, *Une école de théologie*, p. 137. 'Le Fils de Dieu est un personage de l'histoire. C'est donc sur une histoire que le théologien travaille. Son donné, ce ne sont pas les natures des choses ni leurs formes intemporelles; ce sont des événements, répondant à une *économie*, dont la réalisation est liée au temps, comme l'étendue est liée au corps, par-dessus l'ordre des essences. Le monde *réel* est celui-là, et non pas l'abstraction du philosophe. Le croyant, le théologien croyant, entre par sa foi dans ce plan de Dieu, et ce dont il cherche l'intelligence, *quaerens intellectum*, c'est une initiative divine, c'est une série d'initiatives divines, absolues, dont le trait essentiel est d'être sans "raison", tant les initiatives générales de la création, de l'incarnation, de la rédemption, que les initiatives particulières des prédestinations de la grâce: contingences suaves et terribles d'un amour qui n'a aucun compte à rendre de ses bienfaits ni de ses abandons. Le vrai monde de la contemplation et de l'intelligence théologique c'est celui-là livré aux initiatives d'un Dieu libre, qui mène à son gré cette immense et indéfinissable historie, don't il se fait le premier personnage.'

and under Chenu's tutelage, Schillebeeckx discovered for the first time the importance of history for theology, and it was this more than anything else that won him over from his earlier fascination with philosophy to a passion for theology.[61] Theology is both *theologia* and *oikonomia* and therefore it is not *either* a speculative discipline *or* an historical discipline, it is both. Christian faith is grounded in the divine–human relation, and theology is the explication of this relation. This is the characteristic that has given Schillebeeckx's work both its energy and creativity and its continuity and stability – a characteristic that he shared quite profoundly with Chenu.

It follows that one of the most important and interesting questions to explore with respect to the theologies of these two Dominicans is the question: what is the relation between *theologia* and *oikonomia*? How is this relation understood and described? What are the underlying theological or doctrinal presuppositions? What are the methodological decisions involved? These questions that began to come into focus in the earlier chapter on revelation now come into quite sharp focus in this chapter on Christology. For both Chenu and Schillebeeckx, theology has an overarching soteriological framework: the transcendent God is revealed in the events of salvation history. This relation between the revelation of the transcendent within the contingent is governed for Chenu by the 'law of incarnation' by which he means the principle that governs the economy of grace, the economy both of covenant and of revelation – *une économie d'alliance et de communication*.[62] The economy of incarnation gives theology its fundamental structure. The act of faith is a fully human act in which the integrity of the human is sustained, and it is a supernatural act dependent upon grace whose object is not dogmatic proposition but the transcendent God who fulfils human desire. For Chenu this relation between human and divine that gives theology its structure is analogous

---

[61] See Paul Bourgay, 'Edward Schillebeeckx', in *Bilan de la théologie du XXe siècle, II,* ed. Robert Vander Grucht and Herbert Vorgrimler (Paris: Casterman, 1970), pp. 875–890 (p. 876). 'C'est à l'automne 1945 seulement qu'il put se render au *Saulchoir* pour obtenir sa licence en théologie. Ce séjour à Paris est une étape importante dans l'évolution de Schillebeeckx. Le Saulchoir était imprégné de la pensée et de la méthode du P. Chenu. Cette théologie vivante, qui ne se contentait pas de répéter les anciennes formulas mais voulait donner une réponse aux problèmes de notre temps, séduisit le jeune étudiant. Jusqu'alors son désir avait été de collaborer avec De Petter dans la recherche philosophique. Maintenant, il découvre sa vocation de théologien. "Au Saulchoir, dit-il, j'ai appris à aborder les problèmes d'un point de vue historique." C'est, de fait, une des richesses des grands études théologiques de Schillebeeckx: toujours il parcourt l'histoire de la tradition pour en resituer les points saillants dans la problématique actuelle.'

[62] Congar, 'Le Père M-D Chenu', p. 781.

to the human divine relation revealed in the Christological mystery.[63] Yet it is precisely at this point that there is a substantive difference between the theologies of Chenu and Schillebeeckx.

It is perhaps because of the profound similarities between Chenu and Schillebeeckx – the tremendous continuity between their work – that the differences between them are so striking, and certainly one clear difference is the treatment of Christology. Both of these Dominicans describe the relation between *theologia* and *oikonomia* in terms of incarnation. For both of them the structure of theology itself is the logical and necessary outcome of the incarnate nature of revelation: theology is chastened always by the 'given', that is, by God's self-revelation in history. Furthermore, for both of them this structure to their theology is not a question simply of organization, rather it is an analogous and ontological relation, and as such it is the principle in light of which decisions concerning theological method are taken. However, it is at the point where incarnation is related explicitly to the person of Christ that there is a significant difference. Although Chenu develops this theme more generally, Schillebeeckx repeatedly turns to Christology, and where Chenu describes the structure of his theology as being given by the 'law of incarnation', Schillebeeckx describes the structure of his as 'Christological'. This is a significant theological difference.

What essentially is the difference between Chenu and Schillebeeckx, between an 'incarnational' and a 'Christological' structure? Incarnation is quite evidently at the heart of Chenu's theology as even this brief analysis of his treatment of the doctrine of faith and the nature of theology demonstrates. Incarnation is of fundamental importance within Schillebeeckx's theology. This became clear in his analysis of the new trends in dogmatic theology and his evaluation of the strengths and weaknesses of the new philosophies taken up in the preceding chapter on the nature–grace relation; in this chapter on his Christology, incarnation emerges as the key concept in light of which he interprets the entire Christ event, and this is the difference between them. Stated quite generally, for Chenu the relation of *theologia* and *oikonomia* is incarnation where this structure is not often explicitly described or developed with reference to the person of Christ but is elaborated upon more extensively in abstract terms, as in *Une école de théologie* where the focus is the relation between the speculative and the historical

---

[63] Chenu, *Une école de théologie*, p. 145. 'La même loi, qui il y a un instant nous faisait requérir une incarnation de la parole de Dieu dans des paroles humaines au cours de l'histoire, nous presse maintenant d'accepter jusqu'au bout le régime de connaissance qu'implique cette incarnation: la théologie est solidaire du mystère théandrique de la parole de Dieu, Verbe fait chair. Là seulement elle peut trouver une si audacieuse confiance dans la cohérence de la foi et de la raison.'

within the discipline of theology.[64] For Schillebeeckx this is not the case and the relation between *theologia* and *oikonomia* is understood in 'personal' terms – incarnation is personal in Christ – specifically in the personal terms of the kenotic Christology found in *Christ the Sacrament*.

These of course are general statements which deserve to be nuanced. There are certainly quite explicit Christological references in *Une école de théologie*. In particular the analogical relation in which humanity participates in the mystery of God is clearly Christological. The life of faith – grace – makes us *contemporains du Christ*.[65] This grace is not something other than the Christological mystery but participation in this one mystery – *double mystère théandrique, mieux, unique mystère, qui est le mystère même du Christ*.[66] Faith is the grace of the new humanity, the life of *les enfants de Dieu*.[67] However, the contrast with Schillebeeckx's theology is striking. Where the specifically Christological references vis-à-vis incarnation are glancing in Chenu's work, Schillebeeckx's sacramental theology – and indeed all of his theology – is much more self-consciously Christological.[68] There are anthropological consequences that inevitably follow from these different approaches, not least because the decision about Christology affects how they describe human participation in the divine mystery.

One of the questions that has been asked of Chenu's Christology is as follows: what place is there for the personal Christ within his theology?[69] Behind this question lies another question: to what extent does Chenu

---

[64] This is precisely the place, in Chenu's preoccupation with the relation between the historical and the transcendent, where a turn to Christology might most be anticipated. See Potworowski, *Contemplation and Incarnation*, p. 197, who notes 'the modest reality of the Incarnation' characteristic of Chenu's theology. 'There is no doubt that [incarnation] is the all-pervasive structure in his theology. What is its exact status and meaning? Surely it is more than a metaphor or a structural device for organizing his theology. But what exactly is the relationship between incarnation as process or law and the event of the incarnation? Given the centrality of incarnation in Chenu's theology, where the law of incarnation is considered as ruling the whole of history and especially the role of the church in the world, why is there relatively little specific reference to Christ? The issue becomes paradoxical when we consider that Chenu's whole effort was devoted to the integration of the historical dimension of the existence into theology which is precisely where the role of Christ should have its greatest impact.'

[65] Chenu, *Une école de théologie*, p. 135.

[66] Ibid. p. 137. Emphasis mine.

[67] Ibid. p. 150.

[68] This brief analysis of the christological references in *Une école de théologie* reflects a pattern within all of Chenu's theology. See Potworowski, *Contemplation and Incarnation*, p. 229. 'There can be no denying that Chenu fails to clarify in a sufficiently systematic way the precise relationship between the unique event of incarnation in the person of Christ and the actualization of this event in the history of the church.'

[69] Potworowski, *Contemplation and Incarnation*, p. 211.

articulate the uniqueness or particularity of Christ, or is this obscured ultimately in the description of incarnation as the general structure and dynamism of the human–divine relation? Does the incarnation in Christ become an example of a more general principle or is it a unique and particular event?[70] The anthropological question this raises for theology is as follows: in light if this Christological issue, to what extent can he then describe the personal nature of human being? What room is there for the uniqueness and particularity of the human person or is this obscured finally in his overarching concern for the historicity of the human? There are clear benefits from Chenu's treatment of the incarnation. Far from collapsing the human into either a dualistic or reductive theological anthropology, Chenu's theological realism, governed as it is by the law of incarnation, allows him to argue for a theology that takes seriously human integrity. The indivisibility of the human is well established and sustained in his work and his incarnational realism is the ground for his own certain confidence in the coherence between faith and reason, an *audacieuese confiance* that he lived out in his own life – he faced all of the inquisitorial activities of the Holy Office with remarkable equanimity. Yet for all of these strengths, there seems little space for individual particularity and for the personal in his anthropology, a consequence perhaps on the emphasis placed on historicity.[71]

Certainly Schillebeeckx shares with Chenu a fundamental commitment to the historicity of God's self-revelation and of the human person. However, his theology and its incarnational realism have more space for the personal Christ. Hence his theological anthropology overcomes what might be seen as a weakness in Chenu's work – it describes both the historicity of human being and the personal nature of human existence. *Filii in filio* is both an ontological statement and a personal one because it is grounded both in God's self-giving as human salvation and in the kenotic personal relation

---

[70] These are questions for *Une école de théologie* and for his work more generally. Potworowski, *Contemplation and Incarnation*, p. 212. 'The nature of theology, for Chenu, is centred on the task of searching for reasons, for the intelligibility inherent in creation from the point of view of God's plan. Basic to the task is the search for laws manifested in particular events. The emphasis is on the intelligibility of particular events, both in the church and in the world, on the search for a deeper meaning than appears on the surface of things. Chenu is thus always looking at things in terms of the big picture. The danger is that the particularity of the concrete experience or event will be swallowed up in the articulation of intelligibility, that the event will be seen as an instance of law. Chenu is aware of the danger, but is not always immune to it.'

[71] This again is a reflection on both the particular text, *Une école de théologie* and on his work more generally. Potworowski, *Contemplation and Incarnation*, p. 214. 'The question remains whether [the emphasis on historicity] is a sufficient category to encompass all that is meant by the concrete, especially when considering the person. . . . Several traits remain undeveloped in Chenu. . . . Perhaps Chenu's mistrust of a theology focused on the individual and the individual's interiority can account for this.'

between Father and Son. This is the Christology and anthropology that emerges from a reading of *Christ the Sacrament*. Human being is sacramental. That is, it is embodied and situated and at the same time it is transcendent and eschatological. This description of human life is for Schillebeeckx the logical consequence of a Christological sacramental theology. If Christ is the primordial sacrament then theological anthropology, if it is to hold to its Christological structure, gives rise to an understanding of human being as sacramental.

The point to this brief analysis of incarnation as the structure of Chenu's theology is not a critique of that theology. Rather, the intention in this quick study of *Une école de théologie* is simply to draw attention to a difference between the theologies of mentor and student, a difference that pays dividends within Schillebeeckx's theology in a better rounded anthropology. Less a comment on Chenu than on Schillebeeckx, this difference draws attention to the theological foundations that allow Schillebeeckx to assume an anthropology in which human being as person is always a situated freedom; these foundations become clear in the place he gives to Christology. His theology, like that of Chenu, gives rise to a rich description of human action and to the meaning or possibility that grounds action. Yet it allows more space for the particular and personal in its description. If Chenu's work is sometimes lacking in precision, as has been suggested of the rather thin Christological explication of incarnation, this may be attributed to his overriding conviction in the prophetic nature of the activity of the Word in history and to the pastoral practice of theology.[72] Ultimately both the charges of imprecision and of a prophetic and pastoral dynamism integral to theology are traits that Schillebeeckx does indeed share with him. Yet, most significantly, it is Schillebeeckx's interpretation of the fully personal nature of Christ's humanity and the appropriation of this as the theological method – 'Christ who, as man, is for us the way leading to God' – that allows Schillebeeckx to develop a theological anthropology from a Christological ontology.[73]

For Schillebeeckx, Christology provides the 'method' or 'structure' for theology and for theological anthropology, yet it does so not by providing a system or framework. Rather, Christology is the ontological basis (*zijnsgrond*) for the encounter between God and humanity, and hence it is the ontological ground from which we may speak of the fullness of humanity:

This is encounter which would not even be possible did not the God who comes to meet us raise us up from within to an ontologically higher plane. For since Christ's loving gesture brings about a responsive

[72] Potworowski, *Contemplation and Incarnation*, p. 229.
[73] Schillebeeckx, 'Theologia *or* Oikonomia?', p. 97.

love in us, it also brings about the ontological basis upon which we, while remaining men, become capable of the theological act of encounter with God in trusting and loving surrender.[74]

Within this idea of Christology as the ontological basis – the *zijnsgrond* – for theological anthropology there are several ideas that need to be considered more explicitly. Acknowledged only provisionally here, these ideas are significant for understanding Schillebeeckx's Christological ontology. The first of these ideas is that Christology is always done in the context of theology, that is to say, Schillebeeckx's Christology is done against the backdrop of faith in the Triune God.[75] The identity of the God who comes to meet us is given in God's self-revelation and this self-revelation is purposive. It establishes the conditions that make the *theologal* life possible for humanity.[76] The possibility for humanity of participation in the divine life is the work of the Triune God.[77] In the manner in which God

---

[74] Schillebeeckx, *Christ the Sacrament*, p. 78. In this translation of the Dutch text 'ontology' has been used to translate both '*ontologisch*' and '*zijnsgrond*'. See *Christus Sacrament van de Godsontmoeting* (Bilthoven: Nelissen, 1959), p. 81: 'Het gaat om een ontmoeting die zelfs niet mogelijk zou zijn indien de ons tegemoettredende God ons niet van binnenuit optilt tot een hoger ontologisch niveau. Want juist omdat het expressieve liefdesgebaar van Christus in ons het wederantwoord wekt, bewerkt het tegelijkertijd de zijnsgrond van waaruit wij, mens blijvend, toch de theologale akt van de godsontmoeting en gelovige en minnende overgave kunnen stellen'. *Zijnsgrond* can be understood quite literally as the 'ground of being'.

[75] See Leo Scheffczyk, 'Christology in the Context of Experience: on the Interpretation of Christ by Edward Schillebeeckx'. *Thomist* 48 (1984), 383–408. Scheffczyk underlines the Trinitarian strength of Schillebeeckx's Christology in *Christ the Sacrament*. He is however mistaken in his reading of Schillebeeckx's later Christology on this point. Furthermore, it is difficult to follow him when he suggests that Schillebeeckx's treatment of the doctrine of the incarnation cannot bear the Christological weight that Schillebeeckx suggests: 'The thesis of a continuous, progressive incarnation over the whole of Jesus' life cannot ground all that is claimed for it as explaining the growth of Christ's humanity.' p. 384. This dismisses too quickly the importance of the personal nature of the humanity of Christ in Schillebeeckx's Christology.

[76] The term 'theologal' rather than 'theological' is used here following the Dutch text for clarity. See translators note: 'Current today in its Dutch, French and German equivalents, it indicates existential God-centredness as distinct from the abstract-analytic nuance of "theological"'. Schillebeeckx, *Christ the Sacrament*, p. 16 no. 14.

[77] See Borgman, *Edward Schillebeeckx: een theoloog in zijn geschiedenis*, p.65: on the *theandric* nature of reality which leads Schillebeeckx to his ontology. Comprehensive talk about human reality needed to be theological, not in the sense of expounding truths of faith presented by the church, but as talking about the full ontological reality of the *homo deificus*, of our being children of God which embraced all that was natural and human. 'Dit impliceerde dat het omvattende spreken over de menselijke werkelijkheid theologisch diende te zijn, niet in de zin

148

comes to meet humanity as salvation, salvation is revealed as Trinitarian activity. This becomes clear in the second idea contained in this text considering the ontological basis upon which humanity is capable of the theologal act of encounter with God, and that is the particular event that makes this encounter possible.

The particular event that makes the theologal encounter possible is 'Christ's loving gesture', also described as 'the God-man's expression of love', 'the God-man's glance at us'.[78] Salvation is expressed for Schillebeeckx in this image of a 'glance' directed towards humanity, which 'changes our whole life' and at the same time fulfils it in all of its freedom:

> [T]he gesture of Christ's human love, precisely because this human act is a personal act of God the Son enters into the centre of our personal freedom if we but hold ourselves open to it. Christ's gesture of human love is able truly to effect an answering love. The quality of the appeal which does not wish to constrain our freedom remains intact. But it is, in human form, a divine appeal, and in a man of good will this infallibly attains its goal.[79]

Christ's gesture of human love moves in two directions. It flows both from the relation of Jesus to the Father and from the relation of Jesus to humanity.

In the man Jesus is realized the fidelity of the covenant in a twofold way. At last the dialogue that was ever breaking down finds a full and perfect human resonance. In a single person both elements are fulfilled: the invitation and the reply of perfect fidelity, and in such a way that both the invitation and the response constitute the complete revelation of God.[80]

---

van uitleg van kerkelijk voorgehouden geloofswaarheden, maar als spreken over "de vol-ontologische werkelijkheid van de homo deificus, van ons Godskind-zijn", dat al het natuurlijk-menselijk omvatte'. This conviction is in place from the outset of Schillebeeckx's career. It is developed christologically in his treatment of Christ's incarnation. See Schillebeeckx, 'De zin van het mens-zijn van Jesus, de Christus', *Tijdschrift voor theologie* 2 (1962), 127–172. In this chapter it is discussed in relation to Schillebeeckx's sacramental Christology in *Christ the Sacrament*.

[78] Schillebeeckx, *Christ the Sacrament*, p. 79; see *Christus Sacrament*, p. 82: 'de Godmens'.

[79] Ibid. p. 78.

[80] Edward Schillebeeckx, 'The Sacraments: an Encounter with God' in *Christianity Divided: Protestant and Roman Catholic Theological Issues*, ed. D. Callahan (London: Sheed and Ward, 1961), pp. 245–275 (p. 247). 'Sackramentele als Organe der Gottenbegegnung' in *Fragen der theologie heute*, ed. J. Feiner (Einsiedeln: Benziger Verlag, 1957), pp. 370–401.

Jesus is the consummation of the *exitus reditus* movement, creation and redemption, invitation and response, in which human reality is constituted:

> The man Jesus is not only the one sent by the Holy Trinity, he is also the one called to be representative of all humanity. He is not only the visible embodiment of God's wooing of man, but also the representation and highest fulfilment of the human response of love to God's courtship. Jesus, the free man, who in his humanity reveals to us the divine invitation of love, is at the same time, as man, the person who in the name of all of us and as our representative accepts this invitation. As head of redeemed humanity, he is in a sense the whole of mankind.[81]

Contained in this description of Christ's loving gesture is an understanding of the human nature of Christ as personal and dynamic, not passive. In Christ the divine–human gesture of love is directed to human freedom as the fulfilment of human life: the act of surrender to participation in the divine life according to our human nature.[82]

The third idea is the intersubjective aspect of the relation between nature and grace. Although this has been discussed at some length in the preceding chapter, it finds its ground in a Christological structure, one which holds together the integrity of what it means to be human with the reality of humanity's dependence upon the graciousness of the transcendent God. The God 'who comes to meet us' raises humanity to a new life not by adding something to human nature – humanity 'remains human' – but by fulfilling nature from within – humanity becomes 'fully human' – able to share in the divine life, the 'theological act of encounter with God'.[83] Central to Schillebeeckx's account of grace, the theologal act of encounter, is his understanding of intersubjectivity as this pertains to the relation between the Triune God and humanity.

Schillebeeckx develops the theological notion of intersubjectivity within his sacramental theology both by reference to the doctrine of Christ and the doctrine of revelation. Christologically, he draws upon Aquinas' doctrine of the

---

[81] Schillebeeckx, 'The Sacraments: an Encounter with God', pp. 247–248.

[82] Participation in the divine life is developed by Schillebeeckx with reference to the theological virtues of faith, hope, and charity. Described as the *theologal* life it is what Schillebeeckx means when he writes of the life of grace, human life directed towards its goal, of human existence directed *towards* God. See the translator's note: 'By "theologal attitude of existence" we mean a vital human activity of which God himself is the object and the motive, and in the perfecting of which God is coactive: namely the life of grace in faith, hope and love, the only virtues which of their nature bring about a personal relationship with God.' *Christ the Sacrament*, p. 16 n14.

[83] This is the 'humanization of humanity' to which Küng refers in his description of Schillebeeckx's work. See Küng, 'Een theologie met een jong gezicht', p. 357.

incarnation with its emphasis on the personal nature of the Son's humanity.[84] Behind this Schillebeeckx points to the patristic Christologies that place emphasis on the human nature of the Son as active and not merely as passive in relation to the divine.[85] The notion of intersubjectivity is also brought to bear upon sacramental theology via the doctrine of revelation. Schillebeeckx begins a 1957 essay on sacramental theology with a discussion of the 'sacramental principle of revelation'.[86] Revelation is both word and sacrament:

> Precisely because the supernatural saving reality, veiled in historical events, and surrounded by the darkness of mystery, is present to us only in earthly form (*sacramentum*), it demands the revealing word (*verbum*) as the interior aspect of its earthly appearance.[87]

Revelation in both covenant and in Christ is constituted by 'word' and 'sacrament'[88] and has an intersubjective, or 'dialogue structure':

> The burden of all God's revelation in the Old Testament is exactly the course of history which results from the alternation between God's constant fidelity and the ever-recurring infidelity of his people. This revelation, then is accomplished in a dialectical situation: out of the dialogue of struggle between God and his people, in fidelity and infidelity, the concrete content of revelation takes shape.[89]

This intersubjective structure is able to bear the weight of a doctrine of revelation in which the relationship between God and God's people describes both divine transcendence and divine immanence within history, in relation to human freedom:

> In one way, of course, [revelation] arises from a decision of the living God which is completely and sovereignly free. But looked at from the

---

[84] See Schillebeeckx, *Christ the Sacrament*, p. 14 n 10.
[85] See Schillebeeckx, 'New Trends in Dogmatic Theology', pp. 123–127 where Schillebeeckx turns to the patristic emphasis on kenosis. Schillebeeckx draws attention to Thomas' own familiarity with patristic Christologies, clearly situating Thomas as an historian of the tradition and not as 'the tradition' in his own right, abstracted from the biblical and patristic theology which he inherited. Schillebeeckx, *Christ the Sacrament*, p. 14 n 11.
[86] Schillebeeckx, 'The Sacraments: an Encounter with God', pp. 245–246.
[87] Ibid. p. 241.
[88] This corresponds to Schillebeeckx's description of revelation as being always both revelation-in-word and revelation-in-reality. Revelation both makes history and at the same time interprets history via the prophetic word. See Edward Schillebeeckx, 'Revelation, Scripture, Tradition, and Teaching', in *Revelation and Theology*, pp. 2–26. 'Openbaring, Schiftuur Traditie en Leeergezag', in *Openbaring en Theologie*, pp. 13–27. First published in *Kerk en Theologie* 16 (1963) 85–99.
[89] Schillebeeckx, 'The Sacraments: an Encounter with God', p. 247.

viewpoint of history, this revelation remains the result of a dialogue of acts: between the invitation and proposal of love by God and the personal, loving response or refusal of love by God's people.[90]

This history or 'dialogue of acts' finds its intersubjective interpretation in 'the prophetic word': 'I will be *your* God, you *my* people.'[91]

Revelation in this intersubjective structure reveals both the nature of the God who comes to meet humanity and the true nature of humanity itself. The true nature of God is revealed as perfect fidelity in love, and this fidelity establishes the definitive end of human life:

> Through all the vicissitudes of this history God desires to lead his people in spite of everything to a final and definitive fidelity. The revelation which leads up to Christ then, evolves in history as a dialogue in which God wrestles with human freedom in his desire to save mankind. It is an existential, two-way struggle between God who calls and man who resists – until this God who invites to a faithful love, himself personally responds as true man to this courtship, with a return of love whose fidelity knows no bounds – which does not shrink even from the death of the Cross.[92]

Revelation, accomplished ultimately in Christ, is theocentric and anthropocentric. In God's self-revelation the true nature of both God and of humanity is given.

In God's self-revelation Christ becomes the *zijnsgrond* for humanity in a specific manner. Christ is 'true humanity' in his response to the Father's love. This response is described by Schillebeeckx as 'faithful love'. It is love conditioned by a boundless fidelity and in this sense the true nature of humanity is given by the Cross. The end of human life is accomplished in the 'final and definitive fidelity', which is Christ's act of surrender to the Father. This is the fourth point that follows from Christology as *zijnsgrond*: the description of human life and activity as response, a 'responsive love', which is both an expression of human freedom and at the same time an expression of dependence upon God's graciousness.

Human life is described by Schillebeeckx as the 'vocation to faithfulness'. In Christ God has realized the 'concentration' of this vocation.[93] In other words in Christ, God has given humanity to itself, has realized humanity's vocation to be human by establishing the ground for human faithfulness in

---

[90] Ibid.
[91] Ibid. pp. 246–247.
[92] Ibid. p. 247.
[93] Schillebeeckx, *Christ the Sacrament*, p. 13.

relation to the divine. Human life, if it is described as a vocation to a particular relationship with God, has a Christological structure:

> God's ultimate purpose was to call a faithful people into life. Broadly speaking, there would be continual failure, until God himself raised up a man in whom was concentrated the entirety of man's vocation to faithfulness, and who would himself keep faith with the Covenant in the perfection of his fidelity. This man was Jesus. In him there was a visible realisation of both sides of faith in the Covenant. In the dialogue between God and man, so often breaking down, there was found at last a perfect human respondent; in the same person there was achieved the perfection both of the divine invitation and of the human response in faith from the man who by his resurrection is the Christ. The Covenant sealed in his blood, found definitive success in his person. In him grace became fully visible; he is the embodiment of the grace of the final victory, who appeared in person to the Apostles. Christ himself is the Church, an invisible communion in grace with the living God (the Son made man with the Father) manifested in visible human form. For this is what he is as the 'first-born' and Head of all creation. Consequently the whole of humanity is already, in its Head, assembled into communion with God.[94]

The ground of being for the human vocation to faithfulness is the perfection of Christ's fidelity. This perfection of fidelity is found for Schillebeeckx in Christ's human adoration of the Father, an act of worship to which the Father responds definitively. Christ's perfect fidelity, his Passover, leads to the glorification of the Son by the Father and to Pentecost.[95] In Christ the relation between human and divine gives ultimate expression to the relation between human freedom in all of its integrity and the 'untramelled freedom of God's mercy'.[96]

In summary, for Schillebeeckx Christology is the ontological basis for the encounter between God and humanity because it is the sacramental revelation of the mystery of God and of the human in relation to this mystery. God's self-revelation is the invitation and the response that defines humanity in its

---

[94] Ibid.

[95] Ibid. p. 71.

[96] Schillebeekcx develops this Trinitarian and christological sacramental theology as grounds for understanding the free gift of grace present in the sacraments. The 'infallible working of grace in the sacraments' is grounded in the 'sacramental mystery of Passover and Pentecost.' Sacrament, as the mystery of Christ's worship, is an expression of divine generosity, and hence grace preserves its gratuitous character. Essential to sacramental theology is the 'sacramental reality of the redeeming Trinity in Christ.' See Schillebeeckx, *Christ the Sacrament*, pp. 68–73.

vocation to intimacy with God. This is an intersubjective relation – creative, salvific, sanctifying, participative and personal. It is revealed and established in the 'God-man's glance at us':[97]

> What does the Word of God say about man? *How does God see man?* That God sees man does not mean simply that he knows what man is making of his life here below. On the contrary, it is the gaze of one who is personally interested, who calls us to salvation and participates with us in a personal, creative and sanctifying way: he is involved in the fortunes of man (so much so indeed that in the *theophania* of the man Jesus he personally devotes himself in solidarity with human beings to the formation and construction of the 'essence of man in himself').[98]

Right at the very centre of Schillebeeckx's sacramental Christology is 'the essence' of humanity in God, and this is the basis for Christology as the ontological ground – *zijnsgrond* – for humanity. This implies that Schillebeeckx is interpreting the Chalcedonian definition of incarnation in a particular manner: the 'doctrine' of the incarnation expresses the fully personal nature of Christ's humanity – the 'essence' of humanity – in the divine – in God's self.

Schillebeeckx's Christology and the Christological structure of humanity's vocation to intimacy with God are dependent upon his interpretation of the incarnation. There are two features of this that are significant here. The first is that the Chalcedonian definition of the union of the divine and human natures in Christ is a soteriological statement, and this soteriology – salvation history – is sacramental:

> The humanity of Jesus is concretely intended by God as the fulfilment of his promise of salvation; it is a messianic reality. This messianic and redemptive purpose of the incarnation implies that the encounter between Jesus and his contemporaries was always on his part an offering of grace in a human form. For the love of the man Jesus is the human incarnation of the redeeming love of God: an advent of God's love in visible form. Precisely because these human deeds of Jesus are divine deeds, personal acts of the Son of God, divine acts in visible human form, they possess of their nature a divine saving power, and consequently they bring salvation; they are the 'cause of grace'.[99]

---

[97] Schillebeeckx, *Christ the Sacrament*, p. 75
[98] Edward Schillebeeckx, 'Dialogue with God and Christian Secularity', in *God and Man*, trans. Edward Fitzgerald and Peter Tomlinson (London: Sheed and Ward, 1969), pp. 213–214.
[99] Schillebeeckx, *Christ the Sacrament*, p.14.

Christology has primarily a soteriological context, a 'messianic and redemptive purpose', and this 'purpose' has a sacramental structure: the messianic reality is human and historical. This is the first point. Related to this sacramental soteriology, is the second point: the mystery of the incarnation, and the specific interpretation of this, determines Christology.

Christology is concerned with the 'redemptive purpose of the incarnation' and because of this redemptive purpose, it cannot emphasize the divinity of Christ at the expense of his humanity, a tendency Schillebeeckx saw in much contemporary Christology. Schillebeeckx sought to redress this tendency within Christology by turning to Thomas' Christology and especially to its treatment of the incarnation.[100]

The dogmatic definition of Chalcedon, according to which Christ is 'one person in two natures,' implies that one and the same person, the Son of God, also took on a visible human form. Even in his humanity, Christ is the Son of God. The second person of the most holy Trinity is personally man, and this man is personally God. Therefore Christ is God in a human way and man in a divine way. As a man he acts out his divine life in and according to his human existence. Everything he does as man is an act of the Son of God, a divine act in human form, an interpretation and transposition of a divine activity into a human activity. His human love is the human embodiment of the redeeming love of God.[101]

Set within a sacramental soteriology, the Chalcedonian definition is the starting point for the Christology of *Christ the Sacrament*. Schillebeeckx's treatment of this definition begins from the '*mysteria carnis Christi*': even in his humanity Christ is the Son of God.[102]

Incarnation: Christology as Sacramental

For Schillebeeckx, Christology is quite simply a reflection upon the *mysteria carnis Christi*: even in his humanity Christ is the Son of God. The place to begin an analysis of Schillebeeckx's Christology is his doctrine of the incarnation. The point is not that Schillebeeckx collapses Christology into the doctrine of the incarnation, rather, what is of interest is his interpretation of this doctrine and how he develops this in relation to the Christ event in its entirety. His understanding of the incarnation and his discussion of its place within Christology leads to an appreciation of Christology as the *zijnsgrond* that opens out into a sacramental anthropology.

It is entirely consistent with his overall theological endeavour that Schillebeeckx should have a sacramental theology that has a Christological

---

[100] Ibid. p. 14 n 10.
[101] Ibid. p. 14.
[102] Ibid. p. 16 n 15.

structure: this reflects fully the relation between *theologia* and *oikonomia*. It is the fullest expression of God's graciousness as it is constitutive of human reality: the God who is transcendence and difference is the God for humanity in human and historical form. The Christological structure of Schillebeeckx's theology attests to the essentially sacramental nature of the divine–human relation. Hence sacramental theology, by its very definition, takes as its starting point the 'analysis of the visible presence of grace which Christ is personally':

> For a sacrament is a divine bestowal of salvation in an outwardly perceptible form which makes the bestowal manifest; a bestowal of salvation in historical visibility.[103]

The sequence of ideas here is important, as is the introduction of the term 'historical' – *historische*.[104] The theology of sacrament follows from a Christology which in Schillebeeckx's analysis is at the same time a soteriology. The doctrinal definition of Chalcedon concerning the union of the human and divine in Christ is at the same time the definitive statement of God's saving activity on behalf of all humanity. The manner of this saving activity gives rise to a sacramental theology:

> Because the saving acts of the man Jesus are performed by a divine person, they have a divine power to save, but because this divine power to save appears to us in visible form, the saving activity of Jesus is sacramental.[105]

This Christology is not grounded in an abstract relation between the divine and human or between nature and grace. Rather it is grounded in the personal and visible presence of grace – grace present in and for human history. It is because of this christoform structure that a sacrament may be described as a bestowal of salvation in historical visibility. Implicit in this definition is the idea that human history is not incidental to salvation. Rather, at its core, sacramental theology is a confession that in Christ all of human history has been taken up into God's salvific act.

The emphasis on the incarnation in Christ as the human visible form of grace, the incarnation of the redeeming love of God, conditions both 'sacrament' and 'encounter', the two terms Schillebeeckx incorporates into the title of his text. Christology gives to the term 'sacrament' its structure

---

[103] Ibid. p. 15.
[104] Schillebeeckx, *Christus Sacrament*, p. 24. 'Sacrament' betekent immers een goddelijke heilsgave in en door uiterlijk waarneembare, grijbare gestalte die deze aanschouwelijk maakt: een heilsgave in historische zichtbaarheid.'
[105] Schillebeeckx, *Christ the Sacrament*, p. 15.

and definition by being its *zijnsgrond*. Christology does not provide sacramental theology with a structure that can then be applied in a parallel fashion to the sacraments. Christology does not function in this way within Schillebeeckx's sacramental theology or within his theology as a whole. The relation between the divine and human in Christ is not a model which, if applied to sacramental theology, provides a definition of sacrament. Rather Christ is the relation between the divine and human in which he is in himself *the* sacrament that grounds any sacramental theology:

> If the human love and all the human acts of Jesus possess a divine saving power, then the realisation in human shape of this saving power necessarily includes as one of its aspects the manifestation of salvation: includes, in other words, sacramentality. The man Jesus, as the personal visible realisation of the divine grace of redemption, is *the* sacrament, the primordial sacrament, because this man, the Son of God himself, is intended by the Father to be in his humanity the only way to the actuality of redemption. 'For there is one God, and one mediator of God and men, the man Christ Jesus' (1 Tim 2:5).[106]

Because it is in his humanity that Christ becomes the way to the actuality of redemption, language of encounter between humanity and divinity within history is possible.

Implicit in this understanding of Christ as *the* sacrament is the fully personal nature of Christ's humanity. As the 'personal visible realization of the divine grace of the redemption', Christ incarnates the divine will to redeem in his human will. Hence Christ's personal freedom and will – the relation between divine invitation and human response incarnate in him – is the *locus* in which the human vocation to faithfulness takes visible and historical form:

> Because the inward power of Jesus' will to redeem and of his human love is God's own saving power realised in human form, the human saving acts of Jesus are the divine bestowal of grace itself realised in visible form; that is to say they cause what they signify; they are sacraments.[107]

Christ's incarnation is sacramental for Schillebeeckx because the divine is revealed in the fully personal nature of Christ's humanity. It is this sacramental nature of human salvation that gives best expression to the historical consequences of Schillebeeckx's treatise on God: 'creation and

---

[106] Ibid.
[107] Ibid. pp. 16–17.

covenant – these form one divine structure, and this is also seen in its historical consequences'.[108]

It is important to recognize the way in which Schillebeeckx understands and interprets the relationship between divine grace and human history. History is quite clearly the arena of human activity. For Schillebeeckx humanity is a 'situated freedom'. Freedom and contingency are both, and at the same time, constitutive of humanity. That is to say, contingency is constitutive of humanity in a manner which does not impede human freedom, rather human freedom is realized in and through its historical contingency. To be human is to be an historical agent: human beings act upon history and in doing so humanity 'makes' history. Yet human history is also the arena of divine activity. It is at this juncture, in the configuration of the relation between divine and human activity in the midst of history, that sacramental theology becomes of interest for anthropology. In constructing a sacramental theology that follows from the fully personal nature of Christ's humanity, Schillebeeckx is developing a sacramental theology that is coherent with the non-dualistic, non-reductive and hence non-competitive relation between the divine and human: this relation – the sacramental relation between personal humanity and divine grace – is creative, salvific, sanctifying, participative and personal.

Sacramental theology points to the activity of divine grace within human history by first attesting to the truth that grace is active *in* history. Sacraments, by definition are visible, and this visibility itself points to the historical nature of God's gracious activity. Secondly, sacramental theology points to the activity of grace in history by patterning itself on the 'saving activity of Jesus'. Hence the manner in which this saving activity itself is described – the relationship between the divine and human in the saving activity of the human Jesus – is definitive. The decisions that Schillebeeckx makes vis-à-vis Christology are indicative of the manner in which he understands grace to be active within human history.

The understanding of human life as 'vocation' is predicated for Schillebeeckx upon one 'simple fact' – the 'simple fact of encounter with God'.[109] Encounter with God is constitutive of human nature and so it follows that there is a 'properly human mode of encounter with God', and for Schillebeeckx the sacraments are this 'properly human mode of encounter with God'.[110] Sacramental theology is then concerned with intimacy with God as constitutive of humanity from the outset: sacrament is a term for the 'intimateness of God's personal approach' to humanity.[111]

---

[108] Schillebeeckx, 'Christian Faith and Man's Expectation for the Future on Earth', p. 54.

[109] Schillebeeckx, *Christ the Sacrament*, p. 3.

[110] Ibid. p. 6.

[111] Ibid. p. 3.

The term 'encounter' raises again the question of the relation between the formal and material aspects within theology. For Schillebeeckx these aspects are distinct yet related. The material questions of doctrine and the formal questions of method are related. Consistently the formal questions of method are determined by the material questions of the content of faith. This is not to suggest that questions of method are arbitrary for him. It is clear from his consideration of the relationship between theology and philosophy in the essay 'New Trends in Dogmatic Theology' that questions of method are taken up very seriously. They are placed at the service of theology. This holds for the relationship of the formal and material aspects of his sacramental theology. The phenomenological category of 'encounter' and the personalist account of 'nature' are placed at the service of the 'simple fact of encounter with God':

> One cannot help remarking that the theology of the manuals does not always make a careful distinction between the unique manner of existence which is peculiar to man, and the mode of being, mere objective 'being there,' which is proper to the things of nature. The absence of this distinction, particularly in treating of grace or of the sacraments, occasionally obscures the simple fact of encounter with God. The intimateness of God's personal approach to man is often lost in a too severely objective examination of that which forms the living core and centre of religion, the personal communion with the God who gives himself to men.[112]

The reference here to the 'intimateness of God's personal approach' to humanity is conditioned by the phrase 'the God who gives himself' to humanity, hence the ground for personal communion with God – and this is what Schillebeeckx means by 'encounter' – is Christ.

In the study of the sacraments, the consequence of this tendency towards a purely impersonal, almost mechanical approach, was that they were considered chiefly in terms of physical categories. The inclination was to look upon the sacraments as but one more application, although in a special manner, of the general laws of cause and effect. Inevitably the result of this view was that we appeared to be merely passive recipients of sacramental grace, which seemed to be 'put into us' automatically.[113]

In place of the older 'mechanistic' understanding of how a sacrament 'worked' – we appeared to be merely passive recipients of sacramental grace – there is now a sacramental theology that reflects the fully personal nature of humanity and the insights this has brought to an interpretation of the incarnation. Just as creation is not the treatise on how the world works – a

---

[112] Ibid.
[113] Ibid.

cosmology – so too sacramental theology is not a description of a mechanistic relation of cause and effect. Grounded in the incarnation, it is the description of human intimacy with God that has been established in the fully personal nature of Christ's humanity. Most particularly, sacramental theology, as encounter between God and humanity, is predicated upon the relation of divine invitation and human response incarnate in Christ: the sacramental encounter between God and humanity reveals humanity's essential vocation to faithfulness.

Schillebeeckx's understanding of the meaning of human life as fundamentally a 'vocation' attests to an anthropology that is at its heart theocentric and christoform. The description of human life as 'vocation' is not something added to an almost self-sufficient account of human nature, as if a philosophical anthropology can take the description of human life only so far and then to this is added, only at the end, a theological postscript. Theocentric anthropology that holds to a Christological structure is an anthropology caught up in describing the 'humanization of the human': the ultimate meaning of humanity is fulfilled in human nature itself. It is not the negation of the human but the fulfilment of the human, according to the nature of what it means to be human.

This is the soteriological and sacramental significance of Schillebeeckx's interpretation of the incarnation – the fully personal manner of Christ' humanity. The anthropological implications of this relation between nature and grace, what Schillebeeckx describes as 'graced nature', come to full expression in his description of the sacramental structure of divine activity within human activity, a description that depends on his interpretation of the incarnation. Incarnation is, for Schillebeeckx, the *zijnsgrond* of humanity that finds its definition in the vocation to intimacy with God. For Schillebeeckx it is possible to speak about the participation of human being in the life of God because it is possible to speak of the divine life – God's saving will – incarnate in the personal freedom and will of Christ: 'because the inward power of Jesus' will to redeem and of his human love is God's own saving power realized in human form, the human saving acts of Jesus are the divine bestowal of grace itself realized in visible form'.[114] Ultimately, in light of this Christology this is what Schillebeeckx's sacramental theology attempts to express: the incarnation of God's call to salvation in the free human response of love.

The sacramental nature of Christ's humanity means nothing less than in Christ's human nature humanity's vocation to intimacy with God has been achieved:

> If the human love and all the human acts of Jesus posses a divine saving power, then the realisation in human shape of this saving power necessarily includes as one of its aspects the manifestation of

---

[114] Ibid. pp. 16–17.

salvation: includes in other words sacramentality. . . . Because the inward power of Jesus' will to redeem and of his human love is God's own saving power realised in human form, the human saving acts of Jesus are the divine bestowal of grace realised in visible form; that is to say they cause what they signify; they are sacraments.[115]

Here the full force of Christ's incarnation as *zijnsgrond* comes to expression. In the incarnation, humanity is defined in a fully creative, salvific, sanctifying, participative and personal relation to God as *filii in Filio*.

In the relation between redemption and the fully personal nature of Christ's humanity – the sacramental reality of human salvation – the fully personal nature of humanity's relation to God is established. This means that humanity is fundamentally defined for Schillebeeckx as *filii in Filio*:

> The result of the redeeming incarnation, as an enduring heavenly reality, is that we are children of the Father in Christ. By the incarnation of his divine life of love, Christ earned for us that his Father should also be our Father, and by the same incarnation, but now through its fulfilment in glory, Christ in actual fact bestows upon us the Spirit which makes us children of the Father, so that we, too, truly are children of the Father. Thus we become by grace what Christ is by nature: Son of God. As *filii in Filio* we are thus caught up in the special providential relationship which holds between the Father and the incarnate Son, and the Father proves himself, in his Son's continual sending of the Holy Spirit, truly our Father all our life long.[116]

The theological definition of humanity is the description of what humanity has become by grace: *filii in Filio*. In other words, the meaning of humanity is conditioned definitively by Christ: 'We become by grace what Christ is by nature'. To understand what Christ is by nature, and logically therefore to understand what humanity has become in grace, means for Schillebeeckx the description of the incarnation, both in 'the incarnation of the divine life of Christ's love' and in the 'fulfilment' of this 'same incarnation now in glory'.

For Schillebeeckx humanity is definitively understood as *filii in Filio*, because we are in grace what Christ is by nature, and this means that the *zijnsgrond* for our redeemed human existence is the enduring redemptive event of incarnation. 'The foundation of all this,' Schillebeeckx maintains, 'is the incarnation', but not incarnation as an isolated moment, rather

---

[115] Ibid. pp. 15–17.
[116] Ibid. p. 39.

incarnation as a 'reality which grows':

> The foundation of all of this is the incarnation. But this incarnation of
> God the Son is a reality which grows. It is not complete in a matter of
> a moment; for example at Jesus' conception in Mary's womb or at his
> birth. The incarnation is not merely a Christmas event. To be man is a
> process of becoming man; Jesus' manhood grew throughout his earthly
> life, finding its completion in the supreme moment of the incarnation,
> his death, resurrection and exaltation. Only then is the incarnation
> fulfilled to the very end. This mystery of Christ or of redemption we
> can call, in its totality, a mystery of saving worship[117]

There are two ideas here with which this chapter will end and this study
will turn towards the final chapter. The first of these is what Schillebeeckx
means by the following: 'The foundation of all of this is the incarnation . . .
this mystery of Christ or of redemption is a mystery of saving worship'. The
second of these ideas is the meaning of, 'This incarnation of God the Son is
a reality which grows . . . finding its supreme moment in death, resurrection
and exultation'. [118] In essence, for Schillebeeckx the incarnation that establishes our human existence as *filii in Filio* is the ultimate revelation of the
intrinsic relation between humanity's metaphysical and moral significance.
Human meaning is defined as both 'that adoration of God for which we are
intended' and the 'radical love of the other in self-emptying'.

These two expressions of the incarnation – Christ's love of the Father and
Christ's love of humanity are related. For Schillebeeckx, the first means simply that in his humanity Christ makes incarnate the perfect love of the Son
for the Father. Christ's human actions are acts of worship and in this he is
the incarnation of the human vocation to adoration of God. Crucially for
Schillebeeckx this perfect love of the Father is expressed in Christ's human
nature. Christ's human actions:

> [Show] their character as acts of worship; these acts are a true adora-
> tion and acknowledgement of God's divine existence . . . in a word they
> are the man Jesus' love of God. Thus Jesus is not only the revelation of
> the redeeming God; he is also the supreme worshipper of the Father.
> Jesus became the redeemer in actual fact by freely living his human life
> in religious worship and attachment to the Father. . . . [I]f we now con-
> sider that this humanity of Jesus represents us all, then it also becomes
> clear . . . that Jesus is the supreme realisation of human love to [the]
> divine offer . . . [t]he foundation of all of this is the incarnation.[119]

---

[117] Ibid. pp. 18–19.
[118] Ibid.
[119] Ibid. p. 18.

By binding together Christ's human adoration of the Father with the events of redemption, Schillebeeckx makes it abundantly clear that if the incarnation is the *zijnsgrond* for human existence then this existence – the human vocation to intimacy with God as *filii in Filio* – is described as adoration or worship. Here the nature of intimacy reflects and coincides with the nature of God as transcendence and difference and at the same time personal. In light of the incarnation, the definition of humanity in relation to the mystery of God – 'I am myself in dependence on God' – leads to a definition of humanity as the vocation to adoration and worship.

The second of these ideas – 'This incarnation of God the Son is a reality which grows . . . finding its supreme moment in death, resurrection and exultation'[120] – indicates the manner in which Schillebeeckx interprets the relation between Christ's love of the Father and Christ's love of humanity. In other words, Christ's passion is the result of his free surrender of self in love of the Father and in love of humanity. This becomes clear from Schillebeeckx's description of the death, resurrection and glorification as the 'supreme moments of the incarnation'. Here, if the incarnation is the *zijnsgrond* for human existence then this existence – the human vocation to intimacy with God as *filii in Filio* – is described as radical love of the other. Here the nature of intimacy reflects and coincides with nature of God as immanent within history. In light of the incarnation, the definition of humanity in relation to the mystery of God – 'I am really myself in of this world, becoming myself more and more therein' – leads to the definition of humanity as the vocation to love of the other. In short, the incarnation establishes humanity's metaphysical and moral significance in an intrinsic relation. Schillebeeckx's description of the death, resurrection and glorification as Christ' human acts of both adoration of God and love of humanity is illustrative of this. Here the centrality of incarnation as the description of the mystery of human redemption comes to the fore.

This incarnation of God the Son is a 'reality which grows . . . finding its supreme moment in death, resurrection and exultation'. This is the key concept which governs Schillebeeckx's sacramental soteriology. 'We can', he suggests, 'distinguish four [moments] of this redemption'.[121] His description of the first 'moment' indicates the relation between trinitarian theology and Christology: the theocentric and Christological character of his theology:

First: The initiative of the Father through the Son in the Holy Spirit. This initiative is the trinitarian background within the Godhead which,

---

[120] Ibid. pp. 18–19.
[121] See Schillebeeckx, *Christus Sacrament*, p. 28. 'In deze verlossing kunnen wij vier momenten onderscheiden.'

though veiled, can be discerned through the temporal order of salvation in the incarnate Son, 'who through the eternal Spirit offered himself without blemish to the Father' (Heb. 9. 14).[122]

There are clear parameters here to Schillebeeckx's Trinitarian theology and these parameters are indicated by the way in which the key terms – trinity, revelation, salvation, temporality, Christology – condition one another. He takes for granted the maxim that the economic and immanent Trinity are the same, hence the reference to the 'Trinitarian background within the Godhead'. Yet theology must remain modest in its Trinitarian doctrine: Trinitarian theology is bound entirely to God's self-revelation within history, 'discerned' only 'through the temporal order of salvation'.

This of course is not to say that revelation exhausts the reality of God. Even God's self-revelation is 'veiled', a situation that Schillebeeckx often describes as a 'mediated immediacy'. God's immanent personal involvement in human history, the *Deus salutaris*, is at the same time God's transcendence and otherness, the *Deus sub ratione Deitatis*. God's aseity and the fundamental dignity of humanity are never in competition. The reference to the inner triune life and to the temporal in the same phrase underlines the consistency with which Schillebeeckx holds together the divine and the human in a non-dualistic, non-reductive and non-competitive relation. The conditioning of these terms by the word 'veiled' suggests that there is a particular relation between these two terms, a relation that is clarified by the soteriological reference, 'the temporal order of salvation in the incarnate Son'. God's salvific activity as it is revealed ultimately in the incarnate Son is normative for the description of the human–divine relation. This points to the eschatological significance of the term 'veiled'. Salvation is both an historical and an eschatological reality in Schillebeeckx's theology.

The 'temporal order of salvation' is described by Schillebeeckx in *Christ the Sacrament* as the dynamic between humiliation and exaltation: 'Jesus' humiliation in the service of God and his heavenly exaltation.' The 'humiliation' is the second 'moment' of the redemptive mystery:

> *Second*: The human response of Christ's life to the Father's initiative in sending him: '… becoming obedient unto death, even to the death of the cross (Phil. 2. 8) – in other words, the religious obedience of the 'Holy One of Yahweh' or the 'Servant of God'.[123]

Christ's human response to the Father is consistently referred to by Schillebeeckx as 'obedience'. It is an obedience that flows from a life centred in Christ's awareness of the Father, a 'religious obedience' that finds

---

[122] Schillebeeckx, *Christ the Sacrament*, p. 20.
[123] Ibid.

expression in self-emptying. This description of religious obedience as self-surrender attests to the particular nature of Christ's relation to the Father: Christ's response to Father is grounded in the relation of trust and love.[124]

It is Christ's obedience and attachment to the Father that are the ground for human salvation. This is the meaning of the cross within Schillebeeckx's Christology. Christ's obedience to the Father is the 'gift of himself to God' as 'essentially an act of love'. Schillebeeckx's Christology is a kenotic Christology. Furthermore, as he suggests in his 'Christological outline' of 1961, the concept of kenosis applies not only to the inner triune life, or only to the moment of suffering and death but to the entire mystery of redemption, 'embracing the whole of Christ's human life'. This is important for Schillebeeckx because he uses the Christological idea of kenosis to describe the personal and human relation between Christ and the Father. He turns to a fuller kenotic Christology, one that stretches from incarnation to exaltation, to redress the balance in the debate between Alexandria and Antioch, a debate that had too long favoured Alexandria.[125] In *Christ the Sacrament* the same kenotic Christology is at play: the redemptive mystery of Christ is found in the humiliation and exaltation. In dispossessing himself of himself, Jesus hallowed himself to the Father in whom he finds his exaltation and glory. Behind all this there lies a mystery of unfathomable depth.[126] In other words, the saving mystery is the relation of humiliation and exaltation between Jesus and the Father.

The second moment of the redemptive mystery, Christ's humiliation, gives way to the third moment:

> *Third*: The divine response to Christ's obedience in the humiliation of his life. 'For which cause also God [i.e. the Father] has exalted him exceedingly and given him a name which is above all names', (Phil. 2. 8) that is, given him might above all powers: Jesus has become the Lord, the *Kyrios*, meaning 'the Mighty,' he who exercises lordship – 'God has made him *Kyrios*.' (Acts 2. 36)[127]

The exaltation of Christ is the Father's response to Christ's self-surrender in obedience. This gives a particular interpretation of Christ's death on the cross in which what is at stake is the loving attachment between Christ and the Father. This is the 'perfection of fidelity', the 'concentration of

---

[124] This description of obedience and self-emptying as attestation of Jesus' relation of trust and love to the Father is equally prevalent in the later *Jesus* books.

[125] Schillebeeckx, 'The New Trends in Present-day Dogmatic Theology', in *Revelation and Theology, II*, pp. 125–126.

[126] Schillebeeckx, *Christ the Sacrament*, p. 27.

[127] Ibid. p. 21.

humanity's vocation to faithfulness' through which Christ becomes the 'embodiment of the grace of the final victory'.

It will become clear from a more extended analysis of Schillebeeckx's understanding of the death of Christ and its place within the redemptive mystery that this is not an attempt to 'spiritualize' the sacrifice of the cross. Rather, it is an attempt to describe 'the visible presence of grace that Christ is personally'; and to describe Christ as grace Schillebeeckx must describe Christ in terms of the relationship between the human and the divine. It is the relationship between Christ and the Father – humiliation and exaltation – which is the prism through which the saving mystery has to be seen if it is to be understood as the final victory of grace. The exaltation by the Father becomes therefore a moment in the redemptive mystery: it establishes the graced reality that is redeemed human existence. That is, Christ, exalted by the Father as Lord, becomes the first-born and head of all of creation and 'consequently the whole of humanity is already, in its head, "assembled" into communion with God'.[128]

From the third 'moment', the exaltation, follows the fourth:

> *Fourth*: The sending of the Holy Spirit upon the world of men by the glorified *Kyrios* or Lord. Christ, 'having reached the consummation [only now] became . . . the source of eternal salvation' for us (Heb. 5.9). The force of the redemption came fully into operation only when Jesus was exalted at God's right hand. 'And I, when I am lifted up . . . will draw all things to myself.' (Jn 12.32) The last phase of the mystery of Christ, between the ascension and the *parousia*, is therefore the mystery of the sending of the Holy Spirit by Christ as the climax of his work of salvation.

The sending of the Spirit, as work of the glorified Christ is the moment in which the full force of redemption is realized: God's response to Christ's humiliation in perfect fidelity is exaltation. From this exaltation follows the sending of the Spirit. The exaltation of Jesus is not simply a statement made by God ratifying the human actions of the Son, although it is this. It is at the same time the definitive statement concerning the hope and promise of human salvation. Christ's exaltation by the Father is the exaltation of all humanity, and this exaltation of humanity is assured, not in the memory of past event, even of the death of Christ. It is assured in the presence of Christ *now*. It is the work of the glorified Christ, the sending of the Spirit, which Schillebeeckx identifies as the climax of the redemptive mystery.

Schillebeeckx's decision to describe the 'temporal order of salvation' as the movement from humiliation to exaltation, and the manner in which he

---

[128] Ibid. p. 13.

develops this description, is the key to understanding how Christology becomes the *zijnsgrond* for theological anthropology. There are two critical features to this description: one is the emphasis placed on the personal humanity of Christ as the *locus* of the perfect human response in fidelity to the divine call to salvation; and the second is the 'enduring nature' of the incarnation which extends to death, resurrection and glorification. In this manner Schillebeeckx identifies the presence of the glorified Christ within human history now with the fully personal actions of the human Christ. In this, the historical and eschatological nature of redemption, and hence of the meaning of human life, are grounded in the person of Christ:

> The Passover brought about a change of emphasis; the Christ *lives* now, at this moment. His glorious body continues to fulfil the function it had during his earthly life. But because this sign of Christ's life-giving redemptive act has become invisible to us, this body of the Lord is prolonged in a form which is visible on earth – in the sacramental Church. In this sense, the church is the prolongation primarily of the heavenly Christ, and therefore it prolongs the function of the earthly body of Jesus. In many a treatise on the church this point is out of perspective, and consequently one is inclined to forget that Christ's 'sitting at the right hand of the Father' was the centre of the primitive Christian faith, which was more a confession of the Christ who lives now than what he had achieved for us in the past, although the latter was the foundation of the former, and in this sense fundamental. Precisely because of this awareness of the presence of the living Christ, the first Christians longed for the fullness of his presence, the *parousia*. 'Christ is the Lord, sitting at God's right hand, is the fundamental confession of faith in both past and future *parousia*.[129]

Quite clearly, for Schillebeeckx, it is the 'enduring mystery of redemption' which is at the heart of Christology, and 'the crux' of humanity's 'definition is precisely' the reality that the 'Christ *lives* now, at this moment'.[130] Theology must be conditioned by 'the primitive confession of faith in the lordship of Jesus, sitting at God's right hand'. Theological anthropology, which defines humanity in relation to the mystery of God who is both transcendence and difference and personal immanence within human history, must be a reflection on the meaning of humanity in relation to 'the Christ who lives now at this moment'. This is what Schillebeeckx means when he describes the exaltation of Christ by the Father as the 'full force of redemption'. Any theological treatise loses perspective if it forgets the centre of the primitive Christian faith: 'the confession of the Christ who lives now'. Theological

---

[129] Ibid. p. 63.
[130] Schillebeeckx, 'Dialogue with God and Christian Secularity', p. 215.

anthropology is a description of humanity in its relation to 'the *Kyrios*, the risen and glorified lord and so also to the Holy Spirit'; hence Christology forms the *zijnsgrond* for anthropology as the 'enduring mystery of redemption', a mystery which is best described by the movement from humiliation to exaltation.

At the centre of Schillebeeckx's Christology and his sacramental theology of salvation history is a particular interpretation of the incarnation: 'the incarnation of God the Son is a reality which grows'. The advantage to this understanding of the incarnation is a Christology that redresses the balance between those Christologies that had too long emphasized the divinity at the expense of the humanity. The personal nature of Christ's humanity is given full scope in Schillebeeckx's Christology without placing the account of Christ's divinity at risk. This gives Schillebeeckx's Christology its full sacramental force and hence it is a Christology that structures theological anthropology. Nowhere perhaps is this expressed more clearly than in the self-emptying of Christ in death. Christ's death in light of the growing reality of incarnation is an act of human freedom and will undertaken in obedience to the Father and in love of humanity. At the centre of Schillebeeckx' interpretation of the death of Christ is the fully personal nature of Christ's humanity and hence the relational nature of his self-emptying. It is this that makes Christ's death salvific: it establishes the dialogue of faithfulness between God and humanity.

Schillebeeckx founds his Christology on a particular understanding of incarnation. This understanding of incarnation as the growth towards the fullness of redemption is considered in detail by turning to its completion:

> We must look closely into this growth towards the fullness of redemption, for in it we are confronted with the mystery of Christ's life, which is this: the man Jesus, as 'Servant of God', by his life of obedience and love on earth, even unto death, earned for us that grace of salvation which he, in glory with the Father, can himself as Lord and Christ, bestow upon us in abundance. This saving reality calls for the closest consideration.[131]

Schillebeeckx begins his description of the growth towards the fullness of redemption by linking together incarnation with Christ's Passover, subsuming the whole of Christ's ministry within this idea of human development: 'Christ's manhood grew throughout his earthly life, finding its completion in the supreme moment of the incarnation, his death, resurrection and exaltation'. By implication Christ's loving obedience to the Father in death stands in continuity with his entire ministry and a lifetime practice of trust and attachment to the Father.

---

[131] Schillebeeckx, *Christ the Sacrament*, pp. 19–20.

This is exactly the implication that gives way to lengthy and full description of Jesus' ministry in the later *Jesus* books. In *Christ the Sacrament,* it is present only by implication, yet Schillebeeckx's understanding of the meaning of the Passover of Jesus, the death and resurrection, is consistent between his early and later Christology. In both *Christ the Sacrament* and *Jesus* the death of Jesus stands in continuity with his life: it is the free obedience and fidelity to the Father even in accepting death that is essential to the redemptive event, and the Father's response to this fidelity is resurrection. Schillebeeckx describes this as the 'fundamental *credo* of the primitive church: we have killed Jesus of Nazareth, but God has raised him to life again.'[132]

'We have killed Jesus of Nazareth'. Schillebeeckx interprets this death of Jesus as a sacrifice insofar as it was a free act of love. He neither spiritualizes Christ's death – 'we are redeemed *in sanguine*, through the blood of Christ, this we find on almost every page of scripture' – nor does he attribute saving significance to death as such – 'this gift of himself to God was essentially an act of love'.[133] Death for Schillebeeckx, even Christ's death in itself, can only be negative. It is the fact that Christ's attachment to the Father embraces even death which allows death 'an essential part to play in the redemptive event'

Because of Christ's free acceptance of it, death has an essential part to play in the redemptive event. For the incarnation through which we are redeemed is not something that was complete all in one instant. It embraces the whole human life of Christ, including his death. And in this human life, and thus also in this death, Christ lives his sonship of the Father in fidelity and loving attachment to the Father.[134]

Insofar as Christ's death is described as the Son's self-surrender to the Father in perfect fidelity, Schillebeeckx can speak of Christ's death as sacrifice: 'there was indeed the act of love, but it was embodied in the sacrifice of blood'.[135] For the same reason Schillebeeckx can speak of death as playing an essential part in the redemptive event.

Christ's death is a sacrifice of reconciliation because it is perfect fidelity. This is what Schillebeeckx has in mind when he describes Christ as the concentration of the human vocation to faithfulness.[136] It is Christ' fidelity that reinstates the covenant with God:

At the Last Supper, Christ clearly gave his death the significance of a sacrifice of himself to God for all. This gift of himself to God was essentially an act of love. But this was realised and embodied in the

---

[132] Ibid. p. 22.
[133] Ibid. pp. 21–22.
[134] Ibid. p. 22.
[135] Ibid.
[136] Ibid. p. 13.

death he suffered at the hands of sinful humanity. He offered himself sacrificially for us to the Father, and the particular way in which this came to completion was by laying down his life. The words of interpretation which Scripture uses in connection with the bread and wine show us Christ's approaching death as a true sacrifice of reconciliation that reinstates the covenant with God. . . . This death sanctifies mankind, reconciles, establishes peace, redeems, constitutes the Church, and therefore unites man in communion with God and his fellow men.[137]

Christ's death as the ultimate expression of fidelity 'reinstates' the covenant with God and in this reconciliation in faithfulness humanity is sanctified. 'God's ultimate purpose', on Schillebeeckx's account, 'was to call a faithful people to life'. That this ultimate purpose is revealed and accomplished in the manner of Christ's fidelity – 'the particular way in which this came to completion was by laying down his life' – establishes certain parameters within which it is possible to describe the human vocation to faithfulness – the life of sanctified and redeemed humanity. For Schillebeeckx it is through the incarnation that we are redeemed, and this has anthropological implications. Most particularly, it has implications for the theological appraisal of human bodiliness, contingency, and historicity.

For Schillebeeckx the description of the vocation to be human as the vocation to faithfulness cannot be spiritualized. The vocation to faithfulness is embodied, contingent and historical. This follows for him quite simply from the fact that the incarnation is a redemptive event. Christ's fidelity as attachment to the Father even in death is an act of love. Yet 'it is impossible' to understand this love as 'merely' an 'internal act'. It is incarnate love, 'embodied in the sacrifice of blood'. The emphasis on incarnation within his description of the redemptive event makes it impossible for Schillebeeckx to accede to a dualistic anthropology in which body and spirit, worship and ethics and ultimately, history and eschatology, can be separated. Because he holds that 'the incarnation through which we are redeemed embraces the whole human life of Christ, including his death', human life in its entirety, in its bodiliness, contingency and temporality, is embraced, not sidestepped, in the vocation to faithfulness.

The arena in which the redemptive event is enacted is human history. Christ, in the fully personal nature of his humanity, as a 'situated freedom', lives 'his sonship of the Father in fidelity and loving attachment to the Father'. Christ's 'acceptance of death is a free act' and because it is a free act, 'death has an essential part to play' in the redemptive event. 'Christ as free man', lives out his life and his death in 'loving attachment to the Father'.

---

[137] Ibid. pp. 21–22.

In Christ's attachment to the Father even in death, humanity as a situated freedom is redeemed. Sanctified humanity is not humanity 'in spite of' the situated nature of our freedom, rather, sanctified humanity is humanity 'because of' the situated nature of our freedom. Embodiment, finitude, and contingency are not the stumbling blocks between humanity and God. This is not what is overcome in the reinstatement of the covenant. What is overcome is infidelity, replaced now by the possibility of holding fast to the vocation to fidelity in the midst of finitude and contingency. Resurrection for Schillebeeckx, and its relation to the death of Christ and to the sending of the Spirit and promise of the *parousia*, heightens this understanding of the vocation to human faithfulness as the vocation to attachment to God *in*, and not *in spite of*, embodiment, finitude and contingency.

The sacramental reality of redemption and hence the sacramental nature of humanity does not end for Schillebeeckx's theology with the death of Christ. Indeed, in Schillebeeckx's Christology the personal nature of Christ's incarnation does not end with death – it reaches its completion in resurrection and glorification. However Schillebeeckx cautions against speaking of resurrection 'too soon': resurrection is not the consequence of Christ's death; it is the consequence of Christ's perfect faithfulness lived in complete self-emptying – adoration of God and love of humanity. In order then, not to speak of resurrection 'too soon', this chapter ends with Christ's death. The topics of resurrection and glorification are taken up in the following chapter and these in turn set up the conclusion of this study: redemption in light of resurrection and glorification – the recapitulation of creation – and the meaning of human action in light of this sacramental reality.

171

4

RESURRECTION AND
HUMAN BEING

Introduction

Schillebeeckx's treatment of the resurrection in *Christ the Sacrament* is very brief: resurrection is 'the sacrifice of the Cross heard and answered by the Father.'[1] Resurrection is ultimately a statement of God's absolute fidelity to humanity. It is ratification of human life lived as absolute trust and radical love. In essence, resurrection is the most profound expression of the truth that the 'infinite is disclosed in the finite without destroying it'.[2] In more Christological and hence personal language, 'God gives man an insight into his own conditions . . . God reveals man to himself precisely as revealing himself as love to man'.[3] In other words, resurrection is not the negation or the reversal of death. This is a point underlined quite starkly in one of Schillebeeckx's sermons: 'I believe in the resurrection of the body':

> Christian belief in the resurrection gives us something to think about: this is a resurrection of *dead* people. Death is presupposed by belief in the resurrection. This may seem a trivial observation, but it has far-reaching implications. Belief in the resurrection does not argue away the fact of death; it allows death to be death, a radical and definitive ending to the particular historical existence of a human being,

---

[1] Schillebeeckx, *Christ the Sacrament of the Encounter with God* (London: Sheed and Ward, 1963), p. 32.

[2] Schillebeeckx, 'What is Theology?', in *Revelation and Theology, I : Revelation, Tradition and Theological Reflection*, 2nd ed. (London: Sheed and Ward, 1987), p. 109.

[3] Schillebeeckx, 'Christian Faith and Man's Expectation for the Future on Earth', in *The Mission of the Church*, p. 54.

for good. The dead never return to our history; that is and remains definitively past time.[4]

Resurrection is not the negation of human finitude. Schillebeeckx's theology of resurrection is consistent with his understanding of the nature grace relation and consistent with his theology of revelation: resurrection is the fulfilment of the human without negating it. It is the ultimate expression of this – it 'does not argue away the fact of death'. For Schillebeeckx this means it does not argue away the 'radical and definitive ending' of human historical existence. It is instead, the clearest expression of human dependence upon God that cannot be divorced from the definition of human meaning within history. Resurrection is the ultimate consummation of what it means to be human both as absolute dependence upon God: 'I am myself in dependence on God', and as a situated freedom: 'I am really myself in and of this world, becoming myself more and more therein'.[5]

Resurrection: Incarnation and Glorification

For theological anthropology, resurrection, and Schillebeeckx's understanding of this in relation to the meaning of death, reveals the full consequence of the mystery of humanity in relation to the mystery of God. What is at stake in a theology of the resurrection for Schillebeeckx is the completely free and gracious nature of God's fidelity, the tension between immanence and transcendence, between the God who 'comes close to humanity' yet is utter difference. Resurrection is a statement concerning God's 'closeness to humanity' that can only be described as 'grace' – 'free and unmerited':

> I want to confess that I have seldom found any sermon as difficult to write as this one, about the resurrection of the body. Not because I have doubts about it; for me it is an evidence of Christian faith, without which any expression of the heart of Christianity would be utopian. But I feel almost painfully helpless in trying to communicate this evidence of faith in any sense, trying to make it understandable as the incomprehensible, unmerited, free consequence of God's utter

---

[4] Schillebeeckx, 'I Believe in the Resurrection of the Body', in *God among Us. The Gospel Proclaimed* (London: SCM, 1983), p. 131. This sermon was first published: 'Ik geloof in de verrijzenis van het lichaam', *Tijdschrift voor Geestelijk Leven* 28 (1972), 435–451.

[5] Edward Schillebeeckx, 'Dialogue with God and Christian Secularity', in *God and Man*, trans. Edward Fitzgerald and Peter Tomlinson (London: Sheed and Ward, 1969), p. 215.

trustworthiness. It is risky for us human beings to talk in this way about the consequence of divine trustworthiness. If we do, we are acting as though we can know what may be a consequence for God.[6]

Schillebeeckx's reticence to embark on a speculative theology of resurrection echoes his reticence to embark on any speculative description of the nature of God that does not follow closely upon God's self-revelation. Resurrection is a statement about the nature of God: God's self-revelation as divine trustworthiness. This is what he means by 'an evidence of Christian faith'. At the heart of Christian faith is the utter trustworthiness of God revealed in the relation between Jesus and the Father. In both his early and later Christology, Schillebeeckx consistently describes the relation between Jesus and the Father as one of trust: Jesus' lifelong attachment in trust to the Father even in humiliation and death and the Father's faithfulness that redeems this lifelong trust in resurrection and exaltation. This relation of trust is the relation between Christ's personal human freedom and God's absolute graciousness – the relation between humiliation and exaltation.

Set within this relational context of trust between the Father and Jesus, Schillebeeckx develops a theology of resurrection in which resurrection is not a 'consequence' of death, even of Jesus' death. It is, insofar as it is a 'consequence' of anything, a 'consequence' of God's very nature. Resurrection is the 'incomprehensible, unmerited, free consequence of God's utter trustworthiness'. In other words, at its heart, Schillebeeckx's doctrine of the resurrection is grounded in a theological realism. The resurrection is an event of God that is consistent with God's very nature. Furthermore, the importance of the particularity of this event is also clear to Schillebeeckx.

The resurrection of Jesus is an event that happens to Jesus and because it is an event that happens to Jesus, it is an event that has happened for humanity as promise. Two things can be noted here in passing. First, Schillebeeckx's theological realism clearly rests on the understanding that the *Deus sub ratione Deitatis* is revealed by the *Deus salutaris*. That is to say, God's nature is not exhausted in God's self-revelation. Schillebeeckx holds to an

---

[6] Schillebeeckx, 'I Believe in the Resurrection of the Body', p. 130. Schillebeeckx's use of the term 'utopia' in this sermon is a development in vocabulary that postdates *Christ the Sacrament*. However, it reflects a career-long preoccupation with the relation between human striving and divine fulfilment. This preoccupation is found in his earlier work in the contrast between heroic and humble humanism. See Schillebeeckx, 'Humble Humanism' in *World and Church*. In this sermon and in the Christology books that follow, this preoccupation is located in the contrast between utopia and the eschatological kingdom of God. In *Christ the Sacrament* it is found in the relation between Christ the primordial sacrament and the sacramental life of humanity in the world. Consistently, through each change of vocabulary or paradigm, at the heart of this preoccupation is the relation of trust between humanity and God. This is the ground of authentic hope.

appreciation of 'mystery' and the proper place for 'silence' within theology. Yet God does not contradict God's self in revelation. In revelation 'God takes God's identity seriously'. Secondly, Schillebeeckx's theological realism holds to a certain Christological realism: God's self-revelation, and hence theology, has a Christological structure. With respect to the resurrection of Jesus, this Christological realism is sustained for Schillebeeckx in his doctrine of incarnation in which incarnation and resurrection are held together in the redemptive event of God. Schillebeeckx's theology of resurrection hinges on the manner in which he develops the relation between incarnation and resurrection.

Schillebeeckx makes a series of moves within his Christology that are significant to the development of his theology of resurrection. Each of these moves underlines the extent to which he understands resurrection as a revelation of the nature of God and of the nature of humanity in light of its relation to God. In Schillebeeckx's Christology, resurrection is described as the relation of trust between the divine and the human and not described as 'a consequence of death'. Resurrection is the revelation of God's graciousness, that is, resurrection reveals divine freedom as the ground of human salvation. Hence the manner in which Schillebeeckx develops his theology of resurrection is particularly significant for a theological anthropology because it points both to the nature of God and to the nature of God's intervention within human history. Consequently, it highlights Schillebeeckx's characteristic concern to describe divine intervention in a manner that safeguards the dignity of human freedom and which, at the same time, expresses the reality of God's salvific relation to humanity. The moves made by Schillebeeckx in developing his understanding of resurrection carry especial anthropological freight for him because in describing the nature of God he is, at the same time, describing the nature of humanity. The identity of the divine and the consequent identity of the human are inseparable within his theology.

The first of these moves that points to the development of Schillebeeckx's understanding of resurrection has already been alluded to: it is his insistence that the resurrection must be understood in the context of a lifelong relation of trust between the Father and Jesus. Resurrection is not a 'consequence' of Jesus' death, rather it is a 'consequence' of the relation between Father and Son. In this particular sense, it is not the establishment of a new relation but divine ratification of the relationship to which Jesus has been faithful throughout the lifelong process of becoming human. Here again Schillebeeckx's understanding of the incarnation as an event of long duration – 'Jesus' humanity grew throughout his earthly life, finding its completion in the supreme moment of the incarnation, his death, resurrection and exaltation' – is a strength.[7] It provides Schillebeeckx with a description of divine

---

[7] Schillebeeckx, *Christ the Sacrament*, p. 19.

intervention within human history that is both ultimate – there are clear eschatological implications – and that at the same time leaves human freedom within history intact. This work is done for Schillebeeckx by the concept of 'person': the 'personal' nature of the relation between Father and Son reveals the personal nature of God's relation to humanity.

Schillebeeckx's doctrine of incarnation seeks to give full expression to the personal nature of Jesus' humanity. In *Christ the Sacrament*, Schillebeeckx announces this fundamental principle of his Christology that comes later to a much lengthier description in *Jesus*: 'We must look closely into this growth towards the fullness of redemption, for in it we are confronted with the mystery of Christ's life'.[8] By describing the 'mystery of Christ's life' as the 'growth towards redemption', Schillebeeckx indicates that the mystery of Christ's life embraces both human history and the eschaton. Redemption is in history, and it is beyond history as its fulfilment. This is made even clearer by his expansion upon what he means by the mystery of Christ's life: 'the man Jesus, as "Servant of God," by his life of obedience and love on earth, even unto death, earned for us that grace of salvation which he, in glory with the Father, can himself as Lord and Christ bestow upon us in abundance.'[9]

The mystery of Christ's life reveals the personal nature of God's intervention in human history and therefore indicates the nature of the relation between human history and divine fulfilment of this same history:

> According to scripture, the resurrection is an event which is indissolubly bound up with Jesus, whose death was an apparent farce, seen as the historical end-result of his life of trust in God. This trust does not seem to have been justified. But belief in the resurrection of Jesus then says that while the whole of Jesus' life may seem a fiasco, it nevertheless bears God's seal of approval. The reason why in the view of scripture this is no *deus ex machina* is that God does not just become faithful to himself, to this Jesus and to all creation after Jesus' death; he already *was* faithful, albeit tacitly, in Jesus' life and death. Through the resurrection God simply confirms his trust and trustworthiness in which Jesus continued to believe. The resurrection is the divine confirmation of the validity and rightness of Jesus' life and message. The resurrection confirms that God always was with Jesus right through his life, even in the desolation of his crucifixion. The resurrection is not a comforting rescue afterwards. It is the free consequence of God's trust.[10]

'Belief in the resurrection' is for Schillebeeckx not the undoing of history or even its explanation. Belief in the resurrection is belief in the nature of

---

[8] Ibid.
[9] Ibid.
[10] Schillebeeckx, 'I Believe in the Resurrection of the Body', p. 134.

God. At the same time it is a statement about the nature of human history. Because of its Christological structure, the infinite is revealed in the finite without destroying it. Human history remains 'ambiguous', yet its ambiguity is not indicative of divine absence. Human history is fulfilled not in a divine rescue after death. This would render history and human freedom meaningless. Rather, human history is fulfilled as a 'free consequence of God's trust'. The continuity between history and eschatology is grounded in God's nature – 'God does not just become faithful to himself, to this Jesus and to all creation' after death, even Jesus' death. God's sovereign freedom is present in history as divine faithfulness. Hence for Schillebeeckx Jesus' death, the 'desolation' of crucifixion, is not divine absence but silence. 'People talk about the *word* of God as revelation, but through Jesus I am taught that God has revealed himself through *silence*'.[11] Divine silence and not divine absence leaves human history intact precisely in revealing divine faithfulness. Divine silence has a Christological structure for Schillebeeckx: it is the mode of the Father's identification with Jesus. Schillebeeckx describes the Father's identification with Jesus as the revelation of both divine fidelity and divine freedom. Resurrection is neither the negation of death nor the consequence of death and hence resurrection is both a 'human' event and an event of divine freedom.

The second move that underlines Schillebeeckx's insight that resurrection is not understood as a 'consequence' of death is his description of redemption as a 'progressive action'.[12] This illustrates again the extent to which his doctrine of incarnation shapes his Christology:

> The incarnation of Christ is not something static. Christ's redeeming action, though a single reality, grows and develops so that, in the context of his whole life, we can distinguish in it three principal elements: (a) his death and descent into hell; (b) the resurrection from the dead; (c) his glorification or his being established by the Father as Lord and thus sender of the Holy Spirit.[13]

By describing redemption as a 'progressive action' Schillebeeckx is able to articulate redemption as one event, which nevertheless has discrete 'moments'. Thus resurrection is a 'moment' in this event that is distinct from the death of Jesus. The distinct nature of these 'moments' is most significantly underscored by the description of the action of death and of resurrection or more specifically by the description of agency in these two events: 'We have killed Jesus of Nazareth, but God has raised him to life again'.[14] The death of Jesus

---

[11] Ibid. p. 135.
[12] Schillebeeckx, *Christ the Sacrament*, p. 24.
[13] Ibid.
[14] Ibid. p. 22.

is the consequence of sin, the 'utmost effort of sinful humanity to stamp out all that is godly in the world'; resurrection is the consequence of God's fidelity to humanity in spite of this ultimate unfaithfulness. The distinct nature of these 'moments' is also underscored by the passage of time between death and resurrection that Schillebeeckx alludes to by reference to Christ's descent into hell.

Predictably, Schillebeeckx does not have a speculative theology of the descent into hell, and it is acknowledged only in passing. It does serve however to draw attention to the passage of time between death and resurrection. For Schillebeeckx, this is significant because it highlights the distinct nature of the events of death and resurrection. Christian belief in the resurrection is entirely predicated upon God's activity in raising Jesus from the dead. Yet to understand the meaning of the resurrection, and therefore to understand the meaning of Jesus' death, it is important not to speak of the resurrection 'too soon':

> I think that the death of one of us, the historical Jesus of Nazareth, can offer us a perspective on this particular dilemma; light comes, however, not from Jesus himself but from the one whom he called 'God and Father'. There was something special about the death of this man who nevertheless died a death like so many others; a violent, inhuman death, the execution of an innocent person. Of course here too we can mention Jesus' resurrection too soon, so that it becomes a kind of *deus ex machina*. But anyone who looks more closely can see that here there is no desperate expedient, no solution at all, but a deep belief in God.[15]

There are two points made here about the nature of Jesus' death, and in both cases it is important not to speak of resurrection 'too soon'. The first point is that Jesus' death is a human death. It is not the particular historical circumstances of his death, the violence or injustice reflected in the death of an innocent person, which makes his death unique. The simply human nature of Jesus' death, death that is both particular to Jesus and universal to human experience, is emphasized by Schillebeeckx in his hesitation to speak of the resurrection 'too soon'. He draws attention to the reality of Jesus' death as an event independent of the resurrection by referring to 'the dead Jesus': 'The physical resurrection is the eternally new event of God himself who identifies himself with the dead Jesus'.[16]

However, if the first point to be made about Jesus' death here is that it is simply a human death and therefore common to us all, the second point is that his death is unique and therefore redemptive – 'There was something special about the death of this man who nevertheless died a death like so

---

[15] Schillebeeckx, 'I Believe in the Resurrection of the Body', p. 132.
[16] Ibid. p. 135.

many others'. The uniqueness of this death is found not in the death itself but in God, in the relation between Jesus and the Father: 'Light comes not from Jesus himself but from the one whom he called God and Father'.[17] Jesus' death in itself was not 'necessary' to reinstate the Covenant. What was necessary was Jesus' obedience, grounded in trust and loving attachment to the Father even in death. This divine–human relation of fidelity is the relation between the two events of death and resurrection. In this sense Jesus' death offers us a perspective on the dilemma of what ultimately remains an ambiguous human event. Death remains a 'radical and definitive ending to a particular historical existence'. Death is presupposed in resurrection; this holds for the death and resurrection of Jesus, a reality that Schillebeeckx highlights by drawing attention, if only in passing, to the passage of time between death and resurrection. The light that is shed on the human predicament of death is shed not by death itself but by resurrection, by the ultimate expression of the trust that grounds the divine–human relation. The descent into hell underlines the passage in time between death and resurrection, and in doing this, it serves to underline the human and therefore universal nature of Jesus' death. In the same manner it also serves to underscore the fundamental uniqueness and particularity of the death and resurrection of Jesus. Schillebeeckx's understanding of the relation between the death and resurrection of Jesus reveals his understanding of redemption and hence indicates what he means by human existence in the light of redemption

Jesus' death and resurrection is unique and particular as a redemptive event. Christ's Passover is 'our actual redemption':

> The Passover is the mystery of Jesus' loving attachment to the Father unto death itself; it is the fidelity to the Father of the Son made man despite the condition proper to fallen humanity in which he had found himself because of our sinfulness. But at the same time it is the mystery of the divine response to this loving fidelity; the answer of divine mercy to the sacrifice of love, and the nullifying or destruction of the power of sin: the resurrection.[18]

Resurrection, as God's act of faithfulness in response to Jesus' lifelong fidelity, is an act of judgement. In Schillebeeckx's Christology, which places emphasis on the personal reality of Jesus' human nature through the idea of incarnation as an event that progresses through life, death and resurrection, Jesus' death is received by the Father in light of his lifelong fidelity. Resurrection is thus a judgement that destroys the power of sin: 'The Passover is the expression of the "*Ego vici mundum*", "I have overcome the world"'.[19]

---

[17] Ibid. p. 132.
[18] Schillebeeckx, *Christ the Sacrament*, p. 23
[19] Ibid. p. 22.

Hence resurrection is 'the answer of divine mercy' to the entirety of Jesus' life, which culminates in the ultimate 'sacrifice of love'.

The nullifying of the power of sin is a gracious act. It takes place within the dialogue of invitation and response: the invitation to fidelity and the response of perfect fidelity. There is an eschatological tension for Schillebeeckx here: we are 'redeemed' and we are 'on the way to redemption'. Sin has been judged and its power nullified and yet we still face judgement after death, judgement in grace that is the ultimate expression of God's sovereign freedom in relation to each individual human life:

> Scripture says: 'God raised up Jesus.' God did it and his action was specifically concerned with Jesus, and not, for example, with the two others who were crucified with him: on that day there were eventually three dead bodies on Golgotha. Despite the way in which death makes all men equal, God, at least, does not look on the death of everyone in the same way, but sees it in the light of the life preceding that death. If he is not a God who is concerned for mankind, the death of each person indeed has the last word and that fate cynically awaits everyone without exception. If he is a living God, then God's divinity in supreme freedom is the last word over each and every human history. This does not imply that resurrection necessarily follows of itself. But it shows how resurrection must be understood as the free gift of God.[20]

For Schillebeeckx the resurrection of Christ, in its uniqueness and its particularity, reveals and establishes the particularity of each human person in relation to God. Resurrection is a personal event – resurrection is God's response to each particular, personal and historical life preceding death. In this relation of particularity resurrection is both an eschatological and historical event. Human 'identity' is not negated in God's self-revelation as the future of humanity.

The particularity of resurrection is central to Schillebeeckx's interpretation of resurrection. Resurrection is redemption as the 'eternally new event of God himself who identifies himself with the dead Jesus'.[21] In resurrection Jesus is established as the Christ of history: 'Let all the house of Israel know most certainly that God has made both Lord and Christ this same Jesus whom you have crucified.'[22] Resurrection is God's judgement over all past history: Christ's descent into hell; and over all present history: Christ's glorification and the sending of the Spirit; and over all future history: the promise of the *parousia*.

In the resurrection, then, as the eternally enduring act of salvation, there is also included Christ's ascension and establishment as Lord, the sending of

---

[20] Ibid. p.134.
[21] Ibid. p. 135.
[22] Schillebeeckx, *Christ the Sacrament*, p. 22.

the Holy Spirit that is Christ's actual exercise of lordship and to a certain extent the *parousia* as well. In their essential core, all these together form the single enduring mystery of salvation: the person of the humiliated and glorified Christ who is the saving reality.[23]

Christ's Passover is our 'actual redemption' as an 'eternally enduring act of salvation'. 'Actual' and 'eternal' capture the eschatological tension within Schillebeeckx's Christology. This eschatological tension reflects something of the tension that Schillebeeckx understands to obtain between the God who has intervened decisively in human history and the God who 'will not intervene in history'.

Resurrection is an event of 'actual redemption' for Schillebeeckx. This is made very clear for him in his description of the particularity and uniqueness of Jesus' resurrection. The difference is the difference between 'utopian daydreams' and the creedal confession of faith:

> Jesus' death compels us to raise the question of God because of the life which preceded it. On the cross, revelation, reconciliation and faith come together, unless with Jesus we also reject his God. This brings us to the significance of the physical resurrection of Jesus. For without this resurrection Jesus of Nazareth is one of many utopias in which mankind abounds and which in fact can supply the strength by which we can take hold of life despite everything, and work for others with more commitment and more courage – at least as long as this commitment is not overwhelmed by actual death. The fact of death then makes what is definitively good a utopia. It is different with the resurrection, which is something radically other than the projection of a utopian daydream. First of all, Jesus' resurrection is not a return to life as in the story of Lazarus. Nor is it simply to be identified as the origin of Christian belief; it is not simply a miracle of intervention in natural laws to raise a corpse to heavenly life. Of course the creed does not say, 'I believe in the resurrection of a dead body or a corpse' but, 'I believe in the resurrection of the body, eternal life'.[24]

Behind Schillebeeckx's theology of resurrection is a quietly confident theological realism. It is a new event of God – not the returning to life of Lazarus. It is an eternal event – Christ is raised in glory and as Lord of history. It is a redemptive event – 'in and through Christ's rising from the dead, God himself has called the "new earth" into being in this world'.[25] But it is each of these things – new, eternal, redemptive – because it is God's event. In the sermon, 'I believe in the resurrection of the body', Schillebeeckx asks,

---

[23] Ibid. pp. 22–23.
[24] Schillebeeckx, 'I Believe in the Resurrection of the Body', p. 134.
[25] Schillebeeckx, *Christ the Sacrament*, p. 22.

'What is the resurrection?' His response suggests that his reluctance to engage in speculative descriptions of the mechanics of the resurrection of the body – 'The gain represented by functional thinking is in fact accompanied by a loss in the question of meaning'[26] – is not the measure of his theological realism, quite the opposite in fact. 'In that case, what is the resurrection? Scripture says "God raised up Jesus". God did it and his action was specifically concerned with Jesus.'[27]

Resurrection is the fulfilment of the human, but not as an explanation which makes human life meaningful nor as an explanation which gives any positive interpretation of death. It is the fulfilment of the human because it is first of all a statement about God:

> It is not even as if in the last resort we could think meaningfully about our human existence without belief in the resurrection. Evidently many people can do precisely this, and why should our thought be more logical and more consistent than theirs? So something completely different is at stake in belief in the resurrection: belief in God. Paul connects God's demand and desire to be all in all with our resurrection (1 Cor. 15.28). Thus the resurrection is first of all a question of God, of God who takes his identity seriously. Only in this way, and not otherwise, is the resurrection also a question of the identity of our humanity and its ultimate meaning.[28]

To say that resurrection is not 'explanation' is not to say that Schillebeeckx does not believe in the resurrection, an interpretation sometimes made mistakenly in the wake of his *Jesus* book. Quite the opposite in fact: it is the measure by which Schillebeeckx takes seriously the soteriological context in which it is possible to speak of resurrection at all. In this context, 'the question of the identity of our humanity and its ultimate meaning' is predicated upon 'the question of God, of God who takes his identity seriously'.

Schillebeeckx underscores this even further by drawing a comparison between the doctrines of *creatio ex nihilo* and the final consummation of creation, and the doctrine of the resurrection:

> In the wider context of salvation in which resurrection is set, the question 'What really happened when Jesus rose?' is almost misplaced, as misplaced as the question of just how in particular the creation of everything from nothing in fact 'took place', or the world will end. As a believer, I just do not know.[29]

[26] Schillebeeckx, 'I Believe in the Resurrection of the Body', p. 131.
[27] Ibid. p. 134.
[28] Ibid. p. 130.
[29] Ibid. p. 137.

Just as a theology of creation is not a cosmology, so too a theology of the resurrection is not a description of life after death. Resurrection, like creation, in light of the sacramental reality of the incarnation, is a relational and therefore ontological term, not an explanatory term. It is a term concerned with identity: the identity of God and the identity of humanity.

Resurrection is concerned with the identity of both the divine and the human as given in salvation history. This concern with the 'identity' of the human raises the question of embodiment. To sidestep this question would be to surrender to a dualistic understanding of the human as body and soul. Because soteriology has a Christological structure such a dualistic understanding of human being is impossible. Salvation, quite simply, 'is promised to the whole man and not just to his soul.'[30] Here again the strengths of Schillebeeckx's Christology – his insistence on the incarnation as the redemptive event, his understanding of the personal nature of Jesus' humanity and his resistance to those Christologies which emphasize the divinity at the expense of the humanity – are so significant. Because of the nature of his Christology, theology is also anthropology:

> It has always struck me that the Greeks have criticised Christianity for being a *genos philosomaton*, i.e. a kind of people who attach too much importance to corporeality. The first fierce reaction of Christians against a misunderstanding of Jesus was directed against docetism, i.e. the view of those who thought that since Jesus was God's Son, it was impossible for him really to have been a corporeal human being like you or me. Here man prescribes for God what is thought to be compatible with God's majesty and in the end fails to understand himself. For what can human consummation ultimately mean for human beings if it leaves out the corporeality which is so familiar to us? In that case I am no longer 'I', and this 'I' has not achieved definitive salvation.[31]

Within Schillebeeckx's theology on the whole, and as a result of his Christology, God's majesty and the identity of humanity coincide. The relation between divine and human is not competitive because God's majesty is revealed in salvation: human consummation does not contradict or threaten divine glory, rather God's glory is revealed precisely in human consummation. Furthermore, human identity itself is revealed and not negated in the manner of its consummation. In other words, to understand God's majesty is to understand the nature of humanity, and to understand the consummation of humanity is to understand God's majesty. This is the logical consequence of the soteriological manner of God's self-revelation.

[30] Ibid.
[31] Ibid. p. 138.

For Schillebeeckx, the resurrection reveals the reality of God's nature as transcendence – God's majesty – and it reveals the nature of humanity in relation to divine transcendence. Divine transcendence is constitutive of humanity: 'For what can human consummation ultimately mean for human beings if it leaves out corporeality . . . in that case I am no longer 'I', and this 'I' has not achieved salvation'.[32] Resurrection, in other words, is the consummation of the human–divine relation that is creative, salvific, sanctifying, participative and personal. It is the consummation of the relation that is constitutive of the meaning of human life, and hence it is the consummation of human identity. '"I" have achieved salvation' means for Schillebeeckx that 'I am myself in absolute dependence upon God; and I am really myself in and of the world, becoming myself more and more therein'.[33] Resurrection, as a 'moment' of Christ's incarnation, establishes human identity in its consummation.

Within Schillebeeckx's Christology, resurrection is 'the sacrifice of the Cross heard and answered by the Father.'[34] Because the 'sacrifice of the Cross' is understood to be the fidelity with which Jesus lives out the whole of his human life, including death, in 'loving attachment to the Father', resurrection is the Father's definitive approbation of this fidelity and hence of human historical existence. In other words, resurrection as a 'moment' within the redemptive mystery of Christ belongs to the *zijnsgrond* from which a theological description of human existence follows. Resurrection belongs to the event of redemption. It is both a statement about God's self-revelation as absolute fidelity and the establishment of the human vocation to faithfulness within the midst of what it means to be human. Resurrection is not redemption as the negation of human embodiment, contingency or finitude but redemption through embodiment, contingency and finitude. Implicit in this is a particular understanding of human sinfulness and a particular understanding of the relation between resurrection, Christ's glorification and eschatology. Resurrection, as the 'eternally enduring act of salvation', is a statement both of what we have been redeemed 'from', and the promise of what we are redeemed 'to'. Here Schillebeeckx describes resurrection as an event that is constitutive of both humanity's 'metaphysical' and 'moral' significance.

Schillebeeckx's interpretation of the resurrection indicates that the resurrection is the consummation of humanity in manner that consummates both our moral and metaphysical significance:

> Understanding and trusting God on the basis of Jesus' life and death, that is, looking through Jesus to God means coming to terms with our own incompleteness, with the character of our existence which is not justified

---

[32] Ibid.
[33] Schillebeeckx, 'Dialogue with God and Christian Secularity', p. 215.
[34] Schillebeeckx, *Christ the Sacrament*, p. 32.

and reconciled. A Christian who believes in the resurrection is therefore freed from the pressure to justify himself. . . . Like Jesus, the Christian dares to entrust himself and the justification for his life to God; he is prepared to receive this justification only where Jesus did: beyond death.[35]

With resurrection the relation between our metaphysical and moral significance becomes clearer in Schillebeeckx's theology. Resurrection is the sanctification of our human historical existence. It establishes the human freedom *from* 'the pressure to justify' ourselves and this, in Schillebeeckx's interpretation, establishes the freedom and the responsibility *to* live now in history in a particular manner. 'Like Jesus, the Christian dares to entrust himself and the justification for his life to God'.[36] For Schillebeeckx this reality – 'like Jesus' must be interpreted in light of the incarnation.

For Schillebeeckx, the incarnation means that Jesus' self-emptying – his humiliation – and his exaltation are 'moments' of the same redemptive event. This has clear implications for the interpretation of the meaning of human life.

> Therefore because [the Christian] is reconciled with the way of God's action, he is also reconciled with himself, with others and with history; he can forgo utopias, violence and cruelty and devote himself completely to improving this world as far as is possible, and making it a more just and happier world for everyone, for a happy and peaceful world is in fact God's deepest intention which he confirms for eternity in the resurrection. Thus the Christian believing in the resurrection lives unprotected and unguarded, defenceless and vulnerable, like Jesus on the cross. [37]

Human self-emptying as radical love of the other is, in Schillebeeckx's theology, 'the final consequence of the incarnation'.[38]

Schillebeeckx has described Christology as the *zijnsgrond* from which the deepest meaning and possibility for human existence follows. He has developed his Christology in a manner that gives scope to the particularity of salvation in Jesus and at the same time points to the theocentric nature of Christology and hence of all theology, including theological anthropology. This is the strength of his sacramental Christology and it establishes the meaning of human life itself. This sacramental Christology depends upon Schillebeeckx's interpretation of the incarnation. This interpretation has two particular features that are most significant for his theological anthropology. The first is the full interpretation of Christ's personal humanity, and the second is the 'enduring' nature of this personal humanity. The incarnation is best

[35] Schillebeeckx, 'I Believe in the Resurrection of the Body', p. 136.
[36] Ibid.
[37] Ibid.
[38] Schillebeeckx, 'Love Comes from God', p. 195.

understood soteriologically as the mystery that embraces a series of 'redemptive moments' – passion, death, resurrection and glorification. By identifying Christ's glorification in this manner with his human and historical nature, Schillebeeckx underlines the sacramental nature of human life: the meaning of human life is both historical and eschatological. God is the future of humanity both as transcendence and in personal immanence. This is the meaning of Schillebeeckx's interpretation of Christ's glorification as a 'moment' of the incarnation.

Christology is for Schillebeeckx the fulfilment of God 'coming close to humanity in grace', and he has identified as one of the most crucial aspects to the description of this relationship of grace: 'The confession of faith in the Christ who lives now seated at God's right hand in glory'.[39] The place that Schillebeeckx gives to this aspect of his Christology is significant. He locates his discussion of the 'Christ who lives now' within his description of the redemptive mystery; set within this overarching soteriological framework, the doctrine of the redemptive work of the glorified Christ is bound to the redemptive work of Christ's life, death and resurrection. In other words, as a 'moment' of the redemptive mystery, the description of Christ in glory is contained for Schillebeeckx within his doctrine of incarnation. This has a number of Christological and anthropological merits. By tying the doctrine of the lordship of Christ to the incarnation, Schillebeeckx allows for a description of Christ's ongoing redemptive activity that is particular to the relation of the divine and human as revealed in Christ's incarnation. Furthermore, it ensures that the doctrine of Christ in glory is concerned with human history: God's salvific activity present within history. The doctrine of the Christ who lives now expands upon the notion of incarnation: God's definitive self-revelation within history that is constitutive of human meaning. In this way Schillebeeckx develops a doctrine of Christ in glory that serves well his theological realism within its soteriological and hence historical parameters – the description of the redemptive activity of the heavenly Christ finds its locus within an incarnational and not a 'speculative' Christology.

In *Christ the Sacrament* Schillebeeckx places his understanding of incarnation – the incarnation that stretches from Christ's birth to glorification – at the service of both sacramental theology and, by extension, at the service of ecclesiology, and he quite deliberately and self-consciously identifies the primitive Christian confession: 'Christ lives now at the right hand of the Father', as a key insight from which ecclesiology and sacramental theology must proceed. Among other things, the 'Christ who lives now' ensures an ecclesiology in a 'minor key' thus not subsuming all description of divine action within history under the rubric of 'the church', an idea to which

---

[39] Schillebeeckx, *Christ the Sacrament*, p. 63.

Schillebeeckx returns in his much later final book of the Christological trilogy:

> [I]n this book I want to put the church 'in its place' and at the same time give it 'the place which is its due'. The church never exists for its own sake, although it has often forgotten this. For that very reason, in this 'ecclesiological' book I shall not be saying too much directly about the church. We need a bit of *negative ecclesiology*, church theology in a minor key, in order to do away with the centuries-long ecclesiocentrism of the empirical phenomenon of 'Christian religion': for the sake of God, for the sake of Jesus the Christ and for the sake of humankind. And all these three – God, Jesus Christ and humankind – are one in the sense that they may never be set over against one another or made into rivals.[40]

The Christ who lives now seated at the right hand of the Father, is the 'place' that gives ecclesiology its perspective precisely because it takes seriously the incarnational nature of redemption: at the centre of human history is the God who acts as creator and redeemer.

Human history is the arena of salvation history and therefore any theology of the church, as with any other subject of theology, should be both theocentric and Christological. The same of course holds true for Schillebeeckx's anthropology: 'Christ in glory' is the *zijnsgrond* for 'humanity in glory', yet this is neither a 'heavenly' nor a speculative anthropology, or even a separate 'Christian anthropology'. Christ in glory is the first-born of the 'new earth', which 'God has called into being in this world' and hence human nature in glory is *filii in Filio* in the midst of history. A theological anthropology for Schillebeeckx is not an ecclesiocentric anthropology: 'No Christian anthropology, rather God is close to humanity in grace'. Theological anthropology is the attempt to describe the communion in grace that holds between humanity and God, a communion that has been established in Christ and is sustained by the living communion between Father and Son: 'Since all this came to completion in Christ as the first-born and precursor of all mankind, in his ascension we too are already in principle "with the Father"'.[41]

One of the strengths of *Christ the Sacrament* is the manner in which it presses theology not to be forgetful of the very centre of the Christian confession of faith: 'Christ lives now'. The extent to which an ecclesiology or a theology of sacraments 'works' must be judged, in Schillebeeckx's estimation,

---

[40] Schillebeeckx, *Church. The Human Story of God*, trans. John Bowden (London: SCM, 1990), p. xix. Schillebeeckx expresses this same commitment to an ecclesiology in a 'minor key' in his commentary on *Gaudium et spes*. Ecclesiology is always chastened by the eschatological definition of humanity. See Schillebeeckx, 'Christian Faith and Man's Expectation for the Future on Earth', pp. 70–89.

[41] Schillebeeckx, *Christ the Sacrament*, p. 24.

by asking, 'To what extent has this theology held to the primitive Christian confession: Christ lives now?'[42] The same is true for theological anthropology and at the heart of Schillebeeckx's anthropology lies the 'fundamental confession of faith in both past and future parousia: Christ is the Lord, sitting at God's right hand'. Schillebeeckx's theocentric anthropology – the description of humanity as *filii in Filio* – is conditioned by his theology of the presence of the living Christ.

There are two parts to this Christological conditioning of human existence: the manner in which the invisible glorified Christ is present and active within human history and the identification of the invisible glorified Christ with the Christ once visible within history. Schillebeeckx is prepared to describe humanity as 'humanity in glory' – indeed, more than prepared and the phase *filii in Filio* receives its full freight here – and to appropriate this description of human life within his theology, it is necessary to press the question: what is the nature of Christ's heavenly act of redemption and what is the relation between this work of the glorified Christ with the work of the earthly Christ? The answer to the first half of this question is predicated for Schillebeeckx upon the answer to the latter half. What Christ 'achieved for us in the past' is the foundation, and in this sense, is fundamental, to the confession of the 'Christ who lives now'.[43] The extent to which this holds for Schillebeeckx is clear from the link he makes between resurrection and glorification: resurrection and glorification are mutually conditioning terms within the Christology of *Christ the Sacrament*.

Here Schillebeeckx's description of resurrection has some very substantive strength, not least when contributing to a theocentric anthropology. The final question that this chapter takes up, before turning to the question of human action in light of resurrection, is the nature of the relation between the Christ who lives now and the Christ once visible in human history.

Two things are at stake within Christology when addressing the question of the work of Christ in glory. The first is the relation between this work and the work of the earthly Christ, and the second is the way – if at all – theology describes the work of the Christ who lives now. It is the first issue that is addressed here, a decision that follows logically from Schillebeeckx's own work; within his Christology he acknowledges both questions and founds the latter upon the former. Several of his Christological commitments are at play here: the centrality of his particular theology of incarnation with its emphasis on the personal nature of Jesus' humanity; the kenotic nature of his Christology, reflected in the movement from humiliation to exaltation; and his decision to locate the meaning of redemption within the relationship of obedience in trust and fidelity between Jesus and the Father, a move that is illustrated most dramatically by his interpretation of the resurrection.

---

[42] Ibid. p. 63.
[43] Ibid.

To take the last of these points first, it is his treatment of the resurrection that demonstrates his understanding of the relation between the work of the earthly Christ and the work of Christ in glory. In other words, Schillebeeckx's description of resurrection will condition his description of the 'redemptive activity of the heavenly Christ'; therefore any constructive theology of Christ in glory must be consistent with a theology of resurrection. Conversely of course, the connection that Schillebeeckx draws between resurrection and glorification serves as a further indication of his theology of resurrection. This link between resurrection from the dead and glorification is clear for him: 'In this resurrection, as the eternally enduring salvific event of Christ, there falls also the ascension, the appointment as Lord, the sending of the Spirit or the actual lordship of Christ'.[44]

The link between resurrection and glorification is the 'eternally enduring salvific event of Christ'; they are two 'moments' of the one redemptive mystery. They are events that take place between Father and Son, and they are events that also contain the fulfilment of all human existence. The implication for a theology of resurrection would seem to be clear: resurrection is not simply the ratification by the Father of Jesus' earthly life that is now past. It is the establishment of Christ in glory, the 'ratification' of Christ's redemptive activity for eternity and hence it is the establishment of redeemed human existence in glory. Resurrection is an event that happens to Jesus by reaching back into the past – the acceptance of a lifetime of obedience and trust – and it is an event that happens to Jesus by stretching into eternity – the establishment of Christ as Lord. All of this is contained for Schillebeeckx in the confession, 'We have killed Jesus of Nazareth, but God has raised him to life.'[45]

With respect to the shape of Christ's existence in glory there are implications as well. By linking glorification quite specifically to resurrection any understanding of existence in glory is conditioned by the parameters within which the doctrine of resurrection functions, namely, within the personal relation between Father and Son. Therefore the work of Christ in glory – at least in so far as Schillebeeckx will attempt a description of the heavenly work of Christ – will be consistent with the personal and free relation of love between Father and Son. Christ in glory does not open out into

---

[44] Schillebeeckx, *Christus Sacrament van de Godsontmoeting* (Bilthoven: Nelissen, 1959), p. 31: 'In deze verrijzenis, als eeuwig-duurzame heilstoestand van Christus, vallen dan ook de hemelvaart, de aanstelling tot Heer, de Gesteszending of de actuele heerschappij van Christus.' Lost in the English text is the deliberate description of the resurrection as a particular event that happens to Christ: 'In the resurrection, then, as the eternally new act of salvation, there is also included Christ's ascension and establishment as Lord, the sending of the Holy Spirit which is Christ's actual exercise of lordship'. Schillebeeckx, *Christ the Sacrament*, p. 23.

[45] Schillebeeckx, *Christ the Sacrament*, p. 22.

a speculative Christology but continues the description of the personal communion between Father and Son. Because Schillebeeckx draws such a deliberate connection between resurrection and glorification it is possible to extrapolate those ideas that Schillebeeckx will want to hold together in communion – and not allow to collapse into opposition – when he attempts to describe the work of the Christ who lives now at God's right hand: human freedom and divine sovereignty; human history and eschatological fulfilment; personal identity and intersubjective dependence.

In other words, by linking any possible description of Christ's work in glory to the work of Christ on earth any subsequent description of the heavenly redemptive activity must be consistent with God's self-revelation as the *Deus salutaris*, as the God of human salvation. Because the resurrection includes both the life and death of Jesus, and because it includes Christ's glorification, any description of the glorified Christ must fall in line with the nature of the life, death and resurrection: the *locus* of this description must be the relation of personal freedom, trust and loving attachment, obedient even in death, which exists between Jesus and the Father. Put simply, any description of Christ's exercise of lordship will be both personal and historical and in this sense the mystery of incarnation circumscribes the work of the heavenly Christ. This is the full force of describing the meaning of humanity as *filii in Filio*: the meaning of human existence is described ultimately only in the relation between Father and Son. Hence the work of Christ in glory is consistent with the description of humanity in glory: free, gracious, personal, incarnate.

The connection between resurrection and glorification points back towards the pattern of Jesus' relation to the Father, and it points forward to the establishment of Christ as 'the eschatological Son of Man'. Thus, another of Schillebeeckx's Christological commitments is current in his theology of Christ in glory and that is the kenotic nature of his Christology:

> The Ascension is (a) the investiture of Christ risen from the dead as universal Lord and King, with which is connected (b) the glorification of Christ which constitutes him definitively and fully the Messiah, and the eschatological "Son of Man". The Ascension is the change from *exinanitio* to *glorificatio*, from humiliation to exaltation.[46]

The soteriological dynamism of Schillebeeckx's Christology is this twofold kenosis that captures for him the twofold relationship to which Christ is ultimately faithful: the Son's relationship to the Father, expressed in the self-emptying of the Son – *exinanitio* – and the relationship of the earthly Christ to humanity – expressed in the humiliation of the death on the cross.

---

[46] Ibid. p. 23.

This kenotic fidelity is acknowledged by the Father – in exaltation from the dead and glorification for eternity. The *exitus–reditus* movement of divine graciousness is revealed through the kenosis of the Son and the ratification of the Father as the personal relation of love between Father and Son into which all humanity is taken up. The redemptive mystery is a personal activity: it is the activity of a personal God and thus it is an activity which establishes humanity as person: free, contingent, finite. The infinite is revealed in the finite without destroying it.

For Schillebeeckx, Christ in glory is the 'first-born' of all creation; the glorified Christ, as the recapitulation of all creation, establishes the meaning of humanity as absolute dependence in a situated freedom. This is the final section of this study: the human vocation to intimacy with God, which is expressed ultimately as *filii in Filio*, calls humanity to radical love of the other.

Resurrection: Mystērion and Human Action

The idea of 'mystery' is a central one to Schillebeeckx's theology. It is given its fullest theological exposition in his work on sacramental theology, *De sacramentele heilseconomie*, and it is a pivotal concept in the Christological exposition of sacrament in *Christ the Sacrament of the Encounter with God*. It is also significant to his epistemological consideration of the relation between conceptual knowledge and non-conceptual realities. In this study it has already been introduced in the chapters on revelation and grace. It is a central concept within Schillebeeckx's treatise on God and his theology of humanity in its relation to God. Beyond the remit of this book, in his later works, the notion of 'mystery' continues and is a key point of continuity that accounts for the overarching coherence of his theological project, both in method and content.[47] Here, at the conclusion of this chapter that takes up the relation between Schillebeeckx's kenotic Christology and his corresponding theological anthropology, which locates the fullness of human life in self-emptying, the idea of mystery particular to his theology can be found right at the heart of this relation. The concept of mystery is integral to his understanding of salvation as the recapitulation of creation. It is used in his theology in the biblical and patristic sense: it is the term used to describe

---

[47] In the Foreword to a recent book that analyses his ecclesiology and its underlying epistemology, Schillebeeckx has written, 'Faith in God without a representation of that faith is meaningless, if not impossible, and moreover is historically ineffective. At the same time, the absolute and grace-filled presence of the divine mystery repeatedly shatters all our images and representations of God.' See, Daniel Speed Thompson, *The Language of Dissent. Edward Schillebeeckx on the Crisis of Authority in the Catholic Church* (Notre Dame: University of Notre Dame Press, 2003), p. x.

God's self-revelation and self-communication within history.[48] Furthermore, it describes what is accomplished in this event of revelation: 'The appearance and the self-revelation of God in human history was called *mystērion*, a mystery: "By mercifully entering the world, he has consecrated this world."'[49] Hence mystery is the term that describes the nature of God, the nature of humanity and the relation between these.

Because Schillebeeckx uses the concept of mystery to describe God's entrance into human history as an act that consecrates this world, it is clear from the outset that this concept is being used in a particular manner. In other words, there are some things that this concept is not doing in Schillebeeckx's theology. First, it is not used to suggest that God is completely unintelligible or to suggest that being human in relation to God is unintelligible. Second, the concept of mystery is not used to suggest a spiritualizing of human life that would divorce any understanding of being in relation to God from being in the world. Third, Schillebeeckx does not use this concept to suggest that human being is absorbed into the mystery of God's self-revelation and thereby loses its distinctiveness and identity. The idea of mystery serves to construct rather than to negate a theological anthropology. It provides a framework that allows him to speak about a relation between two completely distinct realities, creaturely humanity and non-created divinity. At the centre of this concept of mystery is the manner of God's self-revelation, the incarnation, by which 'God accomplished an act of salvation in the earthly happenings of the man Jesus, because that man

---

[48] At the end of *De sacramentele heilseconomie* Schillebeeckx provides a very good summary of the 'structure' of sacramental theology: the relation between '*l' aspect mystèrion*' and '*l'aspect anthropologique*'. Here the relation between God's activity within history and human participation in this activity rests in part on the understanding of divine self-revelation as *mystèrion*: 'La révélation chrétienne n'est pas seulement la communication d'une somme de vérités, prêchées par les prophètes et le Christ, elle est, plus fondamentalement, un *Mystèrion*: c.à.d. une révélation-*réalité*, une histoire de salut dans laquelle la réalité divine, en ce qu'elle intéresse directement l'humanité, se manifeste dans une réalité visible et terrestre.' *De sacramentele heilseconomie. Theologische bezinning op S. Thomas' sacramentenleer in het licht van de traditie en van de hedendaagse sacramentsproblematiek* (Bilthoven: Nelissen, 1952), pp. 665–672 (p. 665).

[49] Schillebeeckx, 'Religion and the World: Renewing the Face of the Earth', p. 10. Schillebeeckx is quoting from the *Dominicaans Martyrologium* for the vigil of Christmas: 'Hij heeft door zijn barmhartig intreden in de wereld, deze wereld geconsacreerd.' See Schillebeeckx, 'Godsdienst en Wereld: het aanschijn der aarde vernieuwen', in *Het geestelijk leven van de leek* (Tilburg: Drakenburgh – conferenties, 1951), p. 65. It is typical of Schillebeeckx rather than incidental that a liturgical reference is appealed to in a piece of theological exposition. Liturgy is a privileged theological *locus* in Schillebeeckx's work, underlining again the commitment to a theology that is non-dualistic. Theology, the development of doctrine, preaching, prayer, liturgy and ethical practice, inform and reflect each other.

was at the same time God.'[50] Hence when Schillebeeckx refers to mystery it takes as its structure the incarnation: it is a reference to the reality of God who both transcends our history and is distinct from it and yet who has also entered into this history in a definitive manner as human salvation and not as negation of the human.

It is the incarnational nature of mystery that Schillebeeckx points to when he describes the relation between being in Christ and being in the world:

> Being in Christ is not one of many ways of being in the world it is rather a dimension in depth which includes all the superficial dimensions of being in the world and not something added to them. A deeper life in God, in *Christ* causes the whole of our being man to enter into a new mystery.[51]

Here, by taking incarnation as the structure of mystery, Schillebeeckx is suggesting that incarnation does not perform an explanatory function, rather it is constitutive of a new reality: the relationship between the divine and human in which the nature of the divine is revealed as mercy and the nature of humanity is fulfilled in redemption. This new reality is the recapitulation of creation.

> In Christ the whole of human existence has commenced a new life. The whole of Christian humanism is contained in this, and it is in her growing awareness of this datum of faith that the church has become sharply conscious, in this biblical view of life, of the real place of humanism within the mystery of Christ, just as understanding of the meaning of man's being in the world has grown and matured in the human mind.[52]

Christian humanism is the 'theological consequence of the dogma of creation in connection with the dogma of redemption'.[53] In other words, the incarnation is the recapitulation of creation, and it is from this 'biblical perspective' that Schillebeeckx proceeds when he outlines his understanding

---

[50] Schillebeeckx, 'Religion and the World: Renewing the Face of the Earth', pp. 9–10. Schillebeeckx describes human participation in the 'once and for all' event of salvation by describing the sacramental nature of that participation. The relation between revelation and incarnation is essential to this description of human participation in the divine life: 'Le sacramentalisme de l'Eglise est donc fondé sur la venue sacramentaire du Christ dans le monde, sur le caractère unique ou l'εφάπαξ des mystères du Christ et, par conséquent, sur la clôture de la révélation-réalité, dont nous devons vivre nous aussi aujourd'hui. Les sacraments sont précisément la célébration mystique ou 'mystérique', cultuelle des 'mysterias carnis Christi': c'est ce qui les constitue en tant que 'mystérion'; un mystère de salut qui n'ajoute rien au mystère du Christ, n'en enlève rien, mais en polarise l'efficacité au profit de tel homme en particulier.' *De sacramentele heilseconomie*, p. 666.

[51] Schillebeeckx, 'Religion and the World: Renewing the Face of the Earth', p. 10.

[52] Ibid. pp. 8–9.

[53] Ibid. p. 10. The whole of Schillebeeckx's theology is a 'consequence' of this connection.

of human existence.[54] It is a perspective which he characterizes as ethical and religious rather than metaphysical.[55] Here the next move is to examine Schillebeeckx's understanding of the recapitulation of creation and the incarnational structure of this, and the contribution made to this by the concept of mystery.

In his essays on humanism Schillebeeckx is clearly concerned to overcome the 'polarity between Christianity and the world', which has had such a long history and had become particularly acute in the twentieth century. Over-coming this polarity is the 'theological consequence' of the relationship between creation and redemption, and it is here that the concept of mystery is of such importance:

> A great deal has already been written, and arguments have long been conducted about christian humanism, but it is doubtful whether man, despite his seeking, will ever penetrate fully to the heart of this reality for the simple reason that he is here confronted with a problem, the two terms of which merge into the mystery, on the one hand, of man's existence as spirit in the world and, on the other, of God's being God, the deeper mystery into which we have been allowed to enter through the mystery of Christ.[56]

What is at stake is the nature of two realities that are distinct and irreducible yet have a particular relation 'in Christ'. At stake too is the particular mode of knowing which is possible:

> Although it is, of course, impenetrable, a mystery does always have a nucleus of openness, of intelligibility – it always presents itself to man's experience and reflection via conceptual, recognisable ideas which at least provide us with some perspective. In this way, we are able, within the mystery, to become more sharply conscious of its content, at least sufficiently conscious to live from it.[57]

The concept of mystery, as has already been noted, does not suggest unintel-ligibility, rather, it gives a particular shape to the knowing which is possible between two realities which are completely other.

---

[54] Schillebeeckx's 1951 essay, 'Religion and the World: Renewing the Face of the Earth', is an attempt to 'illuminate' the 'problem of human existence from evangelical principles'. Schillebeeckx, 'Religion and the World: Renewing the Face of the Earth', pp. 1–18 (p. 5).

[55] Ibid. p. 8. This does not indicate a rejection of metaphysics but highlights a character-istic preoccupation with the relation between history and metaphysics. The rejection of metaphysics either within contemporary strands of philosophy or within theology is a point against which Schillebeeckx argues consistently.

[56] Ibid. p. 1.

[57] Ibid.

Schillebeeckx's commitment to the principle that God's self-revelation is at the same time God's self-communication underlines the essentially Thomistic principle that revelation is intelligible: it is revelation in being received. Following Chenu, Schillebeeckx places emphasis on the historical nature of revelation and thus holds consistently to the idea that revelation 'presents itself' within human experience 'via conceptual and recognizable ideas'. Yet at the same time, by linking the concept of mystery to that of incarnation, Schillebeeckx has indicated that mystery is not only an expression of a particular intelligibility but also an expression of the relation between two realities that are irreducible. Just as in the incarnation the divine and the human exist in relation without detracting from each other in any way, so too in the event of God's salvific self-communication divine graciousness and human freedom exist in a non-competitive and non-reductive relation. Here the distinction drawn earlier between the incarnational structure of Chenu's theology and that of Schillebeeckx comes into even sharper focus. Because Schillebeeckx works out a doctrine of the incarnation within his Christology that rests on the personal nature of Christ and the personal nature of the relation between Father and Son, he has the theological ground well prepared for an anthropology that is both speculative and practical. It is the centrality of the personal structure of incarnation that leads Schillebeeckx to a kenotic Christology, which in turn gives rise to an anthropology that describes the fullness of self as self-emptying. Furthermore, it is an anthropology that gives a rich description of both the life of the individual and the essentially societal nature of human being.

The concept of mystery suggests a particular intelligibility to Schillebeeckx, one which coheres with the idea of 'participation'. It is not an intelligibility or a structure of knowing which is parallel with other structures of knowing. Rather, it is constitutive of our knowing. The task of Christian humanism is therefore not one of reconciling competing or parallel worldviews or realities; it has the task of describing creaturely participation in the divine:

> The biblical and patristic concept of mystery throws a surprising light on to the problem of humanism. It is not directly concerned with reconciling terrestrial and supraterrestrial expectations with each other, but it is concerned with showing a twofold perspective in the one evolving historical event. The kingdom of God comes about in human history.[58]

Revelation in history establishes our participation in the life of God from within this history; hence Schillebeeckx maintains that this mystery is intelligible, and this intelligibility has a practical end: 'We are able, within the mystery, to become more sharply conscious of its content, at least sufficiently conscious to live from it'.[59]

[58] Ibid. p. 10.
[59] Ibid. p. 1.

The biblical and patristic idea of mystery is able to throw 'a surprising light on the problem of humanism' because it is particularly well suited to 'describing the one evolving historical event', the realization of salvation within history. It is a concept that both underlines the intelligibility of revelation and sustains the irreducibility of the divine and the human in relation one to the other. Both this intelligibility and irreducibility find expression in the incarnational structure of mystery: 'He, who, as far as he is concerned, does not form any part of the structure of our world, but transcends it in creative freedom, has himself entered this structure as a fellow-creature. He has become a man in the world.'[60] The problem that confronted Christian humanism in the mid-twentieth century, on Schillebeeckx's reading, was the relation between the transcendent Creator who is completely other from creation, yet who acts in creation in a manner that establishes the meaning of human activity itself. Indeed it is precisely the nature of God's transcendence that is of decisive importance to Christian humanism: the long history in which theology has 'looked for an alibi in the "supernatural" and "supraterrestrial" in order to escape from the harsh terrestrial tasks of a secular plan of life', gives 'evidence of a mistaken view of God's transcendence'.[61] The particular understanding of God's transcendence that lies behind Schillebeeckx's 'humble humanism' is found in his understanding of the biblical and patristic *mystērion* as the recapitulation of creation.

For Schillebeeckx redemption is the recapitulation of creation, the 'recreation of everything in Christ'.[62] The implications of this particular perspective are perhaps best captured by the assertion: 'in Christ', 'the redeemed world is now called the kingdom of God'.[63] Several ideas come together here that

---

[60] Ibid. p. 9. In this context, the Dutch phrase translated as: 'as far as he is concerned' – 'Hij, die voor wat Hem betreft' – is better transposed into English as: 'with respect to his own nature' or 'he, who in himself'. See Schillebeeckx, 'Godsdienst en Wereld: het aanschijn der aarde vernieuwen', p. 64.

[61] Ibid. p. 4.

[62] In his development of this biblical description of redemption Schillebeeckx follows Irenaeus. Schillebeeckx, 'Humble Humanism', p. 30 n 25.

[63] Schillebeeckx, 'Religion and the World: Renewing the Face of the Earth', p. 8. This reference to the 'world in Christ as the kingdom of God' in an essay written over 30 years prior to the *Jesus* book foreshadows one of the dominant themes of that later Christology: the kingdom of God, identified with the person of Christ, transfigures human history while at the same time allows this history to continue. In his early Christology Schillebeeckx develops this idea with more specific reference to the incarnation while in the later Christology it is reflected in the Christological title which dominates his interpretation of Jesus: Jesus as the eschatological prophet of God. The continuity lies in Schillebeeckx's understanding of the relation between creation and redemption: redemption is consistently described as the recapitulation of creation in Christ. Appreciation of the later *Jesus* and *Christ* is sharpened considerably by reading them in light of the earlier *Christ the Sacrament*, especially with respect to the more systematic incarnational structure of the earlier Christology.

make this claim possible: the incarnational nature of recapitulation and the relation between temporality and eschatology.

Turning to the first of these, the incarnational structure of recapitulation, Schillebeeckx can make the assertion that the redeemed world is now the kingdom of God because of the particular relation between redemption and creation to which he holds. That is to say, because he describes recapitulation in light of the incarnation – in Christ – this assertion works precisely because it does not reduce either its divine or human terms. Just as the infinite is revealed in the finite without destroying it, the kingdom of God comes about in human history without destroying this history. The world continues to exist as world with its own history, and at the same time the kingdom of God that transcends it becomes incarnate within it. Because of the incarnational structure of recapitulation Schillebeeckx can hold to an understanding of divine transcendence, which far from threatening humanism actually becomes the ground for it. The theological response to Merleau-Ponty's critique: 'Faith in God kills in us a sense of man and his historicity'[64], is not, for Schillebeeckx, an appeal to a concept of transcendence which absolves Christians from engagement with the world in expectation of the parousia – this is precisely the mistaken view of transcendence which must be avoided. Rather, because God's transcendence becomes incarnate as the recapitulation of creation, the Christian response must be just the opposite of non-engagement, it must be active engagement in the humanization of this world, in its economic, social, political and scientific spheres. Living 'in and through grace and for the kingdom of God' means having 'the most compelling reasons' for accepting the responsibility of 'setting the world in order'.[65]

The anthropological consequence of this relation between creation and redemption is clear. Humanity is redeemed in this world, in the full reality of what it means to be human:

'If anyone is in Christ, he is a new creation' (2 Cor. 5.17), mean[s] not only that man has acquired a new reality, grace, but also that the whole man has, as man in the world, been renewed in and through grace in Christ.[66]

Returning to the idea that grace is not something added to nature yet is something other than nature, the relation between grace and nature in Christ is recapitulation. Being 'in Christ' is not something 'added' to 'being in the world' it is the 'depth' of being in the world, which embraces every dimension of this-worldly human existence.[67] Grace recapitulates nature and hence

---

[64] Ibid. p. 4. See Maurice Merleau-Ponty, *Sens et non-sens* (Paris: Nagel, 1948), p. 191.
[65] Schillebeeckx, 'Religion and the World: Renewing the Face of the Earth', p. 5.
[66] Ibid. p. 8.
[67] Ibid. p. 10.

we live 'concretely in a new world'. This is what Schillebeeckx understands by our 'incorporation into the mystery of Christ':

> The whole of his being man in this world is baptised and christianized. By Christ, the optimistic faith in creation is once again situated in its original sphere of life in which it can freely breathe. As though it were a second day of creation, God pronounces his approval over mankind in Christ 'he saw that it was good'. Paul said this explicitly: 'There is now no condemnation for those who are in Christ Jesus' (Rom. 8.1).[68]

In this paraphrase of Paul and the creation narrative of Genesis, the expression of redemption as the recapitulation of creation could hardly be clearer. Humanity has been incorporated into the mystery of Christ by a 'second day of creation', and the effect of this is freedom to live in the world in hope, free from 'condemnation'. In Christ, in the incarnational nature of redemption, God 'pronounces his approval' over creation. Hence redemption is not the freedom from our creatureliness, rather it is the confirmation and the re-establishment of humanity's created nature. Far from 'killing in us' any sense of humanity's historicity, the understanding of incorporation into Christ as the recapitulation of creation redeems this historicity and grounds it definitively. 'History is not simply a route to the eternal'.[69]

Before turning to the relation between temporality and eschatology, which will further underline the importance of historicity, rather than its negation in relation to the transcendent, and hence the importance of human agency, there is one further aspect of the incarnational structure of Schillebeeckx's soteriology that needs further explanation in this context: the personal nature of creation's recapitulation. Recapitulation in Christ means for Schillebeeckx that redemption is particular to the person of Christ. Christ is 'the content' of redemption in his own personal and historical agency:

> What is absolutely new in Christianity is that God himself has entered the order of our life in this world, or rather, the disorder of that life. Christ, the content of our religiosity, forms a part of history – the son of a Jewish mother, of David's lineage, born in Bethlehem, a little town in Judea, and condemned to death under Pontius Pilate. . . . A man, therefore, who appeared for a limited period of time in the world, and like all men, disappeared again. But – and this is what is new in this episode – a deeper mystery was accomplished in this human history of Christ. God accomplished an act of salvation.[70]

---

[68] Ibid. p. 8.
[69] Ibid. p. 11.
[70] Ibid. p. 9.

This descriptive paragraph that sketches so briefly the events and relationships that locate Jesus in history is not incidental to the essays on humanism but is of significant importance, particularly for theological anthropology. The recapitulation of creation has a personal or particular structure in the incarnation: in the human history of Christ God accomplishes salvation. Partly because its style is uncharacteristic in these essays, this brief description of the human history and situatedness of Christ underlines an important Christological concept: the distinctiveness of Christ's personal history is neither lost nor is it tangential, it is constitutive of salvation. Hence redemption is the affirmation of humanity's created nature, not in a general or abstract manner but in a personal manner that embraces both the social and individual aspects of human nature. Being in Christ then means that humanity realizes its full identity by acting in the world:

> The kingdom of God comes about in human history itself. In being in the world, in which man humanises himself by spiritualising the material world which he recasts for his own use – in this being in the world, a deeper mystery is also accomplished. It acquires its ultimate meaning of a reality which is richer in meaning – being in Christ. Being in the world naturally demands, of itself, humanism. That is to say, as an evolving being that comes into spiritual possession of himself and fully realises himself in all his dimensions in extending the world, man has the task in this world of humanising himself by humanising the world. Being in Christ does not contradict this evolution and task.[71]

The fullness of humanity is expressed in its situated freedom in which both individual identity and social identity are sustained. This is one anthropological aspect of the personal nature of incarnation in relation to creation. A further anthropological aspect is the idea of self-realization or dynamism. Being in Christ does not contradict humanity's self- realization, rather, it becomes the ground for self-realization. This self-realization is best described as 'participation'.

One of the consequences of Schillebeeckx's soteriology is the idea that humanity participates in 'realizing' itself within history, and this participation is defined by the nature of redemption itself, that is to say, it is defined by the incarnational structure of the recapitulation of creation. This means that our human action within our history can be described as participation both in a theocentric sense – we participate in the life of God – and it may be described in a Christological sense – in Christ the fullness of humanity has been revealed in a relation to the divine in which humanity is established and not negated. It is no accident that the term Schillebeeckx uses to describe

---

[71] Ibid. p. 10.

God's saving action within our history is the same term used for our own task within this same history: humanity takes possession of itself and fully realizes itself in extending the world and has the task of *humanizing* itself by humanizing the world.[72] It is this idea of participation to which Schillebeeckx points when he describes our human life as 'sacramental':

> The deepest basis of this definitive humanism which is defiant of time is consequently situated in our 'being in Christ', our sacramental entry into Christ's saving history. It is this way that a deeper mystery is accomplished in human history, a mystery which gives history a more embracing and a definitive meaning. Outside the mystery of Christ, humanism has no lasting meaning. Within the mystery of Christ, however, it becomes an aspect of our redemption in action: 'thou renewest the face of the earth!'[73]

It has already been noted that the idea of 'participation' is coherent with Schillebeeckx's epistemology in which the concept of 'mystery' is especially helpful. The mystery of God becomes intelligible through our participation in this mystery. We are able to become conscious of its content, of God's being God, from within the mystery.[74] This is an incarnational epistemology for Schillebeeckx: we have been allowed to enter the mystery of God's being God through the mystery of Christ.[75] It is also a practical epistemology: consciousness of God that comes from humanity's entrance into participation in the life of God has as its goal human activity in the world. It is a partial knowledge that is at the same time a sufficient knowledge if 'at least' we can live from it.[76] This practical proviso indicates that participation is not only an epistemological term for Schillebeeckx, but it is also an ontological and an ethical term.

In summary, for Schillebeeckx redemption is the recapitulation of creation.[77] This soteriology is brought into sharp relief by the assertion. 'In Christ the

---

[72] 'Het zijn-in-de-wereld vraagt uiteraard, uit zich-zelf, humanisme; d.w.z. als evoluerend wezen, dat in en aan de uitbouw van de wereld, tot geestelijk zelfbezit komt en zijn eigen wezen voluit realiseert naar al zijn dimensies, heeft de mens de aardse opdracht, zich-zelf te humaniseren door en aan de humanisering van de wereld.' 'Godsdienst en Wereld: het aanschijn der aarde vernieuwen', p. 65. Here Schillebeeckx describes the task of humanism as the humanising of humanity – *te humaniseren* - while elsewhere he uses this same phrase to describe God's salvific activity.

[73] Schillebeeckx, 'Religion and the World: Renewing the Face of the Earth', p. 11.

[74] 'Daardoor wordt het mogelijk om ons binnen in het mysterie toch sherper bewust te worden van zijn inhoud, althans in voldoende mate om ervan te kunnen leven'. 'Godsdienst en Wereld: het aanschijn der aarde vernieuwen', Schillebeeckx, p. 58.

[75] Schillebeeckx, 'Religion and the World: Renewing the Face of the Earth', p. 1.

[76] Ibid. p. 1.

[77] Schillebeeckx, 'Humble Humanism', p. 30.

redeemed world is now called the kingdom of God.'[78] A particular theological anthropology emerges from the relation between creation and redemption, between the world and the kingdom of God. This relation is developed in light of the Christological nature of recapitulation, a structure that allows for a theological anthropology that is both incarnational and personal. Such an anthropology is established and not threatened by God's transcendence – the infinite is revealed in the finite without destroying it.[79] Nor is this anthropology threatened by God's immanence – the personal nature of that immanence in Christ becomes the ground for humanity's self-realization and hence it is not the negation of meaningful human action.[80] This self-realization, both individual and social, is best described, on Schillebeeckx's account, as participation, our sacramental entry into the mystery of God's being God. In light of the incarnational reality that recapitulates creation in redemption, human being and action find their ground in the transcendent where the relation between the transcendent and the immanent, the divine and human is described as participation. Here the concept of mystery – *sacramentum* – comes to its full force, and this is further illustrated by a second assertion that expands upon the first: 'Being in the world is not the kingdom of God, but it is part of it'.[81] For Schillebeeckx the redeemed world may be described as the kingdom of God where the relation between the world and kingdom is described as participation, yet here there is an important proviso placed on the nature of participation. This participation is anticipatory.

The anticipatory nature of human action – where human action is understood as participation – introduces the second idea following on from a soteriology that describes redemption as a recapitulation of creation: the relation between temporality and eschatology. To be at all consistent with the incarnational structure of his soteriology and hence with the theological anthropology that results from this, Schillebeeckx must be able to construct a coherent relation between the anticipatory nature of participation and human temporality. He does this by adding a gloss to his first assertion, 'The redeemed world is now called the kingdom of God'. This claim is now conditioned by the eschatological proviso, 'Being in the world is not the kingdom of God but it is part of it'.[82]

Being in the world is not the kingdom of God but it is part of it. Included in this way in the mystery, setting in order and humanizing life in this world

---

[78] Schillebeeckx, 'Religion and the World: Renewing the Face of the Earth', p. 8.
[79] Contra Merleau-Ponty. Schillebeeckx, 'Religion and the World: Renewing the Face of the Earth', p. 4.
[80] Here the significance of the personal nature of resurrection as an event which happens to Jesus is critical to Schillebeeckx's theological anthropology.
[81] Schillebeeckx, 'Religion and the World: Renewing the Face of the Earth', p. 10
[82] Ibid. p. 10.

becomes a hidden beginning of the eschatological redemption, which is also a redemption of the material humanized world. The temporal task of regulating life on this earth is thus, via man's moral and religious life, drawn into the eternal framework beyond the limits of the purely temporal.[83]

The context for this eschatological gloss is a discussion of the biblical and patristic concept of mystery in relation to humanism and the essentially non-contradictory, non-dualistic and non-competitive relation between being in Christ and being in the world. This relation is summarized by the statement, 'A deeper life in God, in *Christ*, causes the whole of our being man to enter into a new mystery,' and it is this statement, 'in Christ', which explains what he means by 'the way' in which being in the world is 'included' in the kingdom of God.[84] The temporal task to which he refers is the humanism he describes as 'humanism of the redemption'. In other words, this eschatological gloss suggests that to develop the Christological structure of human action Schillebeeckx points to the paschal mystery. In light of the eschatological nature of human action, the relation he constructs between incarnation and the paschal mystery is significant: 'in Christ' signifies the Chalcedonian relation between the divine and human, which stretches to embrace the whole event of redemption, from incarnation to parousia.

The non-dualistic nature of redemption is reflected in the relation between the grace of the resurrection and the grace of the cross, and it is here that Schillebeeckx locates his theology of human temporality. This relation indicates the tension between historical failure and meaningful human action, and the tension between temporal event and eschatological event. Essentially, a humanism of redemption is also a humanism of conflict and 'struggle'[85]:

> It is clear that the definitive meaning of humanism, insofar as it is the other side of the coin and the reaction, in man in this world, of the grace of the resurrection, is also conditioned by the grace of the cross. Terrestrial humanism, as the beginning of heavenly humanism, is consequently, through its Christian character, essentially a humanism of the redemption – a struggle, like that between Jacob and the angel of God in Genesis. Jacob won his case. But was lamed. He was nonetheless blessed (Gen. 32.24–31).[86]

---

[83] Ibid. p. 11.
[84] 'Een dieper leven in God, *in Christus*, doet heel ons mens-zijn binnentreden in een nieuw mysterie. Het zijn-in-de-wereld is niet het rijk Gods, maar wordt de aardse humaniserende levensordening tot een verborgen inzet van de eschatologische verlossing, die een verlossing is ook van de stoffelijke gehumaniseerde wereld.' Schillebeeckx, 'Godsdienst en Wereld: het aanschijn der aarde vernieuwen', p. 65.
[85] '[E]en strijd'. Schillebeeckx, 'Godsdienst en Wereld: het aanschijn der aarde vernieuwen', p.71.
[86] Schillebeeckx, 'Religion and the World: Renewing the Face of the Earth', p. 17.

The Genesis reference here that Schillebeeckx inserts into his discussion of the paschal structure of human action seems at first glance to be simply incidental, emerging as it does in a section of text dominated by Johannine Christological references. Yet, deliberate or not, it is clearly indicative of the fundamental importance Schillebeeckx attaches to the conviction that God acts in history. It is also illustrative if the nature of this divine activity: divine action in history does not exclude or circumvent human action but engages with it. This account of the transcendent affirms both human historicity and divine engagement in history, and it does this in a manner that underlines the irreducibility of the distinction between the human and the divine. There are clear echoes here of the liturgical reference by which Schillebeeckx describes the historical reality in which humanity is situated: 'By mercifully entering the world [God] has consecrated this world'.[87]

Utterly central for Schillebeeckx is the truth that redemption is a 'redemption of *people*'. In essence, any 'authentic' account of redemption cannot imply the negation of the human, and therefore of course it cannot negate human temporality and historicity.[88] The irreducible nature of temporality in relation to redemption and the eschatological is expressed in the description of redemption as conflict or struggle, and the structure for this 'conflict' is the paschal mystery. This immediately conditions the reference to Genesis and the nature of 'conflict':

> Christian humanism is a laboriously won fruit of the mystery of grace of the passion in historical humanising and developing mankind. That is the *mystērion* of Christian humanism which, in its deepest essence, merges before our eyes into the mystery of the Godman Jesus Christ, the broken man, in and through his being broken, became the saviour of the *kosmos* (1 Jn 4.14; Jn 4.42). The risen, triumphant Christ therefore bears the stigmata of the drama of his redemption![89]

Several insights recur here that indicate how Schillebeeckx constructs the relation between human temporality and eschatological redemption: the reality of divine activity in history; the irreducibility of the distinction between divine and human; the nature of the relation between human and divine action within the same history. These insights are developed from his Christology – from his interpretation of the death of Christ and the resurrection and of the relation between these two events: 'The risen, triumphant Christ bears the stigmata of the drama of his redemption'. This 'drama of redemption' becomes the ground for the drama of human action.

---

[87] Ibid. p. 10.

[88] 'The whole has to be redeemed. Otherwise our redemption is unauthentic and unsound and not a redemption of *people*.' Schillebeeckx, 'Religion and the World: Renewing the Face of the Earth', p. 11.

[89] Schillebeeckx, 'Religion and the World: Renewing the Face of the Earth', p. 18.

Schillebeeckx describes the relation between human temporality and eschatological redemption by constructing an account of human action that takes its structure from the paschal mystery. This is, in part, a structure of conflict or struggle – conflict between humanity's rejection of Christ and Christ's ultimate fidelity to humanity, and conflict between the utter negativity of death and the fullness of life in resurrection. It is a tension that reflects the incarnational structure of the paschal mystery: 'tension' between the human Jesus and humanity, and between Jesus in his humanity and the Father. The drama of redemption is an historical event, the relative failure of the death of Jesus. It is a meta-historical event, resurrection and glorification of Christ. The relation between these is what Schillebeeckx describes as the 'fundamental eschatological tension', the 'tension between the aspect of mystery and the historical aspect of history'. This is a relation that recapitulates history. The drama of redemption becomes the drama in which human action – the humanism of the redemption – participates:

> The realisation of this possibility and necessity [humanism of the redemption] is directly based in the movement upwards and downwards of human history, insofar as a deeper mystery is accomplished in this in Christ. Because of God's entry into the world, this accomplishment applies to every historical event, including the relative failure of humanism and its constantly recurring situation of conflict.[90]

The non-negation of history is characterized by the continued existence of the 'relative failure' of human action – the upward and downward movement of history – and the reality of recapitulation is characterized by the transposition of the ultimate tension from within the upward and downward movement of history itself to within a more fundamental tension.

> The real problem of the humanist plan, brought about by our waiting for the *parousia* and the continued effect of the ancient situation without salvation, in other words, by the antagonism between good and evil in human development, has its basis however, in an even deeper reality. This is the fundamental tension between the historical aspect of this upward and downward movement in history and the aspect of mystery that is accomplished within it.[91]

Here there is a description of human activity that is not passive, neither in waiting for the parousia nor in the face of the continued failure of history. Human action within history is now transposed into a deeper reality – the recapitulation of creation in the mystery of Christ.

[90] Ibid. p. 16.
[91] Ibid. p. 15.

The place that Schillebeeckx gives to human temporality within his theological anthropology is indicated quite strikingly by the description of human action as a 'humanism of the redemption'. However, this is not a naïve humanism, a fact underlined unambiguously by its paschal structure: just as the 'risen, triumphant Christ bears the stigmata of the drama of his redemption' – stigmata that symbolize the relative historical failure of his life – so too does human temporality continue to bear the relative failure of human action. But this is not in any way a glorification of suffering. The utter negativity with which Schillebeeckx interprets death, and the insistence within his Christology on the reality and negativity of the death of Christ, are substantive provisos against any glorification of suffering or death. This is one clear consequence for a theology of human temporality and action that follows from his interpretation of Jesus' death and resurrection and the relation he constructs between these events. The other consequence which follows from his interpretation of the death of Christ is the active and not passive nature of human action in the face of suffering, and the personal – both individual and relational – character of this action. The death of Christ is interpreted as the ultimate consequence of trust and fidelity in relation to humanity and in relation to God. Christ's drama of redemption is one of tension between 'historical failure' and divine triumph through this fidelity – a tension Schillebeeckx ascribes to humanity's life in Christ and therefore to human action:

> The christian task in society is a beginning, an active commitment to this heavenly humanism. This initial commitment, however, is always influenced by various factors which result in conflict, factors such as man's very situation of being in the world which in itself implies risk, the constant threat of sinfulness in the christians who undertake this task of humanisation. . . . This means that the mystical beginning of this heavenly humanism is always, like the christian life as a whole, a constantly repeated relative fiasco. It is in other words, a humanism which is brought about laboriously in conflict and friction, with the consequence that every new contribution to humanism always contains the possibility of new conflict. Humanity is therefore more the work of man's penetrating more deeply and fervently into the love of God than a question of purely technical and social progress.[92]

The paschal structure of human action grounds temporality in the relation of cross to resurrection. In this way the ongoing conflictual nature of human action attests to a central truth of Schillebeeckx's theological anthropology: 'The nature of our being in the world is not expropriated by our being in Christ'.[93]

[92] Ibid. p. 14.
[93] Ibid. p. 13.

Human temporality is conditioned by a paschal realism in Schillebeeckx's theology. It is a non-naïve construal of human action in light of the redemptive event that takes place within history in a manner which allows the 'historical aspect of history' to continue on its way. This paschal realism also gives Schillebeeckx's anthropology a non-optimistic nature. Precisely because of the depth of its conflictual nature it is an anthropology not of optimism but of hope:

> An even deeper reason is to be found in the fact that Christ's saving history, the source of man's redemption in the world, is not yet complete. Our factual redemption has not yet become evident and visible. The ultimate fact of redemption which has not yet taken place will be inaugurated by a final historical event – Christ's *parousia*. If man's chance of his salvation and that of his humanism as well is to be found in the mystery of Christ, then as long as the final event of this mystery has not become a reality, our redemption will continue to be incomplete. 'In this hope we are saved' (Rom. 8.24). Humanism too is always a humanism on the way, a humanism that is eschatologically stretched.[94]

The paschal structure of redeemed human action – humanism of the redemption – locates the fundamental eschatological tension within history. Schillebeeckx describes this tension as the 'tension between the aspect of mystery and the historical aspect of history', and the theology of human temporality that emerges from this is one characterized both by conflict and hope. The nature of being in the world in Christ is historical: it is situated and it is dynamic. Humanity realizes itself as it acts in history. Because this historicity is recapitulated in Christ and not expropriated, human development or self-realization – the humanization of humanity – is accomplished through deepening participation in the life of God. Humanity 'realises itself as it penetrates more deeply and fervently into the love of God' and not simply through social or technical progress.[95] This is the consequence of a humanism of hope and not of optimism.

In Schillebeeckx's soteriology, being in Christ finds its meaning by being in the world. Being in the world is not expropriated by being in Christ; it is recapitulated in Christ. In this way, being in the world has its *zijnsgrond* in the redemptive event in Christ. There is of course an eschatological tension – 'humanism is always a humanism on the way, a humanism that is eschatologically stretched', but this tension is not a matter of being in this world while waiting for the next. Redemption, as the redemption of people, is redemption of the whole in which this world is recapitulated as the arena

---

[94] Ibid. pp.13–14.
[95] Ibid. p. 14.

of meaningful human action. It is entirely consistent with his soteriology for Schillebeeckx to hold to a description of humanity's historicity in which 'the terrestrial is not simply a route to the eternal'.[96] Humanity comes to its self-realization within history, in a 'constantly repeated relative fiasco'.[97] The conflictual nature of human temporality has been recapitulated in the fundamental tension that belongs to the nature of the redemptive drama itself.

Schillebeeckx sums up his theology of human action as simply 'the theological consequence of the dogma of creation in connection with the dogma of redemption', a summary that is in fact a very apt description of his entire theological project. Here, the implications of his understanding and explication of the 'connection' between creation and redemption for a theology of human action have been analysed by reflecting on two assertions taken from his essay, 'Religion and the World: Renewing the Face of the Earth': 'the redeemed world is now called the kingdom of God', yet, 'being in the world is not the kingdom of God but it is part of it'.[98] Considered in light of his soteriology in which redemption is the recapitulation of creation in Christ, these assertions indicate a theology of human action that can be best described as a sacramental participation in the mystery of Christ.[99] This is a theology of human action that affirms human historicity and temporality. This affirmation is accomplished in a twofold manner: by understanding God's redemptive and self-revelatory activity in history as *mystērion* and by ascribing an incarnational structure to this mystery. Schillebeeckx's own particular handling of these two concepts, *mystērion* and incarnation, yields a rich theological anthropology that is both speculative and practical.

The concepts of *mystērion* and incarnation are so central to Schillebeeckx's theology of human action because he recognizes that any meaningful theological account of human action must begin from, and depends upon, an adequate description of God's transcendence. Any theological anthropology that results in a reductionist description of human temporality and historicity would, in Schillebeeckx's estimation, 'give evidence of a mistaken view of God's transcendence'.[100] A full and theologically plausible account of human action is incumbent upon an understanding of God's transcendence; Schillebeeckx's own theology of human action is so fruitful precisely because of his grasp of the nature of the transcendent. What he says of his theological anthropology – it is simply the 'theological consequence of the dogma of

[96] Ibid. p. 11.
[97] '[E]en telkens herhaald betrekkelijk fiasco', Schillebeeckx, 'Godsdienst en Wereld: het aanschijn der aarde vernieuwen', p. 68. The nature of repetition indicated by the use of 'herhaald' can be interpreted as one of 'recapitulation'.
[98] Schillebeeckx, 'Religion and the World: Renewing the Face of the Earth', pp. 8; 10.
[99] Ibid. p. 11.
[100] Ibid. p. 4.

creation in connection with the dogma of redemption' – may equally be said of his doctrine of God – 'God who in himself does not form any part of the structure of our world, but transcends it in creative freedom, has himself entered it as a fellow creature. He has become man in the world'.[101] The interdependence between a theology of human action and the doctrine of God becomes quite clear in the connection between creation and redemption.

The reference to creation upholds both the absolute difference between Creator and creation and the relational capacity that exists within this difference. Within Schillebeeckx's writings, the doctrine of creation always points towards a distinctiveness in relation between Creator and created, and this lies at the heart of his theology. It acknowledges the sovereign and free nature of God's activity within history and at the same time it affirms the created nature of human action. By identifying this sovereign and free activity within history with the incarnation, this activity accomplishes the recapitulation of creation in which the fully personal nature of the transcendent and the immanent, the human and the divine, are revealed:

> God's entry into human history, his grace in other words, does not cancel out man's history on earth – on the contrary, by entering history God himself becomes, in and for historical man, the most intimate content of man's existence, not in any sense the competitor with man's historical growth. On the other hand he does not become lost in or disappear into this history. . . . It is clear therefore that it is not the historical aspect of human history, but the divine aspect of mystery that is accomplished within this history which is the 'one thing necessary' that gives the historical its deepest meaning. We cannot oppose God to this terrestrial growth, but on the other hand we cannot identify this terrestrial mystery with the supernatural mystery. God despite his deep intimacy with us in history, is completely different.[102]

God's activity in history has a Christological structure and hence it establishes a relation with humanity that is non-identical, non-competitive, non-dualistic, yet is nevertheless redemptive and hence constitutive of humanity.

Schillebeeckx's theology of human action, his humanism of the redemption, is the anthropological consequence of the nature of the relation between God and humanity, a relation that is at the same time one of 'difference' and

---

[101] Schillebeeckx, 'Godsdienst en Wereld: het aanschijn der aarde vernieuwen', p. 64. 'Hij, die voor wat Hem betreft geen deel iutmaakt van onze wereldstructuur, maar haar in scheppende vrijheid transcendeert, is zelf deze aardse structuur binnengetreden als medeschepsel; Hij is een mens-in-de-wereld geworden.'

[102] Schillebeeckx, 'Religion and the World: Renewing the Face of the Earth', p. 15.

one of 'intimacy'. Both the characteristic of 'difference' and the characteristic of 'intimacy' are expressed in the emphasis he places on *mystērion*, a concept that gives rise to a description of human life as anticipatory participation in the life of God. The concept of participation, as the description of the relation of the human to the divine, underlines a series of specific attributes of this relation of intimacy in difference: it is intersubjective and not reductive, active and not passive, personal and not anonymous, embodied and not spiritualized, temporal and not *a*temporal. Two concepts emerge from Schillebeeckx's essays on humanism specifically and from his early writings more generally, which provide a very apt summary of his theological anthropology. These are the concepts of humility and sacrament. Both of these ideas express the Christological structure or *zijnsgrond* of human life. By describing the fundamental nature of human life as self-emptying and as sacramental, Schillebeeckx finds a description of human being that is grounded in both the intimacy and the difference which characterizes the relation between God and humanity:

> The deepest basis of this definitive humanism is situated in our being in Christ, our sacramental entry into Christ's saving history. . . . God despite his deep intimacy with us in history, is completely different, and this imposes on us, in the coming about of the kingdom of God, the fundamental duty of self-dispossession, which is merely the other side of the coin of our loving dedication to God's greater value. [103]

[103] Ibid. pp. 11; 15.

BIBLIOGRAPHY

Alberigo, Guiseppe and Joseph Komonchak, eds *History of Vatican II*, 4 vols (Maryknoll: Orbis, 1995–2002)

Baraúna, G., ed. *De kerk van Vaticanum II: Commentaren op de concilie constitutie over de kerk*, 2 vols (Bilthoven: Nelissen, 1966)

Borgman, Erick, *Edward Schillebeeckx: A Theologian in His History. Volume I: A Catholic Theology of Culture (1914–1965)*, trans. John Bowden (London: Continuum, 2003)

Borgman, Erik, *Edward Schillebeeckx: Een theoloog in zijn geschiedenis. Deel I: Een katholieke cultuurtheologie (1914–1965)* (Baarn: Nelissen, 1999)

——, 'Op zoek naar Maria . . . en verder', *Tijdschrift voor Theologie* **33** (1993), 241–266

——, 'Theologie tussen universiteit en emancipatie: De weg van Edward Schillebeeckx', *Tijdschrift voor Theologie* **26** (1986), 240–258

——, 'Van cultuurtheologie naar theologie als onderdeel van de cultuur', *Tijdschrift voor Theologie* **34** (1994), 335–360

Bourgay, Paul, 'Edward Schillebeeckx', in *Bilan de la théologie du XXe siècle, II*, eds Robert Vander Grucht and Herbert Vorgrimler (Paris: Casterman, 1970), pp. 875–890

Chenu, Marie-Dominique, *Introduction à l'étude de saint Thomas d'Aquin* (Paris: Vrin, 1950)

——, *La Parole de Dieu* (Paris: Éditions de Cerf, 1964)

——, *Pour une théologie du travail* (Paris: Éditions de Seuil, 1955)

——, 'Preface' in *Claude Geffré, Un nouvel âge de la théologie* (Paris: Les Éditions du Cerf, 1987), pp. 7–10

——, *Spiritualité du travail* (Paris: Éditions du Temps Présent, 1941)

——, *St Thomas d'Aquin et la théologie* (Paris: Editions de Seuil, 1959)

——, *La théologie au XXIIe siècle* (Paris: Vrin, 1957)

——, *La théologie comme science au XIIIe siècle* (Paris: Vrin, 1957)

——, *La théologie est–elle une science?* (Paris: Arthème Fayard, 1957)

Congar, Yves, 'Le Père Chenu', in *Bilan de la théologie du XXe siècle, II*, eds Robert Vander Grucht and Herbert Vorgrimler, (Paris: Casterman, 1970), pp. 772–790

de Lubac, Henri, *Augustinisme et théologie moderne* (Paris: Aubier, 1965)

——, *La mystère du surnaturel* (Paris: Aubier, 1965)

——, *Surnaturel: Etudes Historique* (Paris: Aubier, 1946)

Galot, Jean 'Schillebeeckx: What's he really saying about Jesus' ministry?' *The Catholic Register*, October 1983

Geffré, Claude, *Un nouvel âge de la théologie* (Paris: Les Éditions du Cerf, 1987)

——, 'Le réalisme de l'incarnation dans la théologie du Père M–D Chenu', *Revue sc ph th* **69** (1985), pp. 389–399

BIBLIOGRAPHY

Häring, Herman, 'Met mensen op weg, voor mensen op weg. Over het theologisch denken van Edward Schillebeeckx' in *Mensen maken de Kerk*, ed. Huub ter Haar (Baarn: Nelissen), pp. 27–46

Hilkert, Mary Catherine, 'Hermeneutics of History in the Theology of Edward Schillebeeckx', *Thomist* 51 (1987), 97–145

Hilkert, Mary Catherine and Robert Schreiter, eds, *The Praxis of the Reign of God. An Introduction to the Theology of Edward Schillebeeckx* (New York: Fordham University Press, 2002)

Jossua, Jean–Pierre, 'Le Saulchoir revisité: 1937–1983' in *Marie–Dominique Chenu, Une école de théologie*, ed. René Rémond (Paris: Éditions de Seuil, 1985), pp. 81–90

Kennedy, Philip, 'Continuity underlying Discontinuity: Schillebeeckx's Philosophical Background', *New Blackfriars* 70 (1989), 256–277

——, *Deus Humanissimus. The Knowability of God in the Theology of Edward Schillebeeckx* (Fribourg: Fribourg University Press, 1993)

——, *Schillebeeckx* (Collegeville: Liturgical Press, 1993)

Kerr, Fergus, *After Aquinas: Versions of Thomism* (Oxford: Blackwell, 2002)

——, 'French theology: Yves Congar and Henri de Lubac', in *The Modern Theologians*, ed. David Ford, 2nd ed. (Oxford: Blackwell, 1997), pp. 10–117

Kerr, Fergus, ed. *Contemplating Aquinas. On the Varieties of Interpretation*, (London: SCM, 2003)

Küng, Hans, 'Een theologie met een jong gezicht', *Tijdschrift voor Theologie* 22 (1982), 354–359

Lash, Nicholas, *Change in Focus. A Study of Doctrinal Change and Continuity* (London: Sheed and Ward, 1973)

McManus, Kathleen, 'Suffering in the Theology of Edward Schillebeeckx', *Theological Studies* 60 (1999), 476–491

Merleau–Ponty, Maurice, *Sens et non–sens* (Paris: Nagel, 1948)

Potworowski, Christope, *Contemplation and Incarnation: The Theology of Marie–Dominique Chenu* (Montreal: McGill–Queen's University Press, 2001)

Rikhof, Herwi, 'Of Shadows and Substance: Analysis and Evaluation of the Documents in the Schillebeeckx Case', *Journal of Ecumenical Studies* 19 (1982), 244–267

——, 'Thomas at Utrecht', *Contemplating Aquinas. On the Varieties of Interpretation*, ed. Fergus Kerr (London: SCM, 2003), pp. 105–136

Scheffczyk, Leo, 'Christology in the context of Experience: On the interpretation of Christ by E. Schillebeeckx', *Thomist* 48 (1984), 383–408

Schillebeeckx, Edward, 'De broederlijke liefde als heilswerkelijheid, *Tijdschrift voor Geestelijk Leven* 8 (1952), 600–619

——, *Christ: The Christian Experience in the Modern World*, trans. John Bowden (London SCM, 1980)

——, *Christ the Sacrament of the Encounter with God* (London: Sheed and Ward, 1963)

——, 'Christelijk geloof en aardse toekomstverwachting', in *De kerk in de wereld van deze tijd* (Antwerp: Hilversum, 1967), pp. 78–109

——, 'Christelijke identiteit en menselijke integreteit', Concilium 18 (1982), 34–42

——, *De Christusontmoeting als sacrament van de Godsontmoeting. Theologische begrijpelijkheid van het heilsfeit sacramenten* (Bilthoven: Nelissen, 1958)

BIBLIOGRAPHY

——, *Christus Sacrament van de Godsontmoeting* (Bilthoven: Nelissen, 1959)

——, *Christus' tegenwoordigheid in de eucharistie* (Bilthoven: Nelissen, 1967)

——, *Church. The Human Story of God*, trans. John Bowden (London: SCM, 1990)

——, 'Dominicaanse spiritualiteit', *Biekorf* Special Issue: Christmas (1954), 4–74

——, 'Dominicaanse spiritualiteit', *Dominikaans Leven* **31** (1975, 242–246; **32** (1976) 2–7, 54–59

——, *Eucharist* (London: Sheed and Ward, 1968)

——, *Evangelie Verhalen* (Baarn: Nelissen, 1982)

——, 'Evangelische zuiverheid en menselijke waarachtigheid', *Tijdschrift voor Theologie* **3** (1963), 283–325

——, 'Faith Functioning in Human Self–Understanding', in *The Word in History: The St Xavier Symposium*, ed. Patrick Burke (London: Sheed and Ward, 1966), pp. 41–59

——, *For the Sake of the Gospel*, trans. John Bowden (New York: Crossroad, 1990)

——, 'Foreword'in *Daniel Speed Thompson, The Language of Dissent. Edward Schillebeeckx on the Crisis of Authority in the Catholic Church* (Notre Dame: University of Notre Dame Press, 2003), pp. ix–xiv

——, *Gerechtigheid en liefde: Genade en bevrijding* (Bloemendaal: Nelissen, 1977)

——, *God among Us: The Gospel Proclaimed*, trans. John Bowden (London: SCM, 1983)

——, *God and Man*, trans. Edward Fitzgerald and Peter Tomlinson (London: Sheed and Ward, 1969)

——, *God en mens* (Bithoven: Nelissen, 1965)

——, 'God en mens', in *Verslagboek v. d. Theologische week over de mens* (Nijmegen, 1958) pp. 3–21

——, *God is ieder ogenblik nieuw: gespreken met Edward Schillebeeckx* (Baarn: Ambo, 1982)

——, *God is New Each Moment: In Conversation with Huub Oosterhuis and Piet Hoogeven*, trans. David Smith (Edinburgh: T&T Clark, 1983)

——, 'God op de helling', *Tijdschrift voor Geestelijk Leven* **15** (1959), 397–409

——, 'Godsdienst en Wereld: het aanschijn der aarde vernieuwen', in *Het geestelijk leven van de leek* (Tilburg: Drakenburgh –conferenties, 1951)

——, 'Herinterpretatie van het geloof in het licht van de seculariteit', *Tijdschrift voor Theologie* **4** (1964), 109–150

——, 'Het begrip "waarheid"', *Katholiek Archief* **17** (1962), 1169–1180

——, *Het huwelijk, aardse werkelijheid en heilsmysterie* (Bilthoven: Nelissen, 1963)

——, 'Het leed der ervaring van Gods verborgenheid', *Vox Theologica* **36** (1966), 92–104

——, 'Het niet–begrippelijk kenmoment in de geloofsdaad: probleemstelling', *Tijdschrift voor Theologie* **3** (1963), 167–194

——, 'Het niet–begrippelijk kenmoment in onze Godskennis volgens Thomas van Aquino', *Tijdschrift voor Philosophie*, **14** (1952) 411–453

——, 'Het nieuewe mens–en Godsbeeld in conflict met het religieuze leven', *Tijdschrift voor Theologie* **7** (1967), 1–27

——, 'Ik geloof in de verrijzenis van het lichaam', *Tijdschrift voor Geestelijk Leven* **28** (1972), 435–451

BIBLIOGRAPHY

——, *Jesus: An Experiment in Christology* (London: Collins, 1979)

——, *Jezus, het verhaal van een levende* (Bloemendaal: Nelissen, 1974)

——, 'De kerk op drift?' *Tijdschrift voor Geestelijk Leven* **22** (1966), 533–554

——, 'De kyriale waardigheid van christus en de verkondiging', *Vox Theologica* **29** (1958), 34–38

——, *The Language of Faith: Essays on Jesus, Theology and the Church*, ed. Robert Schreiter (London: SCM, 1995)

——, 'Love Comes from God', *Cross and Crown* **16** (1964), 190–204

——, *Marriage: Secular Reality and Saving Mystery* (London: Sheed and Ward, 1965)

——, *Mensen als verhaal van God* (Baarn: Nelissen, 1989)

——, *The Mission of the Church*, trans. N. D. Smith (London: Sheed and Ward, 1973)

——, 'Naar een herontdekking van de christelijke sacramenten. Ritualisering van religieuze momenten in het alledaagse leven', *Tijdschrift voor Theologie* **40** (2000), 164–187

——, 'Nederig humanisme', *Kuulterleven* **16** (1949), 12–21

——, 'Niet–godsdienstig humanisme en het godsgeloof' in *Modern niet–godsdienstig humanisme* (Nijmegen, 1961)

——, 'De nieuwe wending in de huidige dogmatiek', *Tijdschrift voor Theologie* **1** (1961) 17–46

——, 'The non-conceptual intellectual element in the act of faith: a reaction', in *Revelation and Theology, II*, pp. 30–75

——, *Om het behoud van het evangelie* (Baarn: Nelissen, 1989)

——, 'Openbaring, Schiftuur Traditie en Leergezag', *Kerk en Theologie* **16** (1963), 85–99

——, *Openbaring en Theologie* (Bilthoven: Nelissen, 1964)

——, 'Prologue' in *Hilkert, Mary Catherine and Robert Schreiter*, eds *The Praxis of the Reign of God. An Introduction to the Theology of Edward Schillebeeckx*, trans. Robert Schreiter (New York: Fordham University Press, 2002), pp. ix – xviii

——, *Revelation and Theology, I: Revelation, Tradition and Theological Reflection*, 2nd ed. (London: Sheed and Ward, 1987)

——, *Revelation and Theology, II: The Concept of Truth and Theological Renewal*, trans. N. D. Smith (New York: Sheed and Ward, 1968)

——, 'Sackramentele als Organe der Gottenbegegnung' in *Fragen der theologie heute*, ed. J. Feiner (Einsiedeln: Benziger Verlag, 1957), pp. 370–401

——, 'The Sacraments: An Encounter with God' in *Christianity Divided: Protestant and Roman Catholic Theological Issues*, ed. D. Callahan (London: Sheed and Ward, 1961), pp. 245–275

——, 'Theologie' in *Theologisch woordenboek, III* (Roermond: Maaseik, 1958), col. 4485–4542

——, *Theologisch testament: notarieel nog niet verleden* (Baarn: Nelissen, 1994)

——, *Vatican II: The Real Achievement* (London: Sheed and Ward, 1967)

——, *Wereld en kerk*, (Bilthoven: Nelissen, 1966)

——, 'Werkelijkheidsopenbaring en woordopenbaring', *Lumière et Vie* **46** (1960), 25–45

——, 'Woord vooraf' in *Mark Schoof, Aggiornamento: De doorbraak van een nieuwe katholieke theologie* (Baarn: Wereldvenster, 1968), pp. 7–12

——, *World and Church*, trans. N. D. Smith (New York: Sheed and Ward, 1971)

——, *De zending van de kerk* (Bilthoven: Nelissen, 1968)

—— 'De zin van het mens–zijn van Jesus, de Christus', *Tijdschrift voor theologie* 2 (1962), 127–172

Schoof, T. M., *Aggiornamento: De doorbraak van een nieuwe katholieke theologie* (Baarn: Wereldvenster, 1968)

——, *Breakthrough: Beginnings of the New Catholic Theology* (Dublin: Gill and Macmillan, 1970)

Schoof, Ted, ed., *The Schillebeeckx Case*, (New York: Paulist Press, 1983)

Tanner Norman, ed., *Decrees of the Ecumenical Councils*, 2 vols (London: Sheed and Ward, 1990)

Torrell, Jean Pierre, *Initiation à St Thomas d'Aquin: Sa personne et son oeuvre* (Paris: Éditions de Cerf, 1993)

van den Hoogen, T '"Pastoral Theologie": Het theologisch procédé volgens Chenu', *Tijdschrift voor Theologie* 33 (1993), 396–416

Vergauwen, Guido, 'Edward Schillebeeckx – Lecteur de saint Thomas', in *Ordo sapientiae et amoris: Image et message de saint Thomas d'Aquin à travers les récentes études historiques, herméneutiques et doctrinales*, ed. Carlos–Josaphat Pinto de Oliviera (Fribourg: Éditions Universitaires Fribourg, 1993), pp. 655–673

INDEX

CPSIA information can be obtained at www.ICGtesting.com
Printed in the USA
BVOW012222271011

274703BV00002B/1/P

9 780567 036537